IMAGES
of America

GREEN COUNTY

On the Cover: These two unidentified young women dressed in their Sunday best are probably awaiting the arrival of the daily passenger train at Monticello's Illinois Central Railroad depot. Perhaps they are waiting for out-of-town guests or there is a celebration in Monticello, and the women are part of a group of local residents who have come to the depot to welcome the arriving guests and friends to give them a friendly Monticello welcome. (Monticello Historical Society.)

IMAGES
of America

GREEN COUNTY

Kim D. Tschudy

ARCADIA
PUBLISHING

ISBN 978-0-7385-8386-0

Published by Arcadia Publishing
Charleston, South Carolina

Printed in the United States of America

Library of Congress Control Number: 2010924359

For all general information, please contact Arcadia Publishing:
Telephone 843-853-2070
Fax 843-853-0044
E-mail sales@arcadiapublishing.com
For customer service and orders:
Toll-Free 1-888-313-2665

Visit us on the Internet at www.arcadiapublishing.com

I wish to dedicate this book to my grandchildren, Kyle and Mackenzie. You guys have provided me with such wonderful Sunday night breaks from this project. Your laughing and teasing made my weekends working on this book so much easier. One day you will understand.

Contents

ACKNOWLEDGMENTS

I would like to thank all those wonderful people who have helped in any way to bring this book from an idea to its finished form. These include the Albany, Belleville, Brodhead, Browntown, and Monticello Historical Societies for their contribution of photographs and time; Linda and Elda Schiesser were great with helping find answers to obscure questions; Paul Matzke deserves special praise for being the unofficial Juda historian who so graciously helped with providing all the Juda photographs for this book; Dwayne Marty and Ron Pattinson for answering my questions about Exeter; Anna and Bob Keough for finding what seemed to be impossible photographs to find; and the Voegeli family for complete access to their farm photographs. Cynthia Bagley deserves special thanks for her help with Attica questions and the books she so graciously sent me, which gave me a much better understanding of Attica and the English settlement. If I've forgotten anyone I apologize, there were so many of you.

And as always, thanks to my editor at Arcadia Publishing, Jeff Ruetsche, who I see more as a friend than an editor.

Introduction

Green County is my home. Its hills in the town of Exeter have nurtured my ancestors since 1846. Within the next few years, the holding in trust of the land will be passed to the sixth and seventh generations.

It takes a lifetime to understand the emotional power of walking ancestral land. But so often it takes the eyes and mind of a five-year-old to put that emotion into perspective. This past August, my grandson and I camped out on what we lovingly call, "the hill," a treeless, shallow-soiled hilltop.

Our campout was for the purpose of watching the Perseid meteor shower that each August fills the sky with several nights of nature's best light show. This replay of times past brought back memories of three decades ago when my then young sons, their friends, and I slept on the hill under the stars to watch in awe this annual event.

The night's campfire had turned from leaping flames to glowing embers. My son Terry and granddaughter Mackenzie had gone back to town. Kyle and I were now stretched out on our backs to stare at the August sky watching for meteorites.

I wondered as we watched the sky that night if Uncle J. J. took his children up on the hill in the late 1840s to show them the splendor of the August night sky. Did his children talk about the Native Americans that lived in the area? My own grandfather once told me of the periodic reappearance of a family of hungry Winnebago Indians who would work their way into New Glarus asking for food from the people who had taken over their ancestral lands.

Shortly after first light I awoke to find Kyle wide awake. "Grandpa, I have an idea. Let's go out Indian hunting."

"Indian hunting?"

"Yes grandpa, you know, let's hike around and see if we can find things the Indians left behind when they lived here. Grandpa, Indians did live here, didn't they?" The history of the land being what it is, I decided to talk with Kyle about the Native Americans who once called this land theirs.

Kyle's question was a bittersweet one. The people who lived upon these hills before my ancestors arrived have been long forgotten. Precious little remains of their lives—only a few artifacts and the broken dreams of an earlier people.

We broke camp and drove to Attica. As we got into town, Kyle asked, "Where are we now?"

"We're in Attica."

"What's Attica?"

"Attica is a ghost town."

"Grandpa, I think there are ghosts here!"

"There are no ghosts here, Kyle."

"Over there across the river is where the Winnebago Indians had their camp many years ago."

"Were there a lot of Indians here? Did they have children my age? What did they do? Where are they now, Grandpa?"

Kyle's questions haunted me. Why do we ask these questions? Is it out of curious interest? Maybe a sadness at not being able to see the Winnebago people here? Or is it that we know so precious little about our own backyard?

The history of Green County is steeped with quiet people who have made a tremendous impact on humanity, and yet precious little is known of them or their acts. One recent Sunday I photographed the home of Janet Jennings, which is on the National Register of Historic Places. There was nothing significant about her home, and that forced questions: Who was Janet Jennings? What did she do?

Quite to my surprise, she had quite a life story, and her humanitarian acts speak strongly to the notion of quiet and humble people doing great things. Known as the "Forgotten Angel" and the "Angel of Seneca" by those she served, Janet Jennings was one of the true heroes of the Civil War and also the Spanish-American War. Among Jennings's many acts, she worked alongside Clara Barton in establishing the American Red Cross.

Likewise is the story of Robert Bailey, the lone Revolutionary War veteran buried in Green County. Bailey, a humble man of conscience, was one of the early abolitionists. In 1814, while living in the South, Bailey had come to the conclusion that slavery was just not acceptable, and he gave his slaves their freedom.

Kyle was correct: there are ghosts in Attica and in many other places in Green County . . . the good ghosts of our collective past.

— Kim D. Tschudy

One

ALBANY

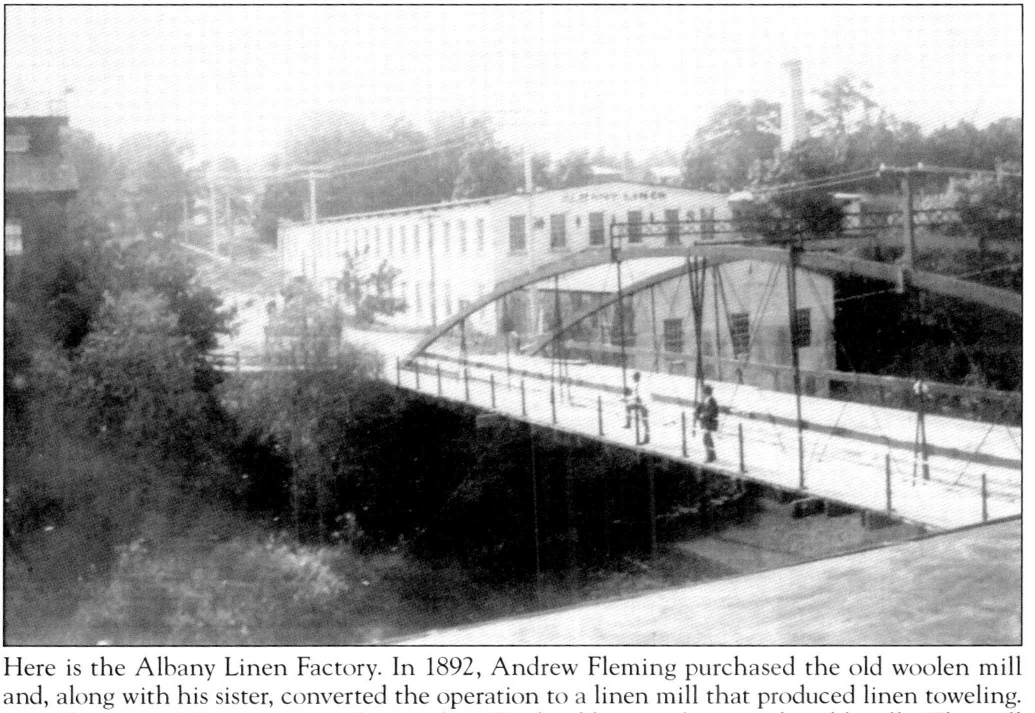

Here is the Albany Linen Factory. In 1892, Andrew Fleming purchased the old woolen mill and, along with his sister, converted the operation to a linen mill that produced linen toweling. Initially some of the raw material came from England but was later produced locally. The mill ceased operations in 1907. (Albany Historical Society.)

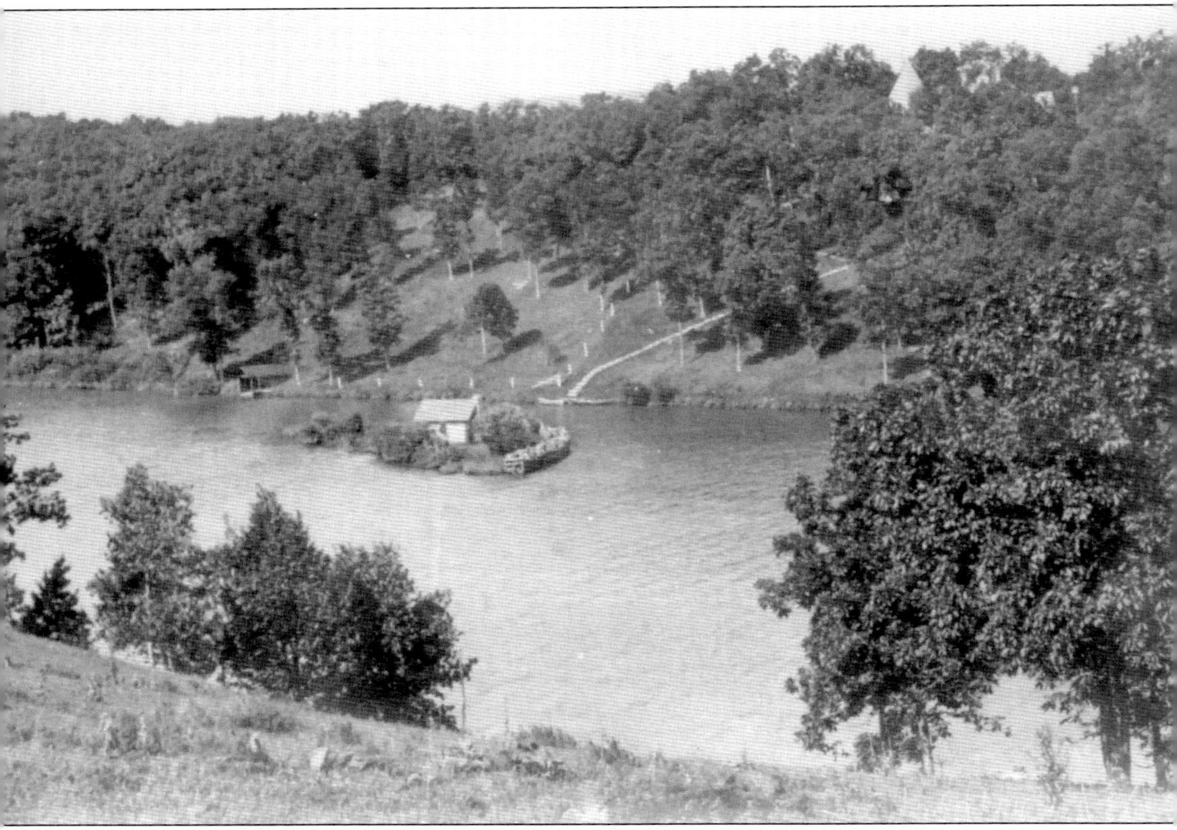

Shown in the middle of this photograph is a small cabin that was built on a small island just upriver from the dam that created Lake Winnetka. Local historians say that this island broke loose from an upper portion of Lake Winnetka during a bad storm, floated downriver, and lodged in this spot. The path leading from the lakeshore directly behind the cabin leads to the Whitcomb home, which in later years became the Whitcomb Sanitarium. That building still stands and recently underwent a major renovation. (Albany Historical Society.)

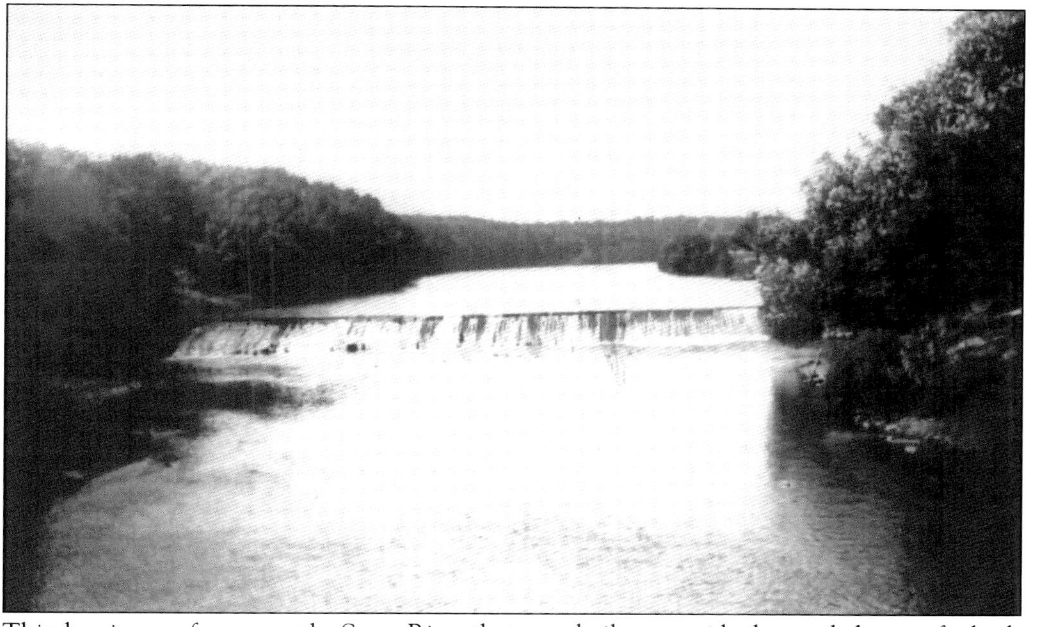

This dam is one of many on the Sugar River that were built to provide the needed power for both gristmills and sawmills as well as turbines that generated early electric power for many of the towns that lined the banks of the Sugar River. At one time, this dam supported five different waterwheels, which in turn provided waterpower for nearby factories. (Albany Historical Society.)

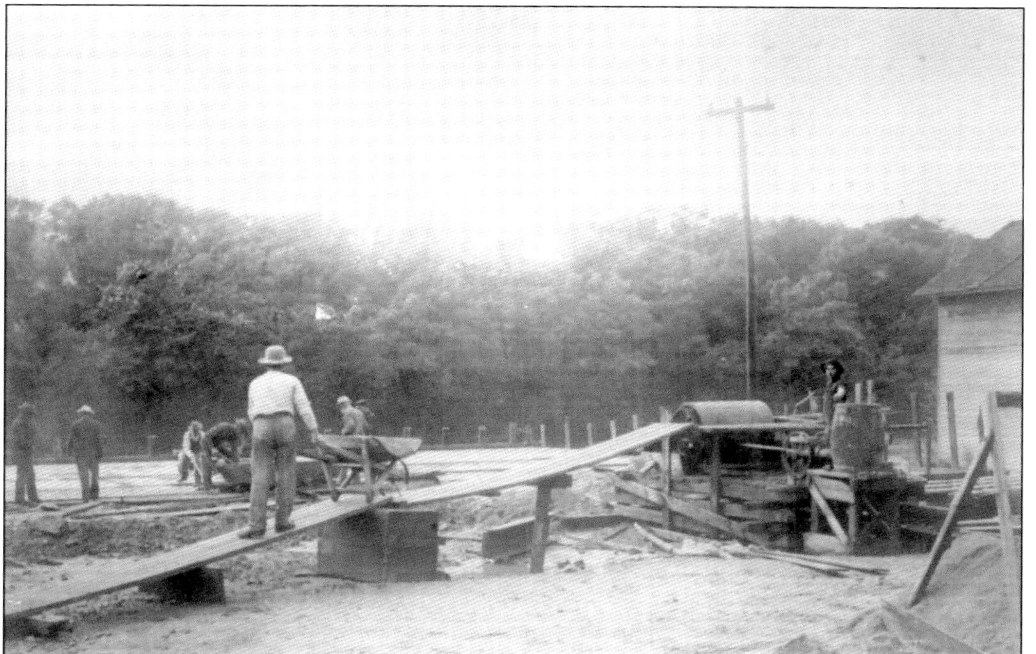

Building a dam is a backbreaking job. Imagine all the hours and manpower consumed to build a dam of the size that was needed to safely hold back the waters of the Sugar River. The necessary concrete for the construction was all hand-mixed on the building site. (Albany Historical Society.)

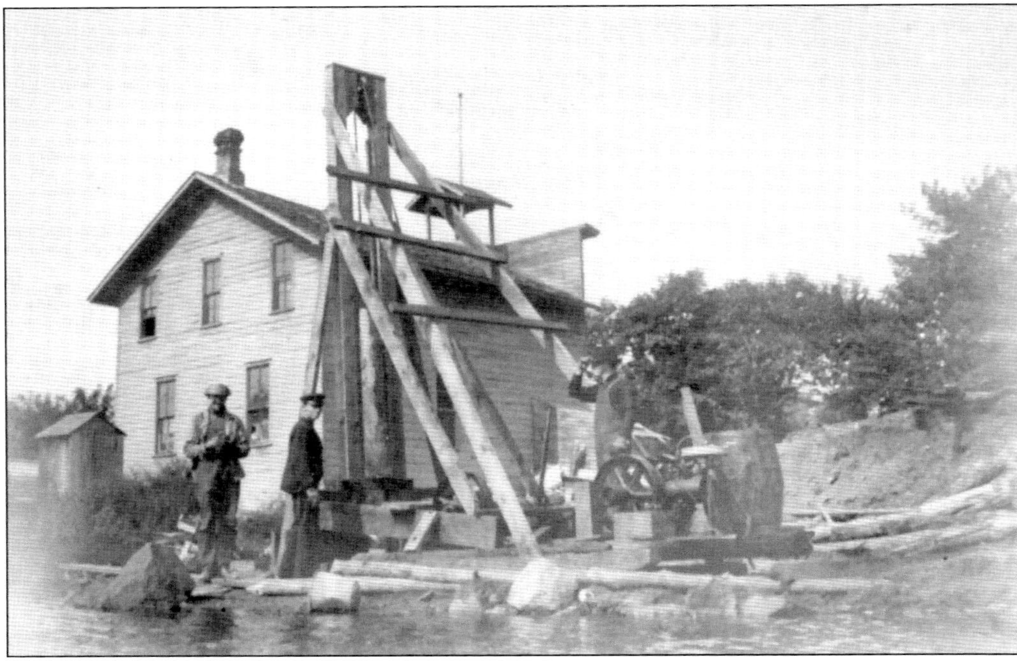

During the building of the dam, many different pieces of equipment were required. The pieces of equipment shown here were hand-built to fit the specific requirements of this project. Notice the rather official-looking hat the man in the center is wearing. (Albany Historical Society.)

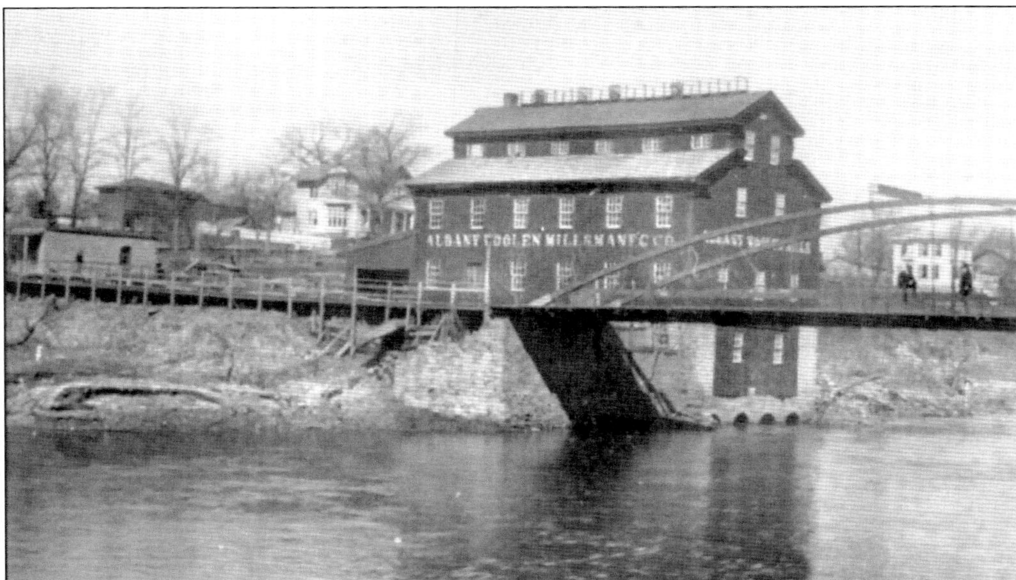

Here is the Albany Woolen Mills and Manufacturing Company. This building was located on the west side of the river that divides Albany, one of two woolen mills located on the Sugar River. Many woolen mills operated on a barter system, which allowed sheep farmers to trade in a certain number of pounds of grease wool (freshly sheared and unwashed) for the blankets and woolen socks they needed. (Albany Historical Society.)

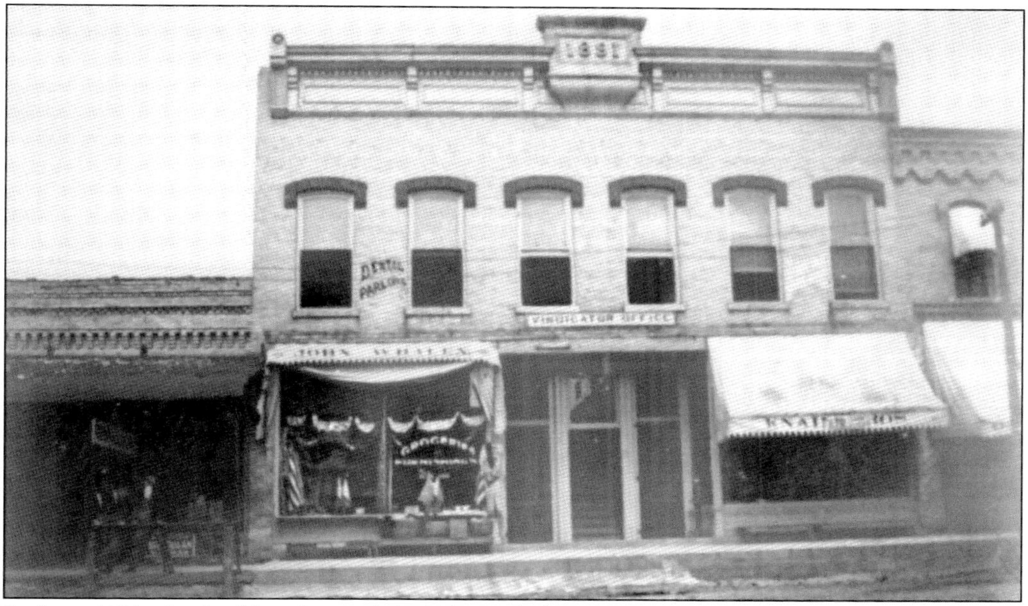

Built in 1891, this building housed the John Whalen Grocery and Furnishings store as well as the *Albany Vindicator*, a pro-temperance newspaper. The second story of this building housed Dr. Osborne, who in addition to his office also had his living quarters here. There was also a dental parlor in the front of the building and the Masonic Hall. Today the building serves as an apartment building. (Albany Historical Society.)

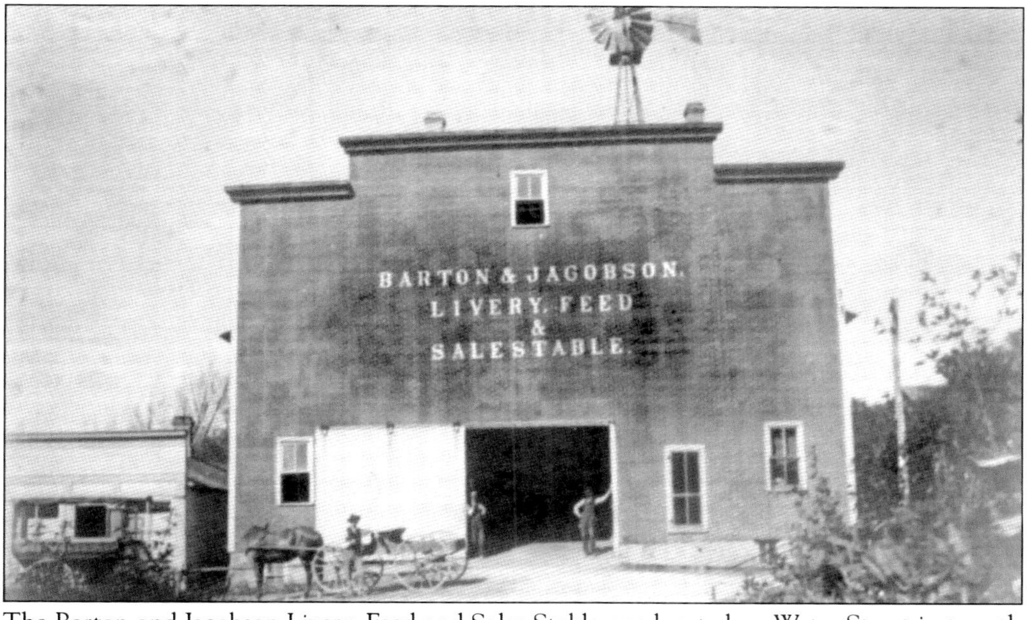

The Barton and Jacobson Livery, Feed and Sales Stable was located on Water Street just south of the bridge spanning the Sugar River. Businesses such as this one were a very necessary part of the local economy that provided transportation services to traveling salesmen who arrived and departed by train and needed a method of moving their sales trunks from store to store in the area. (Albany Historical Society.)

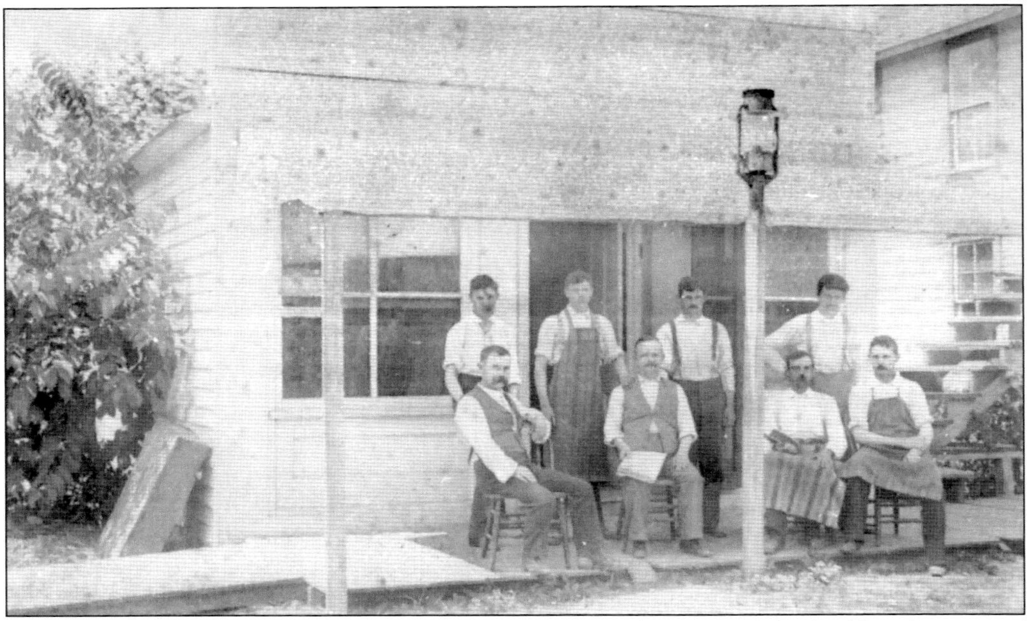

Not much is known about this photograph or the exact location of the building because of modifications and changes in the roofline. Given the heavy aprons several of the men are wearing, they may well have been the local harness makers. Notice the wooden sidewalk and also the kerosene lamp that serves as a streetlight. Many towns had a lamplighter who would nightly make his rounds lighting the streetlights. (Albany Historical Society.)

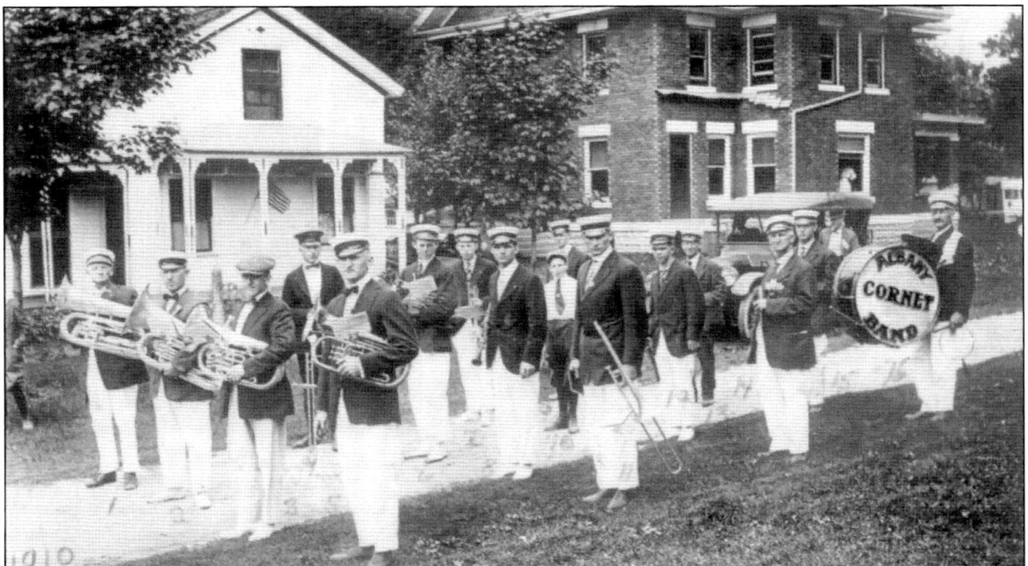

Albany Coronet Band members are readying themselves for the parade that is about to begin. This photograph was taken at the corner of East and Milwaukee Streets. Each small town had one or more community bands that provided much of the town's social activity. It was not unusual for towns the size of Albany to have as many as four different types of bands. Both houses shown in this photograph are still standing. (Albany Historical Society.)

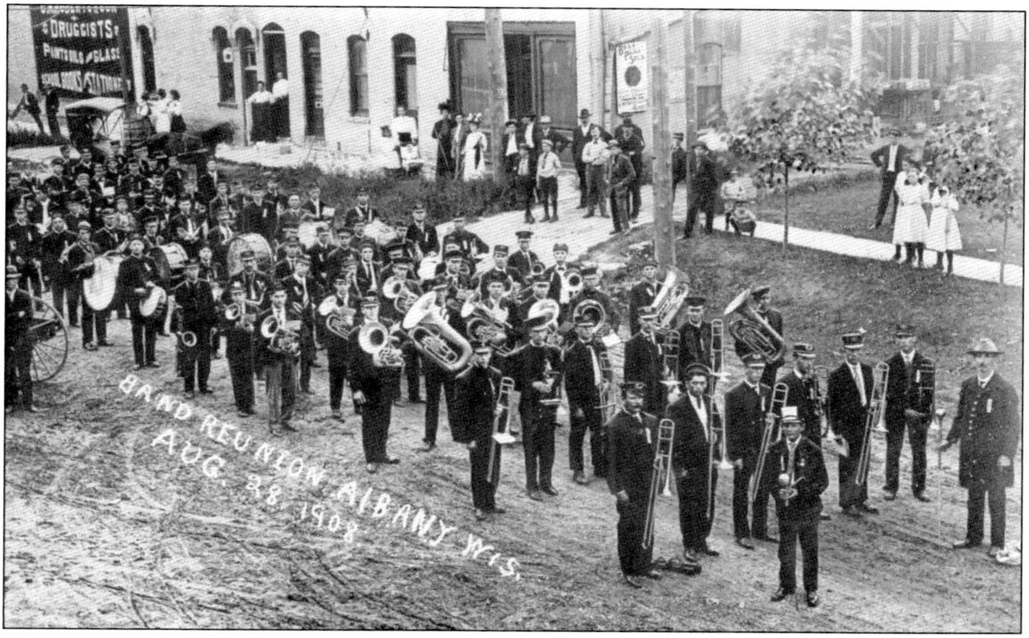

Band reunions such as this one for the Albany Band on August 28, 1908, were commonplace in the first decades of the 20th century. Bands from miles around would board trains early on the day of the reunion and travel to the host town for a day of music, food, and good times. Notice the badges on the band members. (Albany Historical Society.)

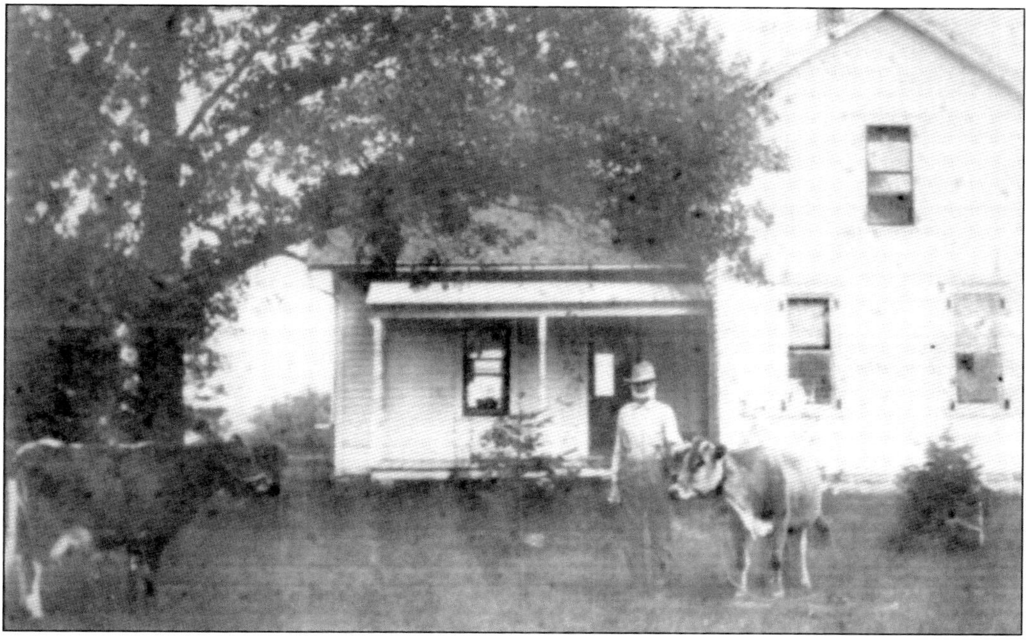

Abner Webb, an Albany area Civil War veteran, enlisted in the Union Army on April 22, 1861, served with Company C, Third Wisconsin Infantry, and was wounded at Resaca, Georgia in a battle that pitted Gen. William Sherman against Gen. Joseph Johnston. Webb took great pride in his livestock; here he shows off a Jersey cow. (Albany Historical Society.)

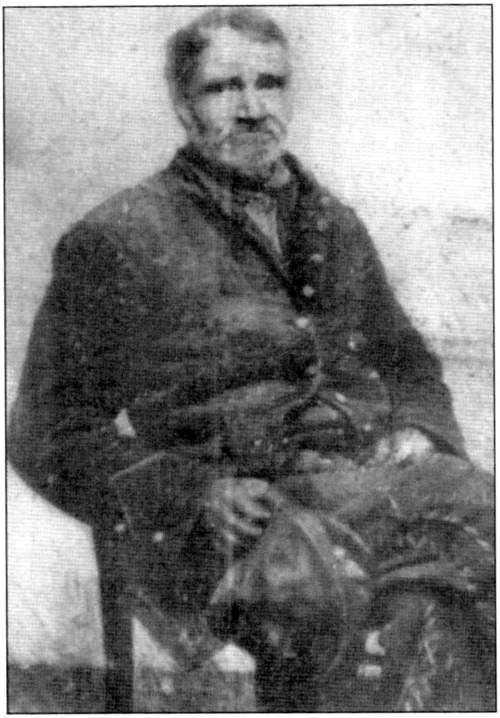

Ruben Folsom was an enigma; little is known about him. He arrived in Green County in 1841 and is thought to have been born in Canada. Ruben lived his life around Albany and spent most of his years here living in a cave, known as Ruben's Cave, which was located on the west bank of the Sugar River. When Ruben died in 1870, he was buried on a hillside between Albany and Monticello. Several years later, the citizens of Albany purchased a marker and moved his body to the Gap Church Cemetery. (Albany Historical Society.)

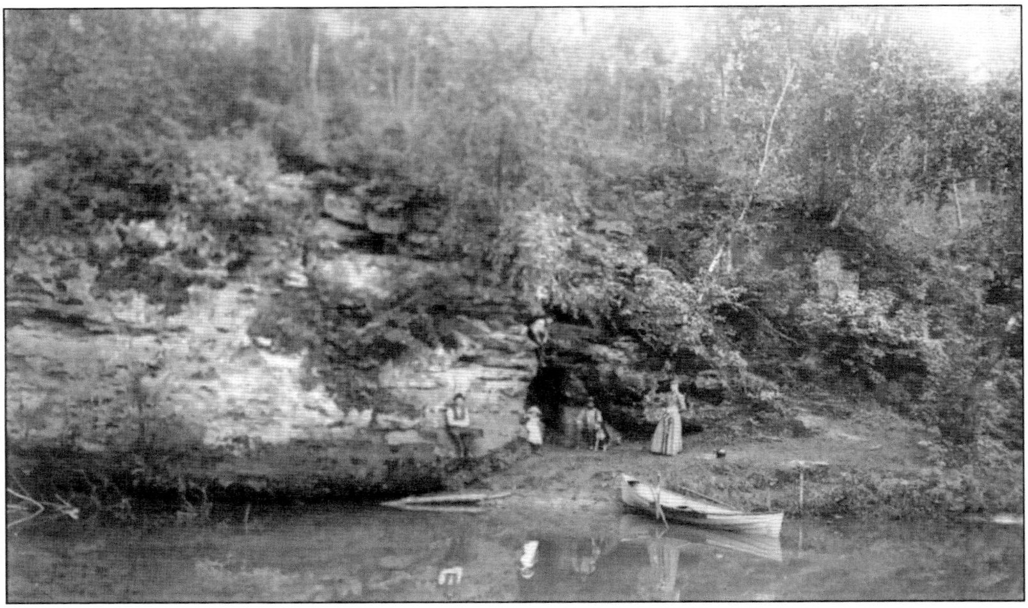

This is the cave that Ruben Folsom called his home for many years. As can be seen in this photograph, Ruben's Cave became a place to explore on leisurely Sunday afternoon canoe and rowboat trips on Lake Winnetka. There is a public access to Ruben's Cave. Ruben, despite being somewhat of a recluse, was well respected in the Albany area and a welcome visitor to most homes in the area. He made his living by hunting wolves for the bounty money. (Albany Historical Society.)

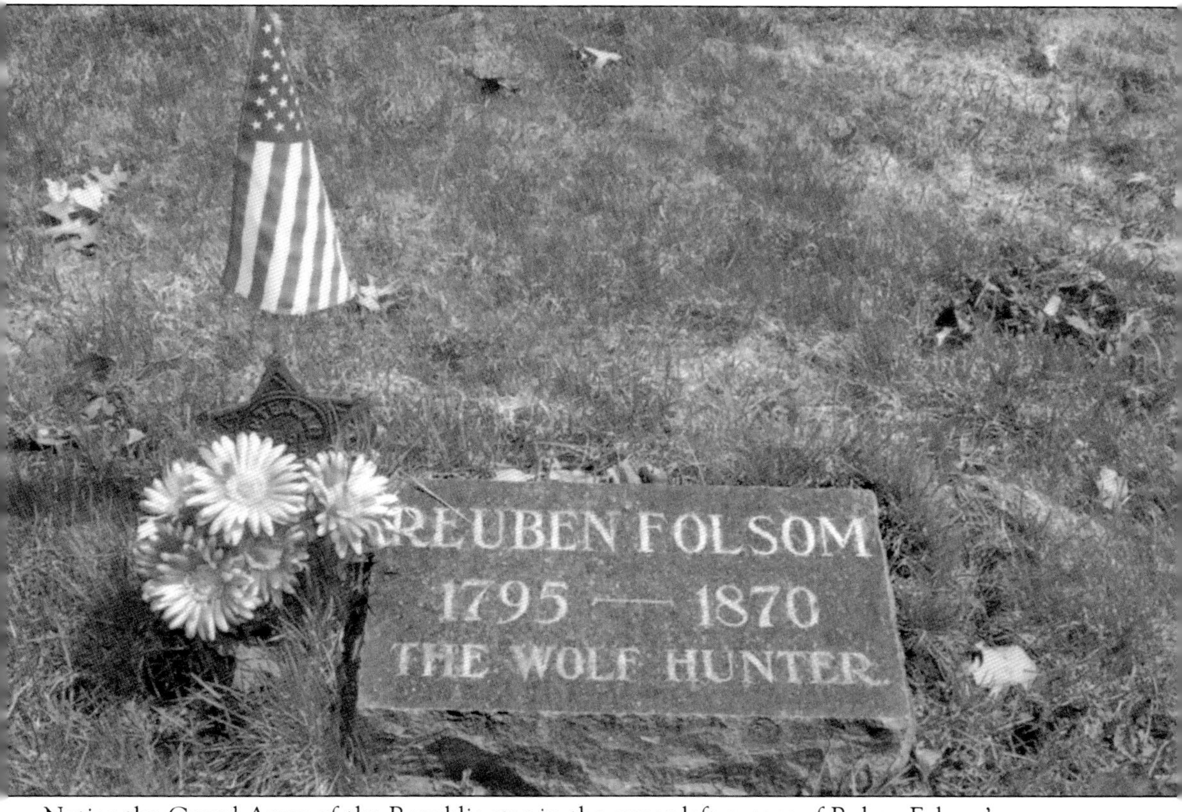

Notice the Grand Army of the Republic star in the upper left corner of Ruben Folsom's grave marker. The photograph of Folsom on the previous page shows him in a military coat. He was at one time in the U.S. Army and also served in the Union Army during the Civil War. He was at least 61 years of age when he enlisted in the latter.

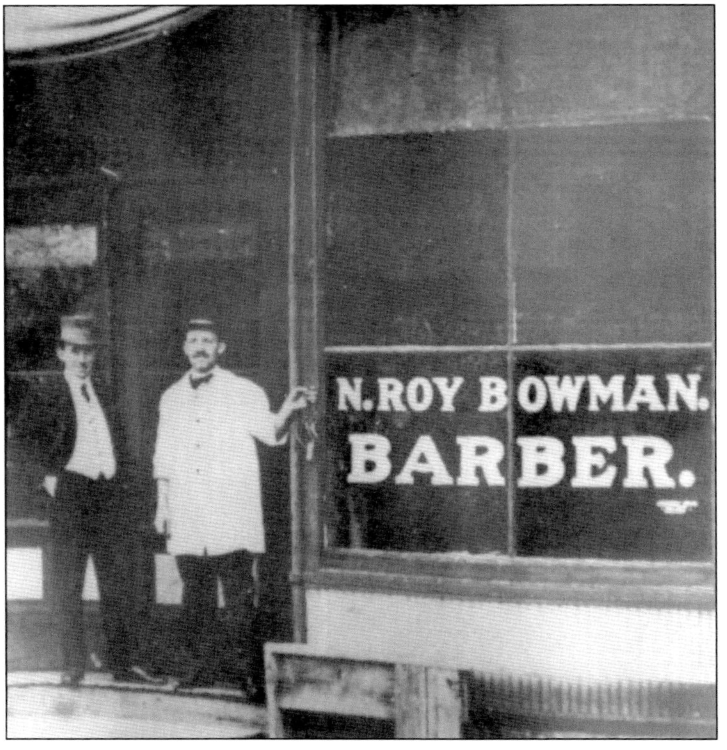

Roy Bowman was a legend in Green County for his 70 years of service to Albany and the surrounding area, not only for his barbershop operation but also for his lifelong community service. Roy moved to Albany from Lodi, Wisconsin, in 1898 when he purchased his barbershop from a Mr. Wagner. Bowman's shop was located on the corner of Main and South Water Streets, but some time later he moved the shop one door south. (Albany Historical Society.)

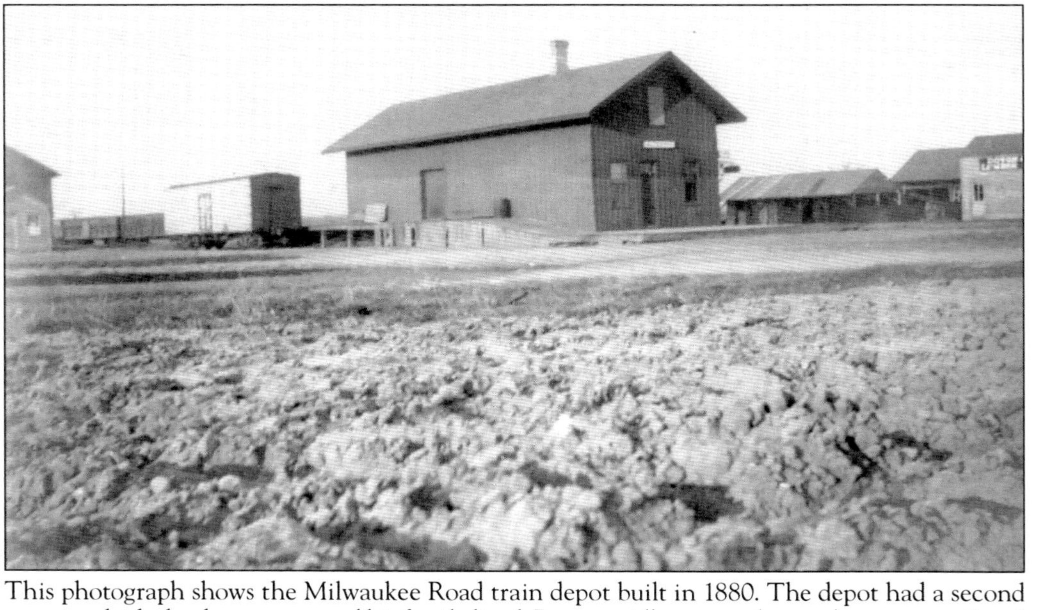

This photograph shows the Milwaukee Road train depot built in 1880. The depot had a second story in which the depot agent and his family lived. Because Albany was the northern-most railroad stop in this part of Green County, the village became an important shipping point for area cattle as well as the final stop for many carloads of hay, grain, lumber, and other necessities needed for the rapidly growing dairy industry in Green County. The depot fell victim to an arsonist after it was sold by the railroad to Robert Atkinson. (Albany Historical Society.)

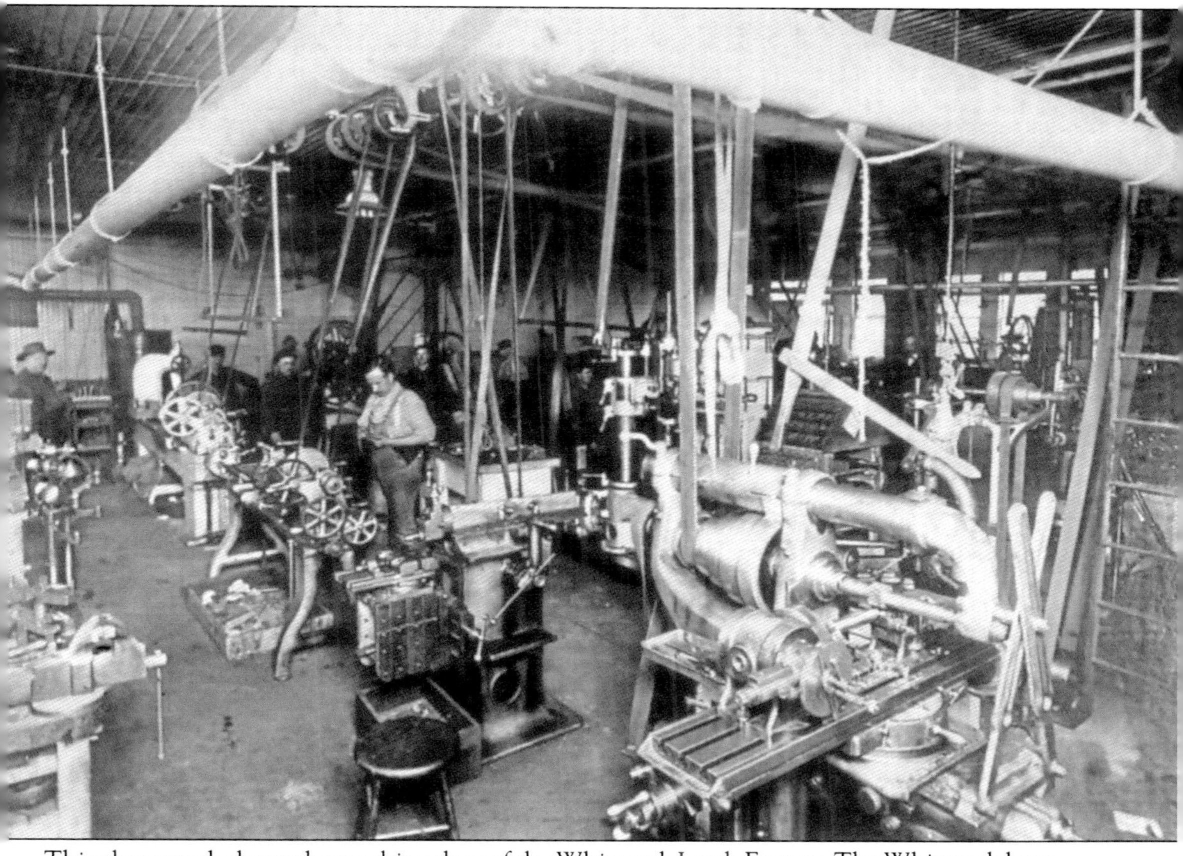

This photograph shows the machine shop of the Whitcomb Latch Factory. The Whitcomb barn-door latch was invented by Dr. Saxxton Morgan and his brother-in-law Harris M. Whitcomb and patented in 1896. Dr. Morgan invented the latch after he regularly came across barn and farm shed doors being kept shut with pieces of wire or twine. The business was sold to Fred Rust in 1957 and moved to Viroqua, Wisconsin, where it was operated by Rust's son Tom. (Albany Historical Society.)

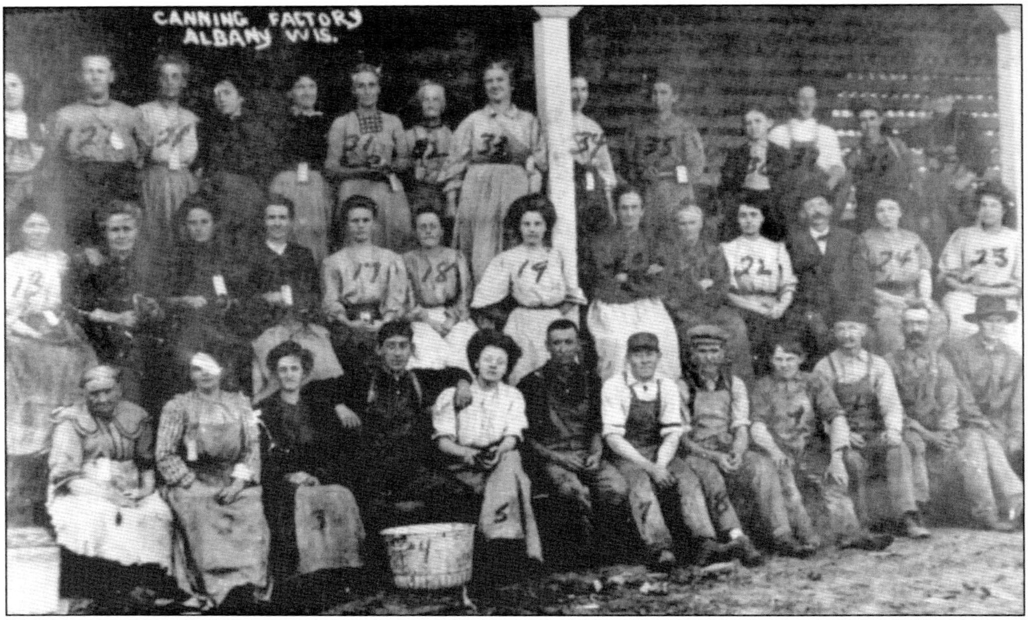

This *c.* 1915 photograph shows the crew at the tomato-canning factory in Albany. Specialty crops such as peas, beans, corn, and tomatoes were often grown on area farms as cash crops. Factories such as this one provided good seasonal jobs for area residents. (Albany Historical Society.)

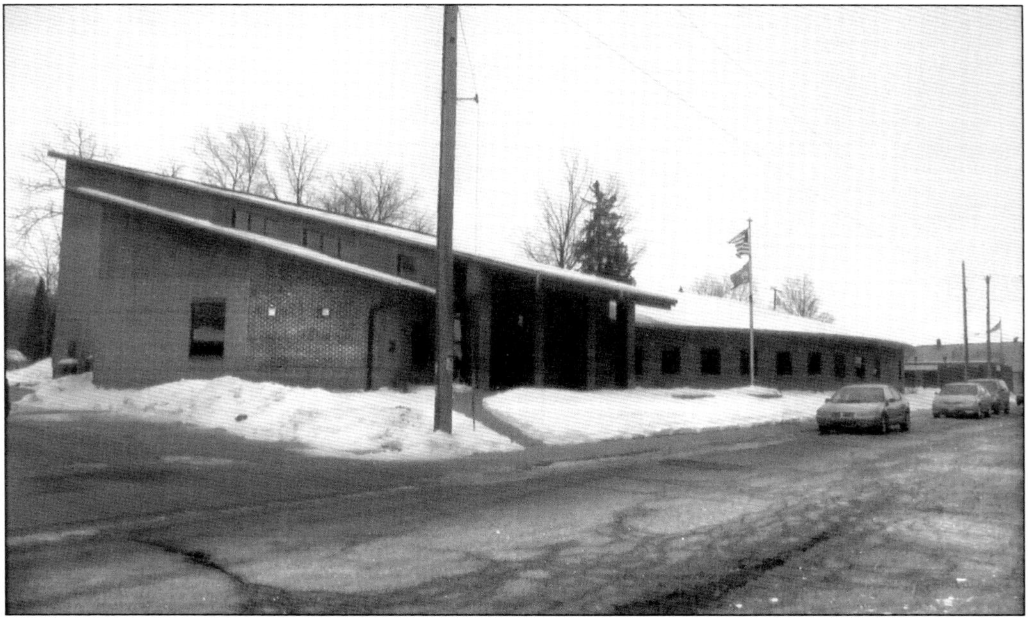

In 2006, the family of Wayne and Eleanor Albertson donated $1 million to fund the beautiful new Albertson Family Public Library, replacing a very old and cramped space. The Albertson family has roots that date back to the early 1850s in what is still known as the Norwegian settlement located northwest of Albany. The Albertson family was successful in their farming, real estate, insurance, and auction businesses. Their contributions to the village of Albany represent the epitome of the true spirit of community.

Two

BRODHEAD

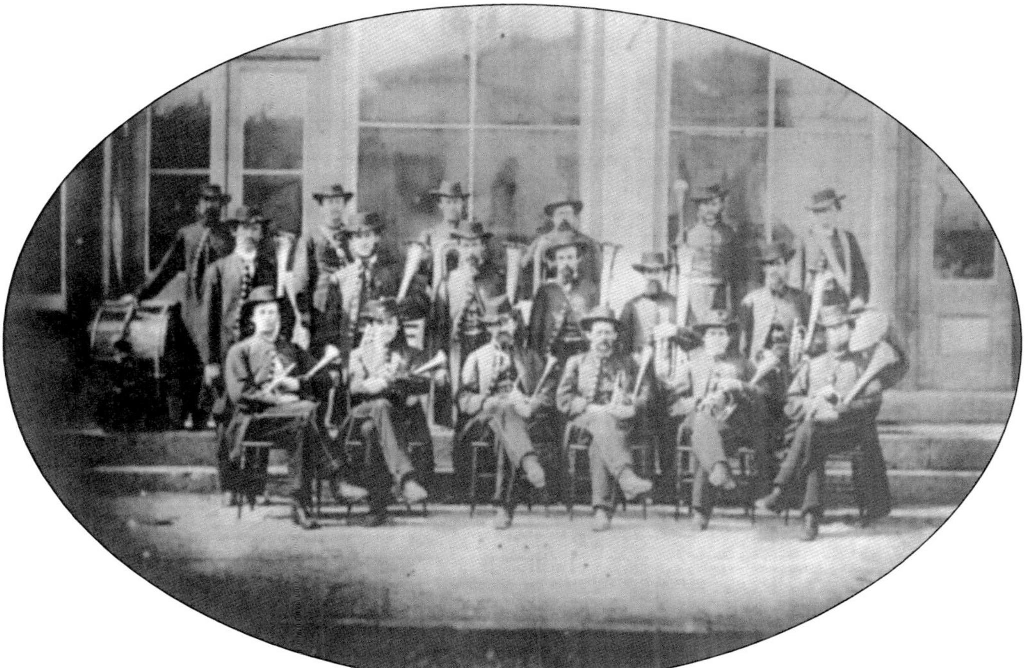

This 1864 photograph shows the Brodhead First Brigade Band members in their new uniforms at Janesville, Wisconsin, just before heading south to join Gen. William Sherman's troops on Sherman's March to the Sea. On the eve of the grand review in Washington after the war, Sherman stated, "My men will march in the grand review as they marched through the South—barefooted and ragged!" They marched proudly to the music of the Brodhead First Brigade Band. Seen here from left to right are (first row) John Faust, Edwin Kimberley, Gerald Kneeland, John Pickering, Thomas Brown, and Theodore Pomeroy; (second row) George Spaulding, Horace Moore, Fred Knickerbocker, Joe Smith, Charles Clark, and Beam Snow; (third row) Emmet Flood, Alfred Mason, C. C. Stone, Norman Hall, John Jackson, and Jacob Brant. (Brodhead Historical Society.)

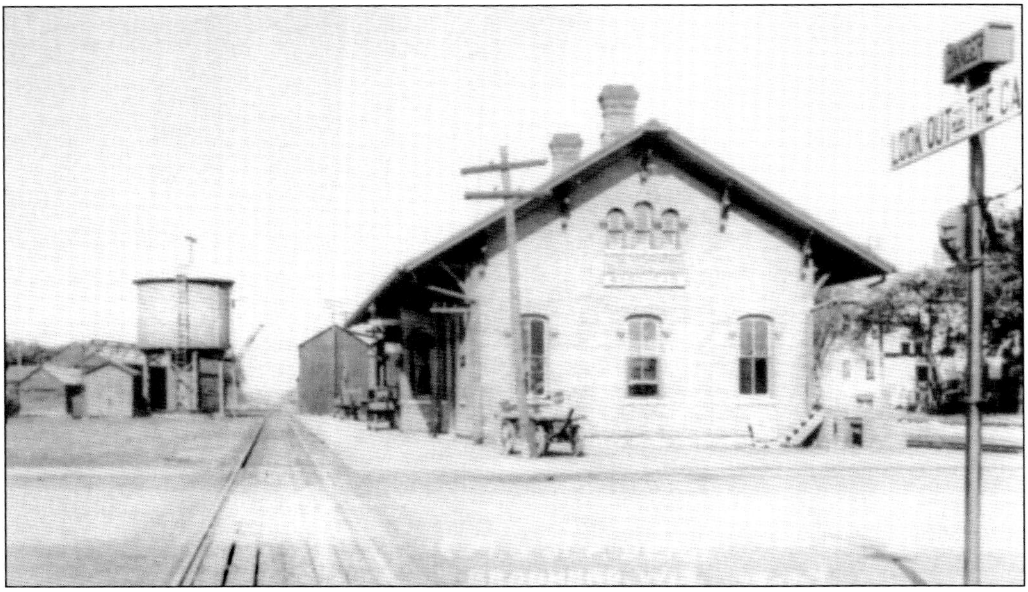

Here is Brodhead's Milwaukee Road train depot. This second depot to serve the area was built in the 1880s. For many years, the depot served the transportation needs of Brodhead and the many manufacturing and agricultural needs of the growing community. After the Milwaukee Road shuttered the doors of this depot, the Brodhead Historical Society purchased and restored it to its original look. Today the depot houses a beautiful museum as well as a Milwaukee Road caboose and a Fairbanks Morse locomotive that was built in nearby Beloit, Wisconsin. Look at the railroad crossing sign on the far right side of the photograph, reading, "Look out for the cars." (Brodhead Historical Society.)

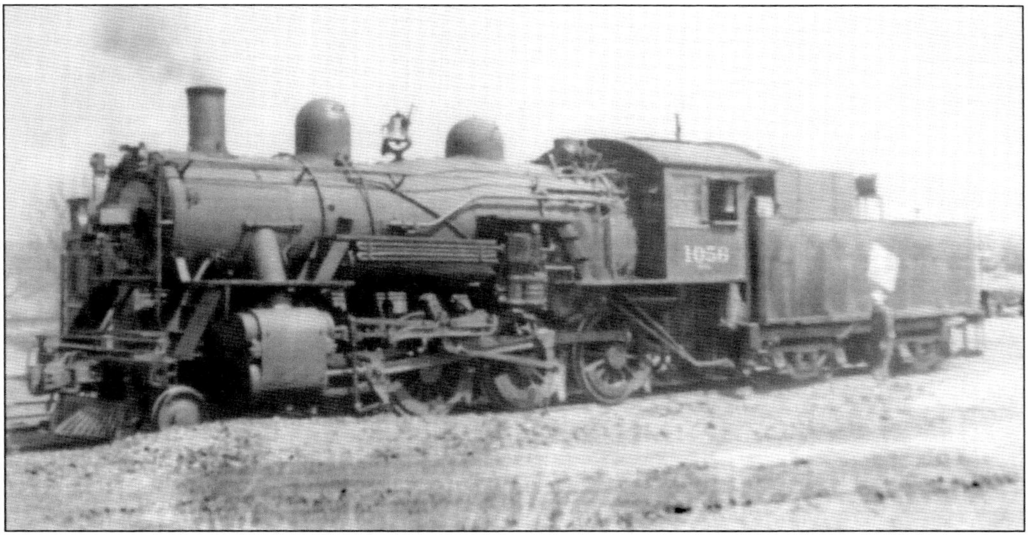

This pre-1918 photograph shows a locomotive built in 1885 at the Milwaukee Road shops in Milwaukee. It served for a number of years on the Pacific Northwest line of the Milwaukee Road. The locomotive was brought back to the Midwest to live out its useful life before being scrapped out. Steam engines such as this one were excellent workhorses on the branchline from Brodhead to New Glarus. (Brodhead Historical Society.)

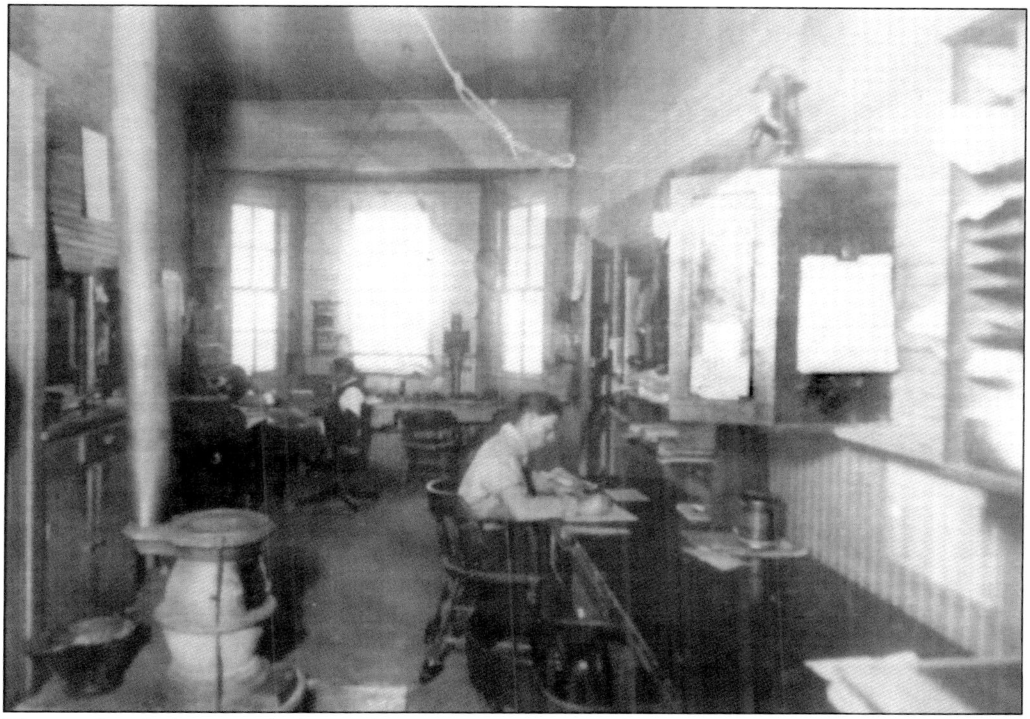

This undated photograph shows the operator's room at the Brodhead depot. The man in the foreground is the station clerk whose job it was to fill out waybills, billing statements, and other necessary paperwork for orderly operation of the railroad. The window area in the photograph was the agent/operator's bay window where he sat and watched the train movements to ensure the safety of train operation. (Brodhead Historical Society.)

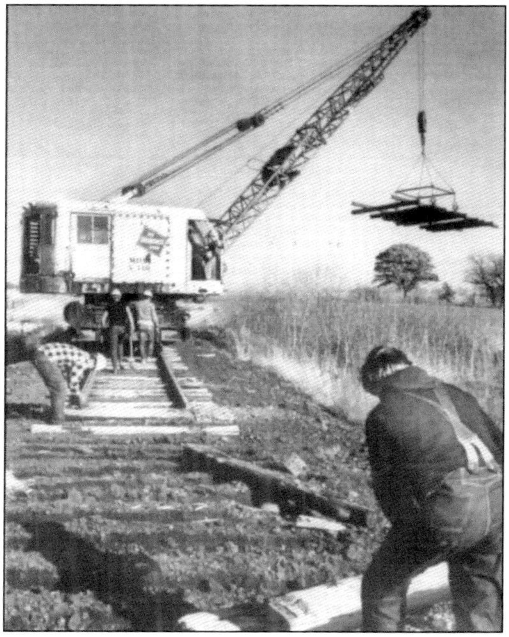

It was a sad day for Green County in the early spring of 1972 when the Milwaukee Road Railroad announced that it was terminating rail service on the Brodhead-to-New Glarus branchline due to a decline in business. In earlier years, because of all the milk and cheese shipped from Albany, Monticello, and New Glarus, this was the second-most profitable branchline operated by the railroad. The Wisconsin Department of Natural Resources purchased the railroad right-of-way and built what would become the Sugar River State Trail. (Brodhead Historical Society.)

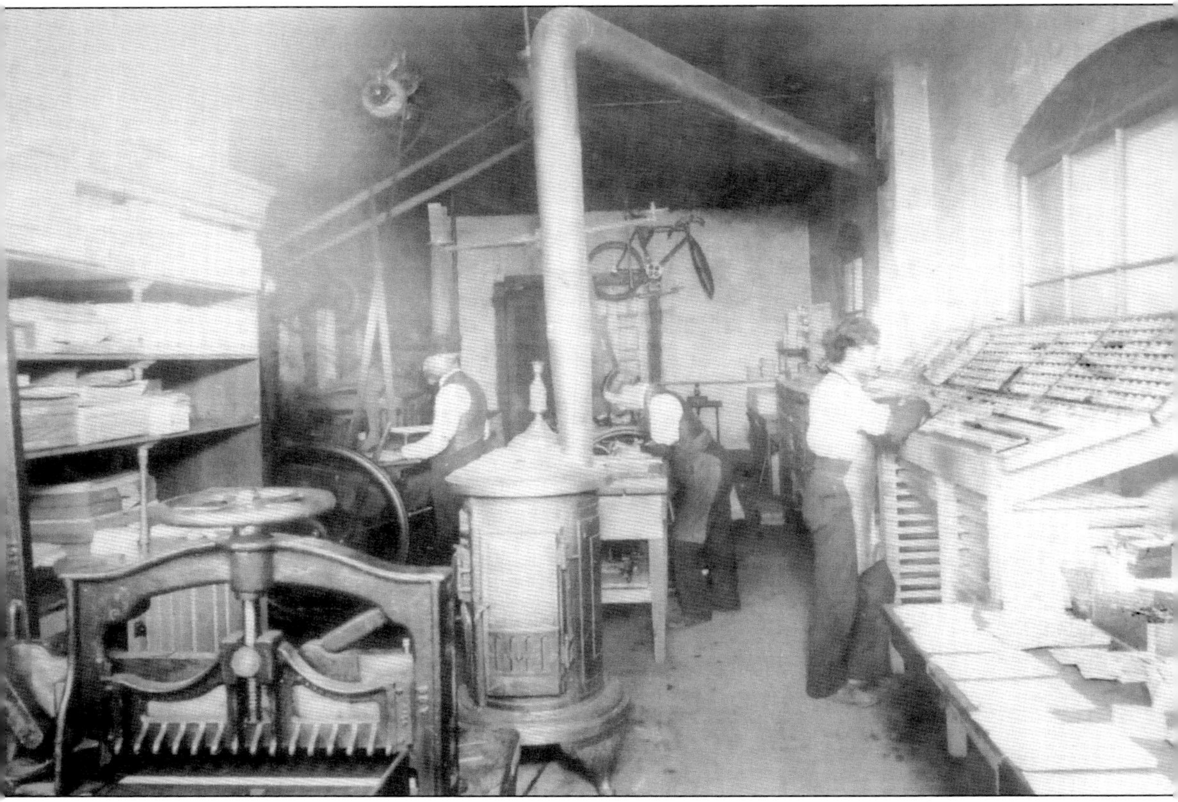

This undated photograph shows the interior of a Brodhead print shop. The machine in the foreground is a large paper cutter used to cut the sheets of paper shown on the shelves on the far left. The man on the right is hand-setting the type. Each letter had to be inserted individually into a lock-up sheet, and it had to be done backward so that it would appear properly on the printed page. Once a person has heard the sound of the press running and smelled printer's ink, he or she will never forget the smell and sound of a print shop. (Brodhead Historical Society.)

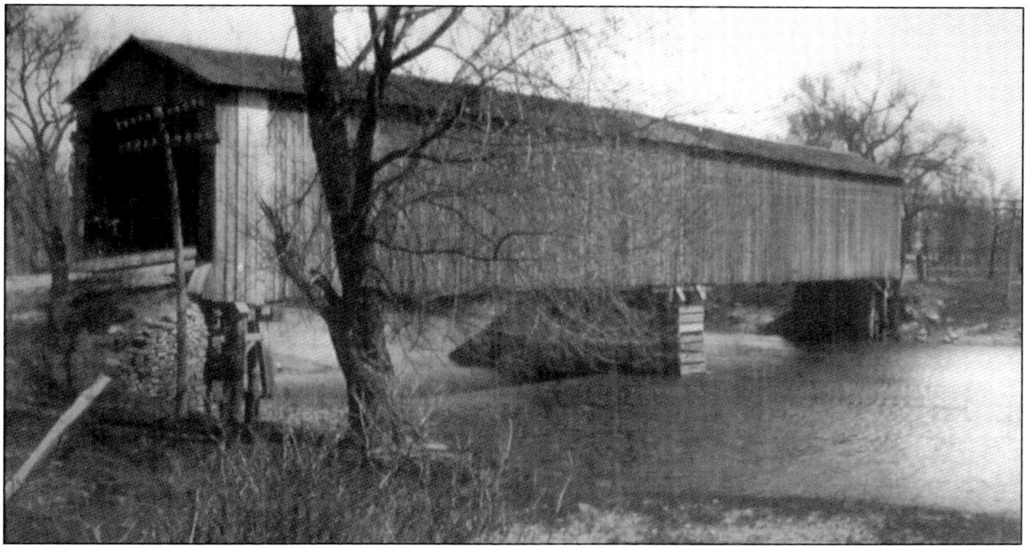

Located west of Brodhead, the Clarence Bridge was probably the longest covered bridge in Green County, stretching 150 feet across the Sugar River on what was Highway 61. Conflicting reports have the bridge built in either 1864 or 1866. In its early years, the bridge was open and later covered but never painted. The Clarence Bridge was replaced with a more modern span by 1927. Clarence Bridge County Park is near where the bridge originally stood. The Brodhead Jaycees built a replica of the Clarence Bridge just north of Brodhead on the Sugar River State Trail. (Brodhead Historical Society.)

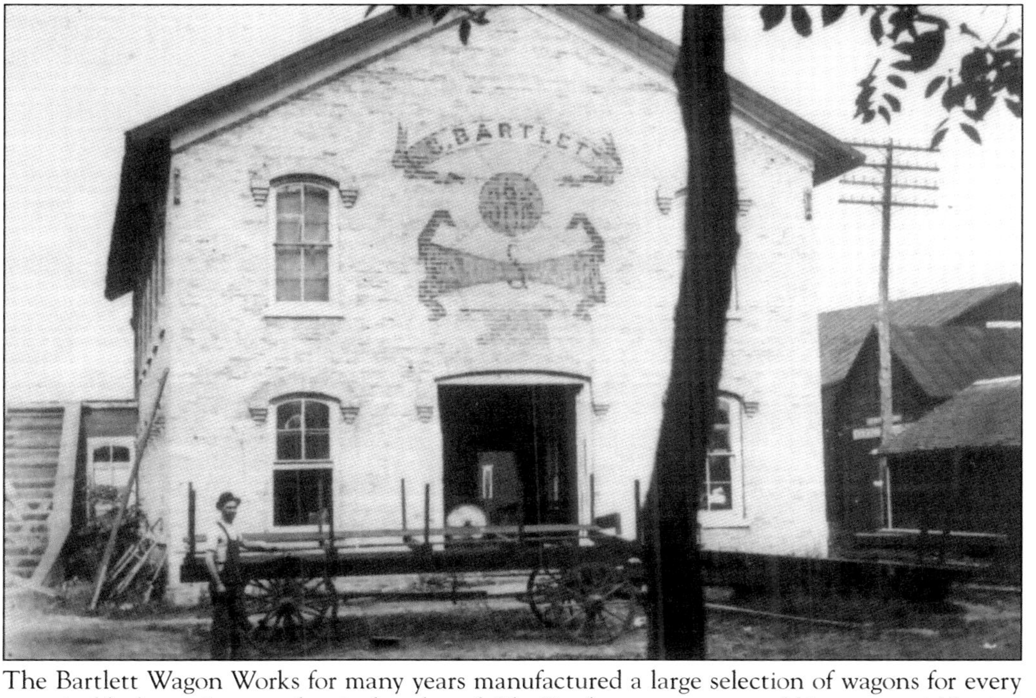

The Bartlett Wagon Works for many years manufactured a large selection of wagons for every conceivable domestic use and agricultural need. The Bartlett wagons were sold in many neighboring towns. This building is still in use today. (Brodhead Historical Society.)

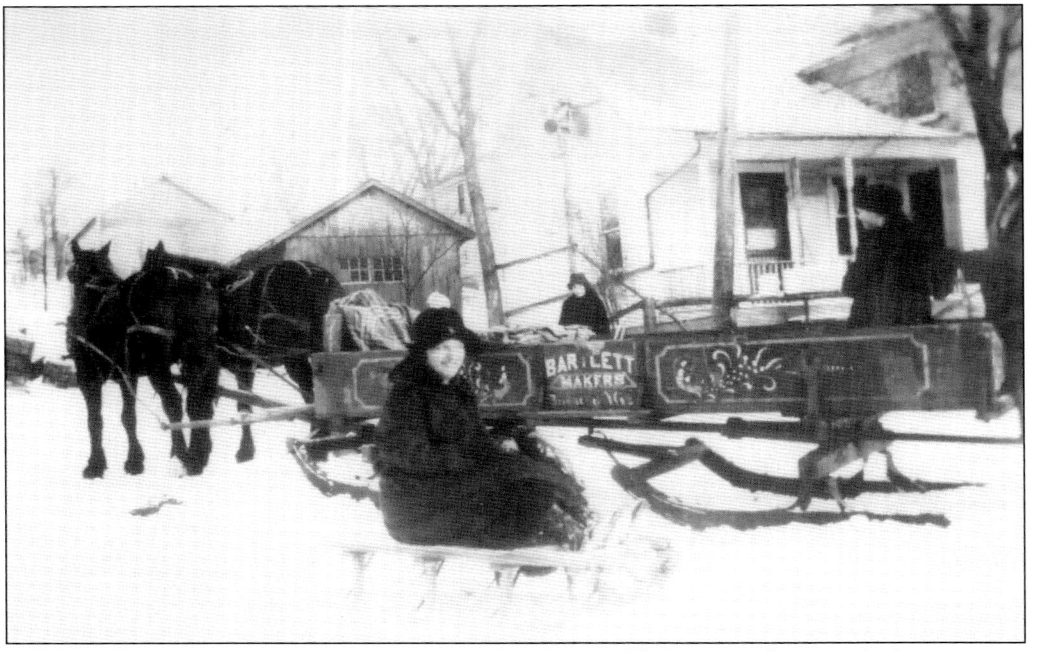

This winter photograph shows a Bartlett Wagon Works sleigh ready for use. Notice the fine artwork on the sides of the sleigh. The artwork that is often found on the sides of old farm equipment such as this sleigh highlights the fine craftsmanship that went into the construction of each wagon built at the Bartlett shop. Judging from their clothing, this family is preparing for a trip to church. (Brodhead Historical Society.)

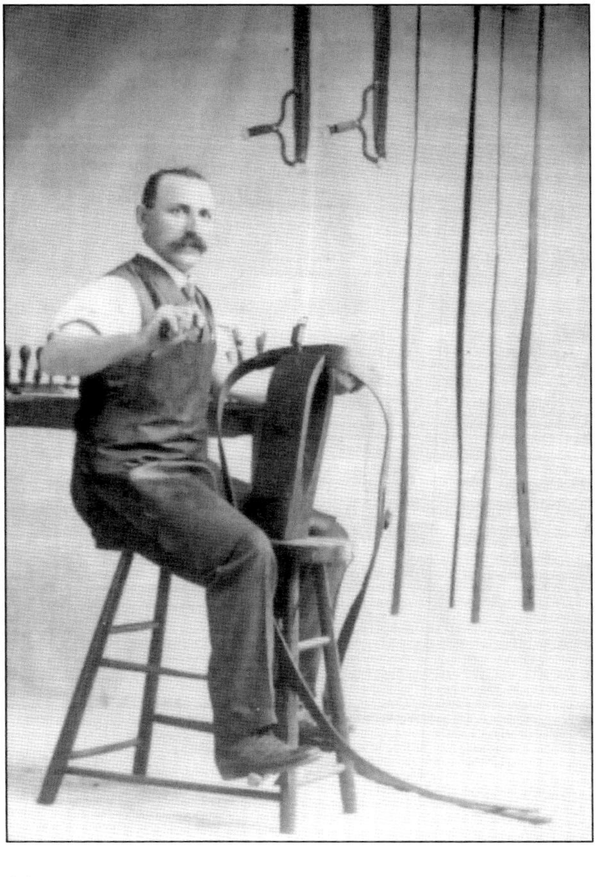

The local harness maker is shown here creating a new set for a customer. Harness makers were artisans in the fine work they produced. It took many years to learn the trade. In most towns, the harness maker is a distant memory in the oldest of the citizens, but an Amish settlement just north of Brodhead has a harness maker still plying his trade. (Brodhead Historical Society.)

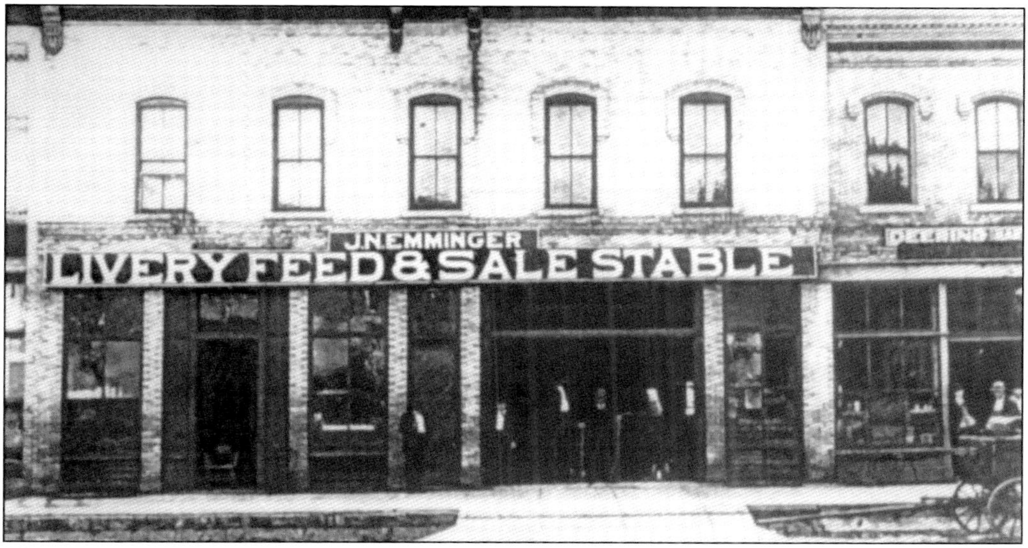

The J. N. Emminger Livery, Feed, and Sales Stable was located in downtown Brodhead. Each town had one or more livery stables to cater to both local needs and those of travelers. With its location just a short walk from the train depot, this Brodhead business was no doubt a hub of activity providing horse and carriage rentals to traveling salesmen and entertainers. This building constructed of cream city brick is unlike most local stables, which were built of wood. No doubt there were several small professional offices located on the stable's second floor. (Brodhead Historical Society.)

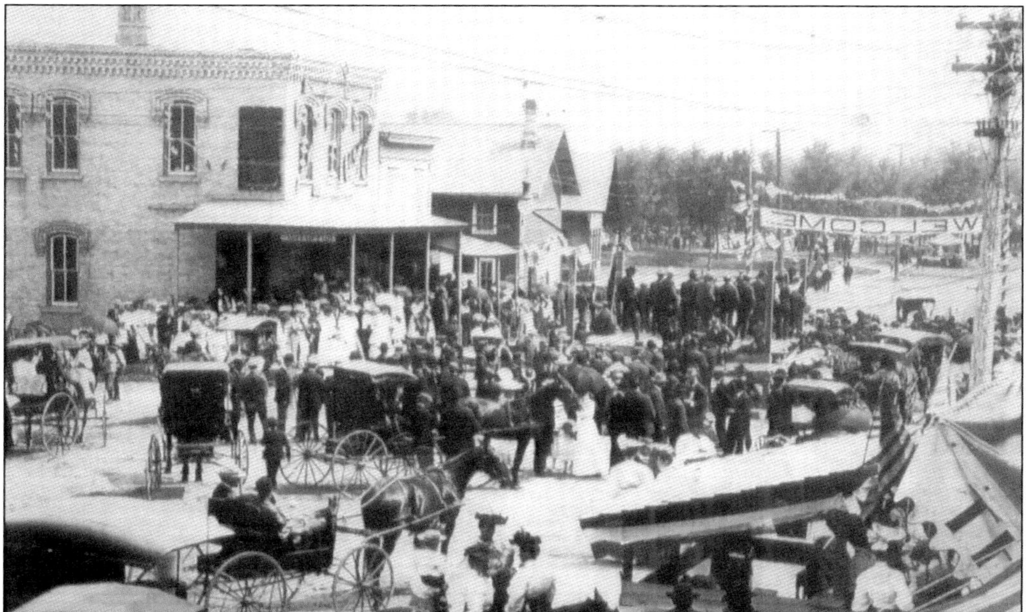

Downtown Brodhead is shown here hosting what appears to be the town's annual Fourth of July celebration. Behind the large welcome banner is the park that appears to have a number of small tents set up for various activities of the day. The Brodhead Post Office was located in the large brick building. Notice also the fancy brickwork at the top of this building. (Brodhead Historical Society.)

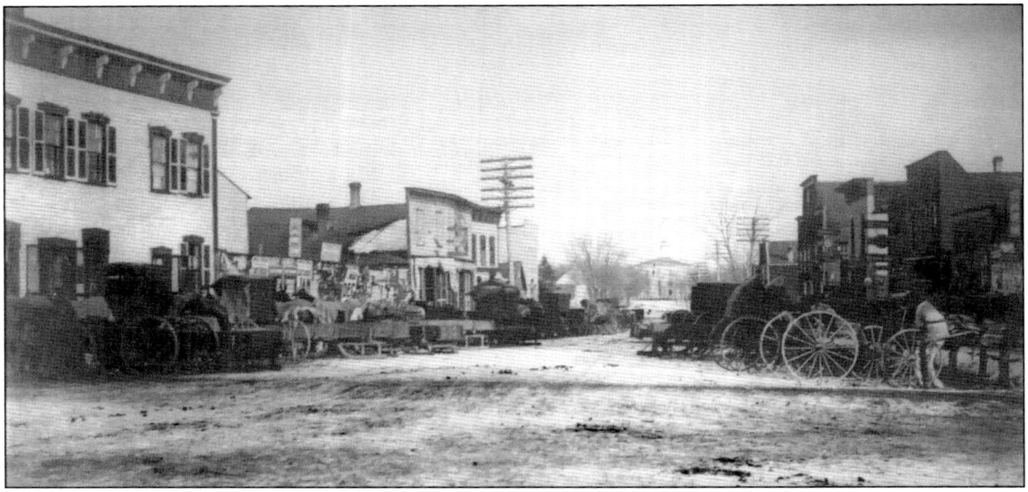

In this image, spring is in the air in downtown Brodhead. The farmers and their wives have come into town for market day. Those having to haul heavy items or live far out in the country have come in sleighs, and those living closer to Brodhead or on more-improved roads have driven a buggy to town. The buildings on the left side of the photograph are older than those on the right. The building on the far left is a rather stylish boomtown-fronted building with shutters on the windows and architectural adornments above them. (Brodhead Historical Society.)

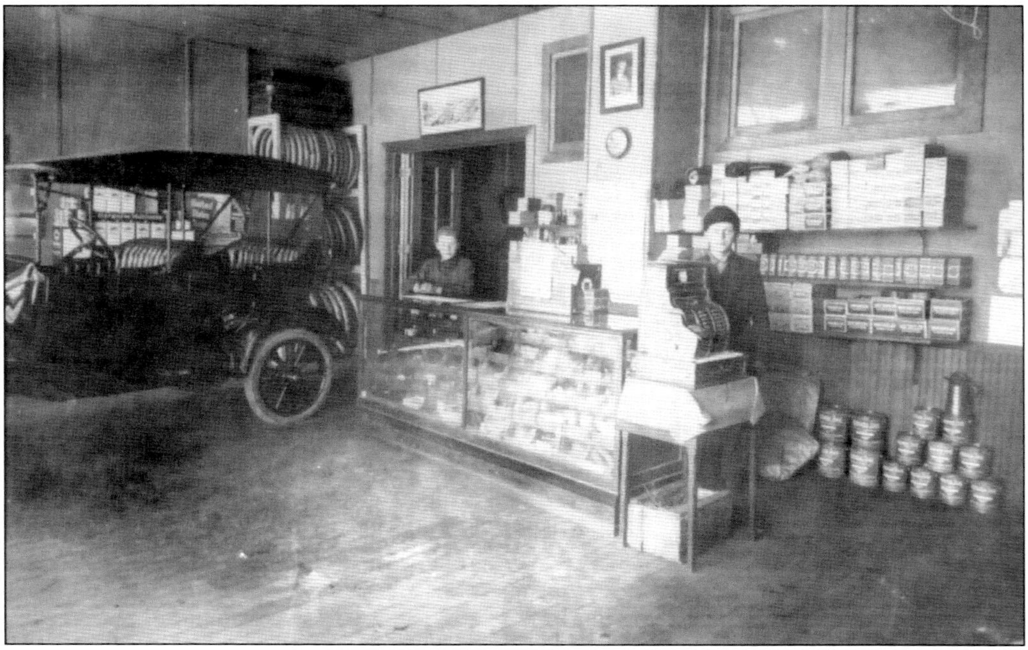

This subject of this photograph is probably the Ford dealership building in Brodhead. At this time, the showroom served not just as the showcase for the new cars but also did duty as the parts department. The large cans on the floor are filled with Valvoline motor oil. The boxes above the motor oil contain Michelin inner tubes, and the racks behind the new car hold tires made by the United States Tire Company. (Brodhead Historical Society.)

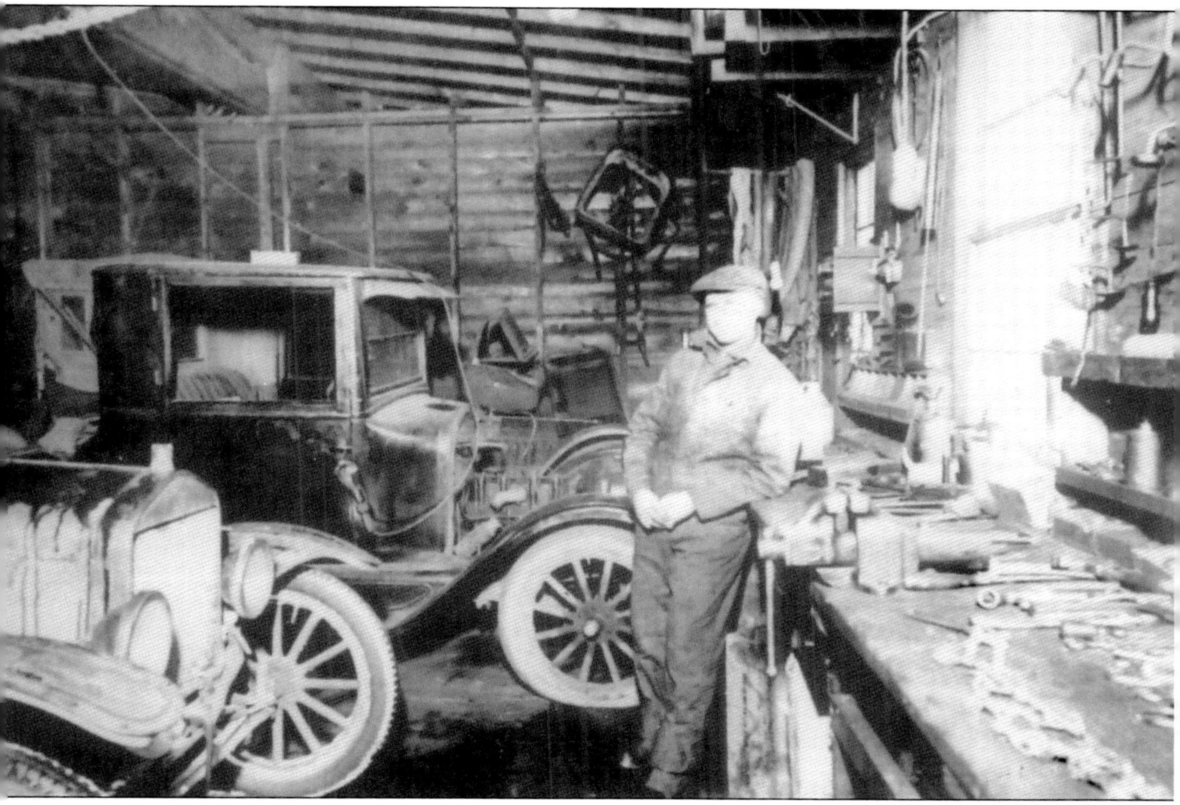

The back shop at the car dealer was an interesting place that was the fascination of every young boy who ever went with his dad to get the family automobile repaired. Automobiles such as the ones shown here often arrived on flatcars at the nearby railroad depot and were moved to the car dealer's back shop to be assembled for sale to the public. (Brodhead Historical Society.)

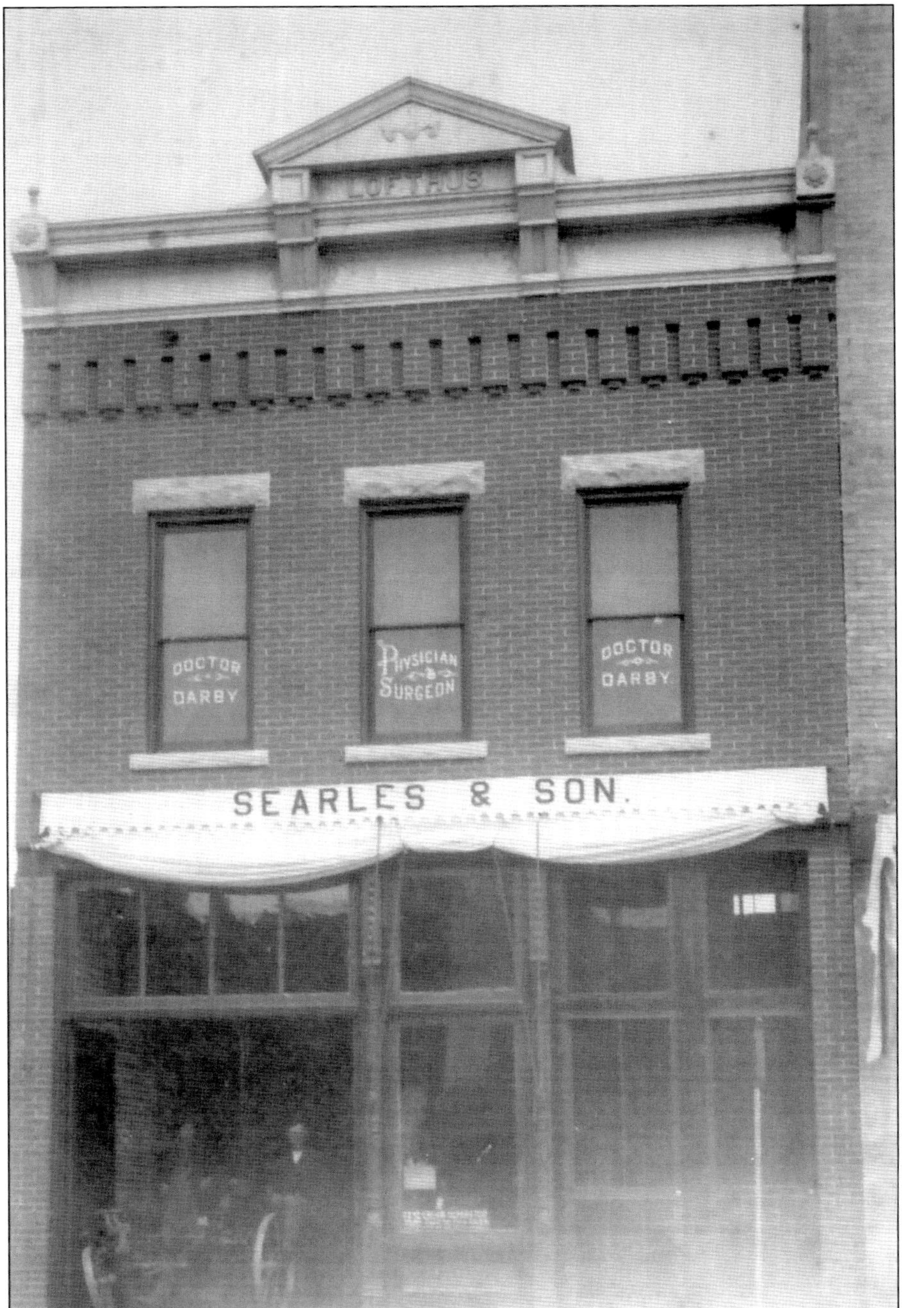

The Lofthus Building served both as an agricultural implement shop and as a doctor's office. The sign on the front door of the building advertises a brand of cream separators. At this time, many dairy farmers sold only their cream, choosing to keep the milk for home consumption and for their livestock. A Dr. Darby, physician and surgeon, had his office on the second-story storefront. In many cases, doctors and dentists lived in apartments behind their professional offices. (Brodhead Historical Society.)

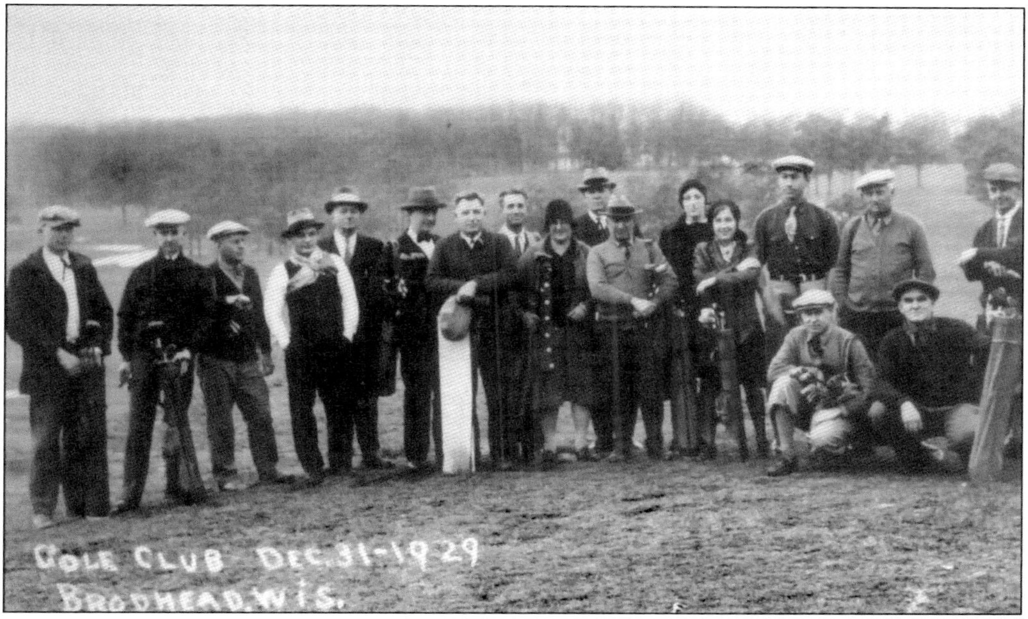

"The Best Golf Course by a Dam Site" is what the sign advertising Decatur Lake Country Club read. The golf club began in 1929 and still plays a major part in the social lives of many residents of Brodhead and the surrounding area. Decatur Lake was formed by damming the Sugar River to provide the power needed to run the businesses and light the homes of Brodhead. (Brodhead Historical Society.)

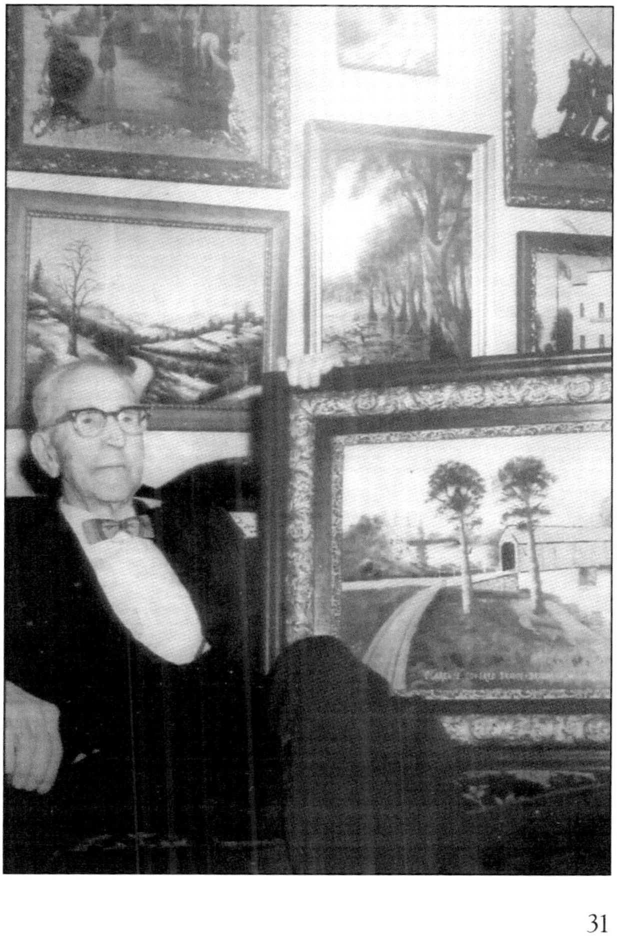

Frank Engebretson, born in 1897 near Gratiot, Wisconsin, made his adult home in Brodhead. He made his living as a home interior painter but became famous for his barn murals in Green and Lafayette County, Wisconsin. His first barn mural was an advertisement at the Jake Winn farm boasting fine Holstein cattle. During his lifetime, Engebretson painted over 2 miles of barn murals. One mural still adorns a barn near Woodford, Wisconsin. (Independent Register Print Center.)

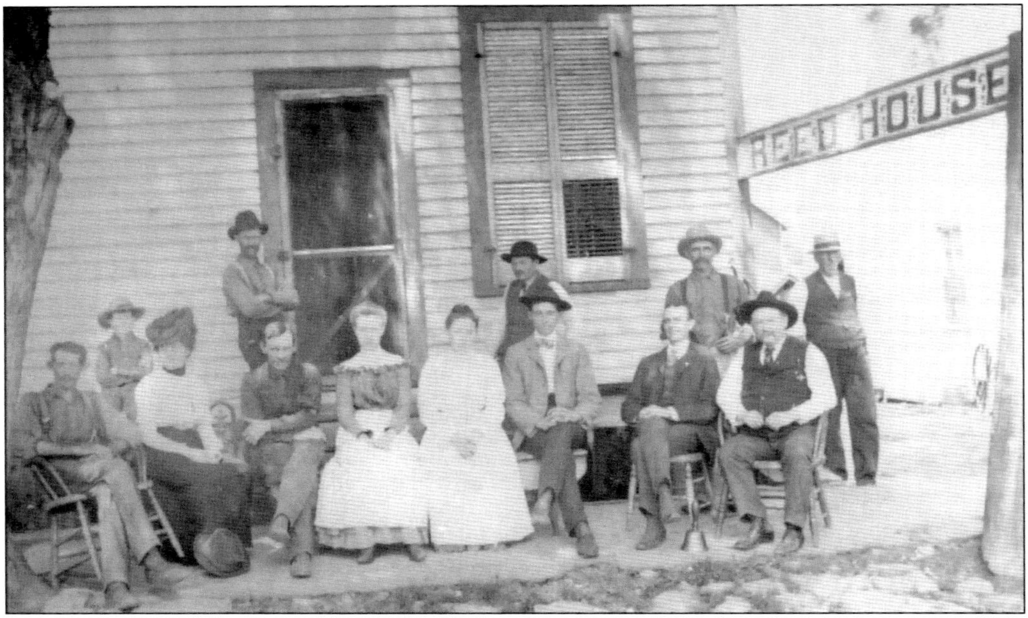

The Reed House Hotel in downtown Brodhead served a very important place in the town's fabric. People arriving via the nearby railroad needed a place where they could eat a good meal and find a comfortable room for an overnight stay. In some cases, hotels like the Reed House also provided rooms for traveling salesmen to use for displaying their wares—the newest items that promised to make life a bit easier. (Brodhead Historical Society.)

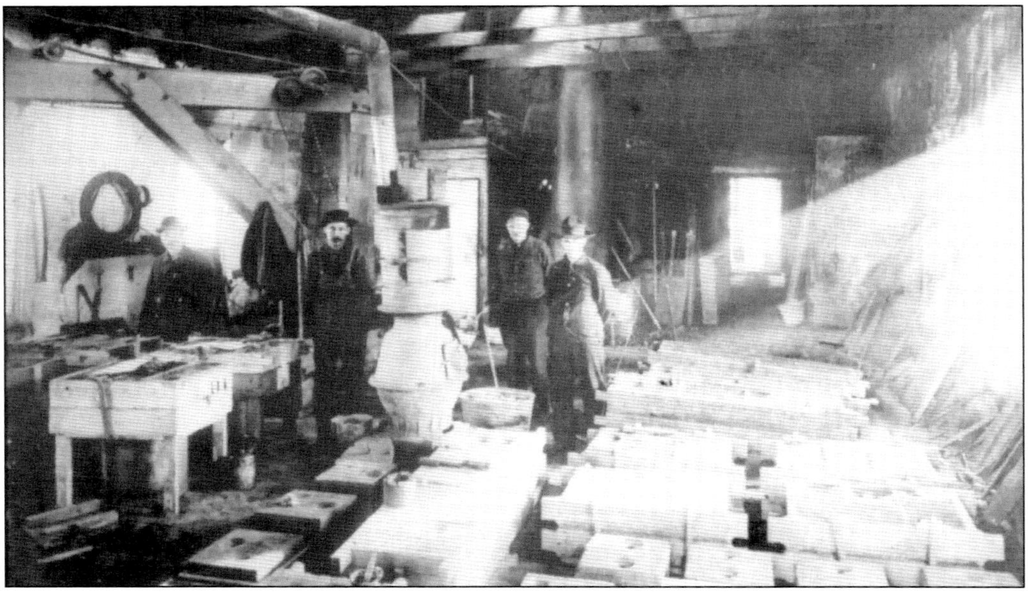

This photograph shows the employees of the Norwegian Plow Company foundry that began business in 1873. When operating at full capacity, the factory could turn out 25 plows each day. Because it was a regional shopping area, Brodhead was able to support a number of factories turning out agricultural equipment needed for the rapidly growing dairy business. (Brodhead Historical Society.)

Three

Browntown

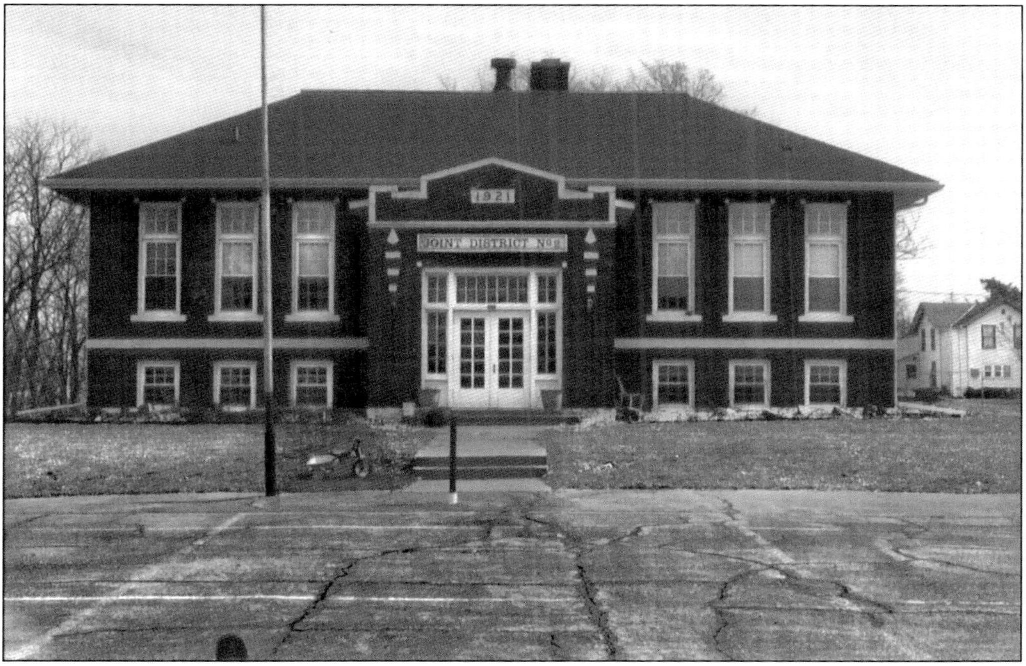

The Cadiz Township Joint School District No. 2 at 214 School Street was the most recent Browntown grade school and was built in 1920. The school this building replaced was used for a village jail for some years. It was constructed using Craftsman-style architecture and is now listed on the National Register of Historic Places. (Browntown Historical Society.)

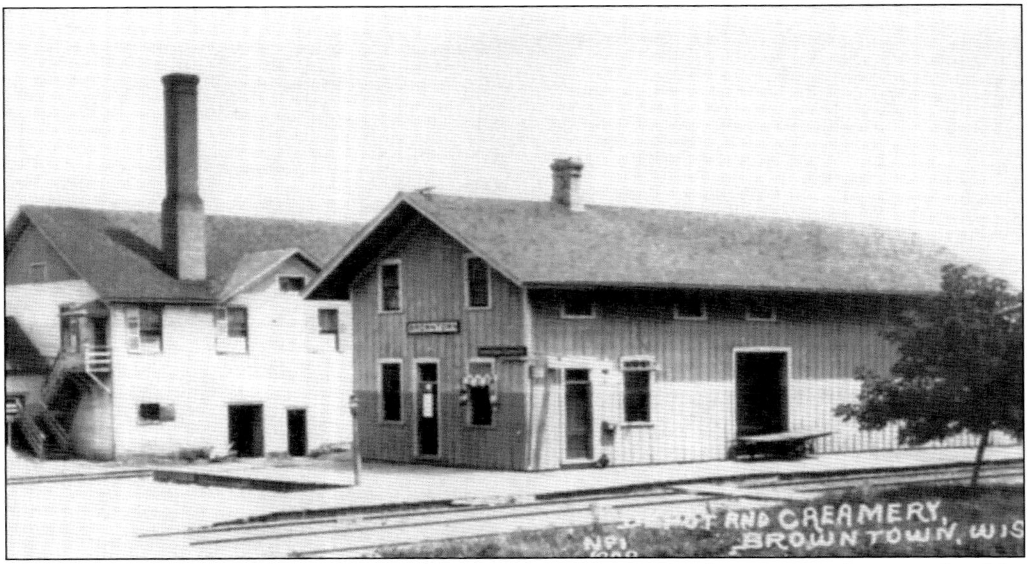

The Milwaukee Road railroad arrived in Browntown in 1882, bringing with it good public transportation and also a means of easily accessing materials and products from faraway places. The Browntown depot was a fairly common small-town depot, built with living quarters for the depot agent and his family. Two other communities on this line, South Wayne and Dunbarton, have similar depots. The building in the background is the creamery. (Browntown Historical Society.)

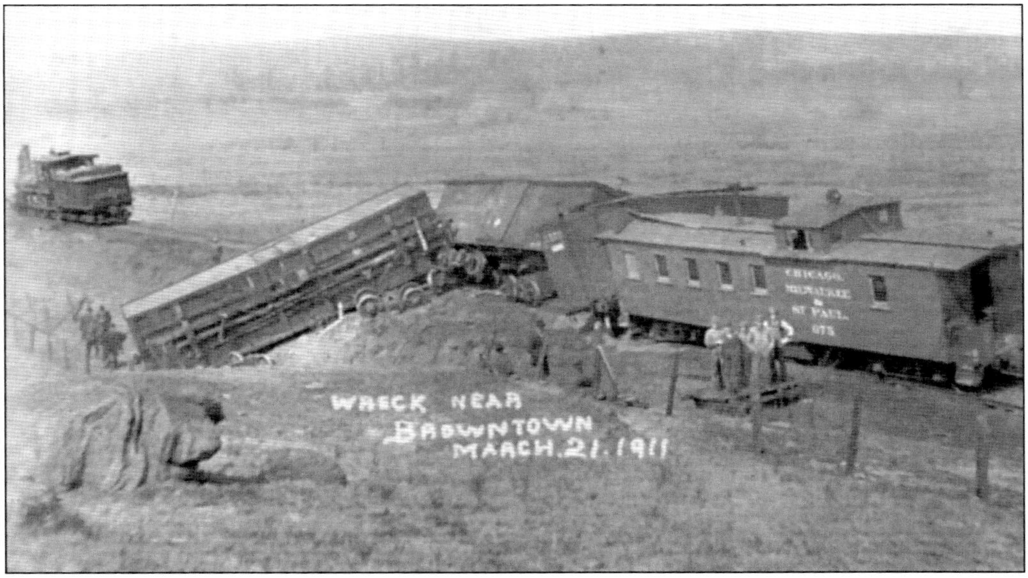

Train wrecks were a cause for excitement; large crowds of spectators came to see for themselves the piled-up cars. The men standing on the small section car next to the caboose are probably the crew that has just arrived to survey the damage and telegraph back to the main office for the necessary cranes and other equipment that will be required to repair the tracks and set the cars back on them so that business will not be interrupted. (Browntown Historical Society.)

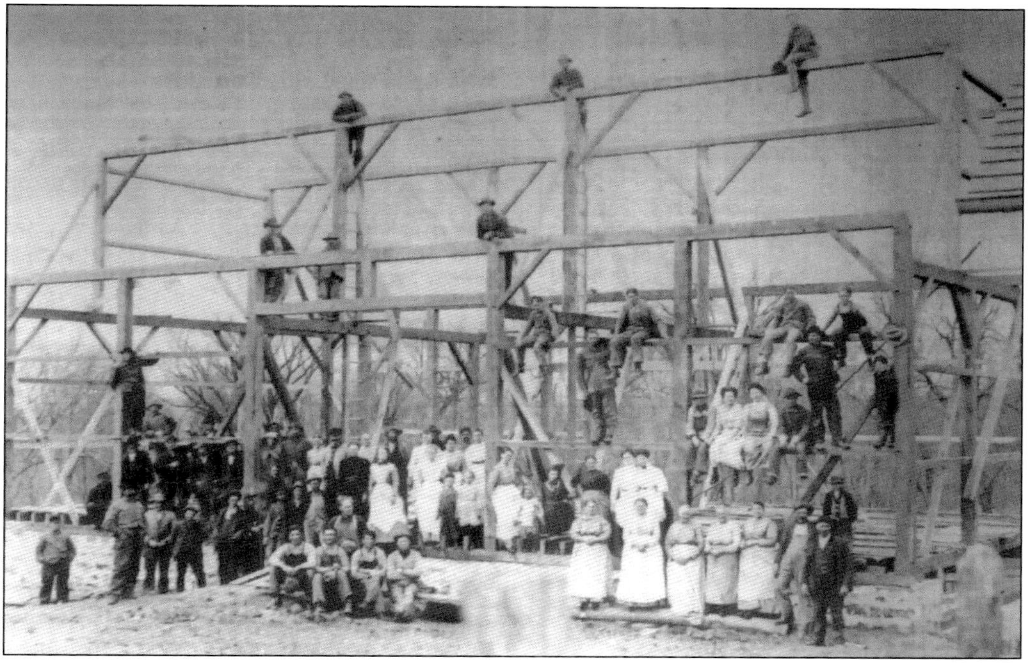

When a farmer needed a new barn, a barn raising was held. The neighbors pitched in for a day or two to get the new barn built. Most of the timbers shown here were pre-cut and drilled so that when the crew arrived the barn would go up quickly. By the end of the first day, the timberwork was completed. The following day, the crews came back to side and roof the barn. The wives gathered in the farmhouse to make a huge meal for their hungry husbands. (Browntown Historical Society.)

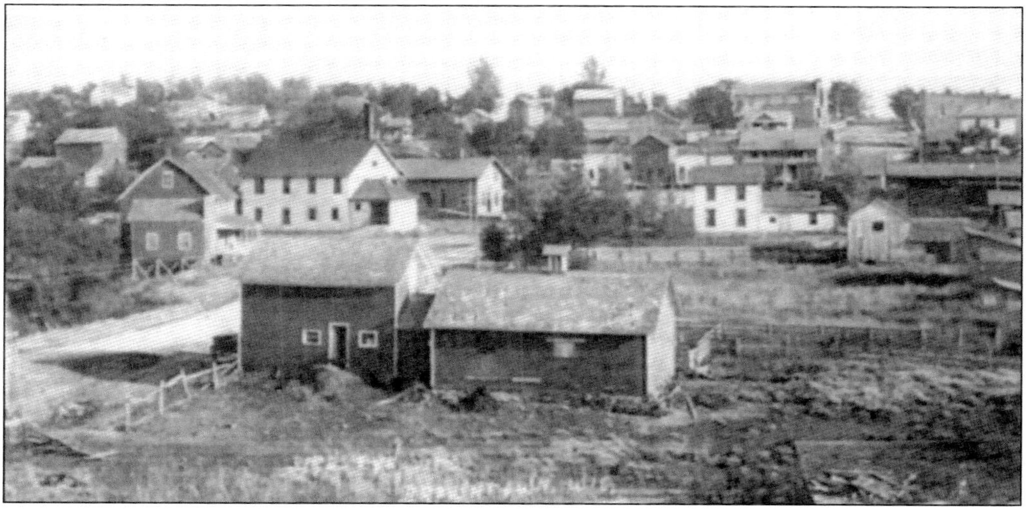

This overview of Browntown shows much of the town as it existed in the early 1900s. The taller half of the barn in the foreground is believed to have been moved to a farm near Monroe. The building on the left side of the road is the mill that was powered by water provided by damming Skinner Creek. (Browntown Historical Society.)

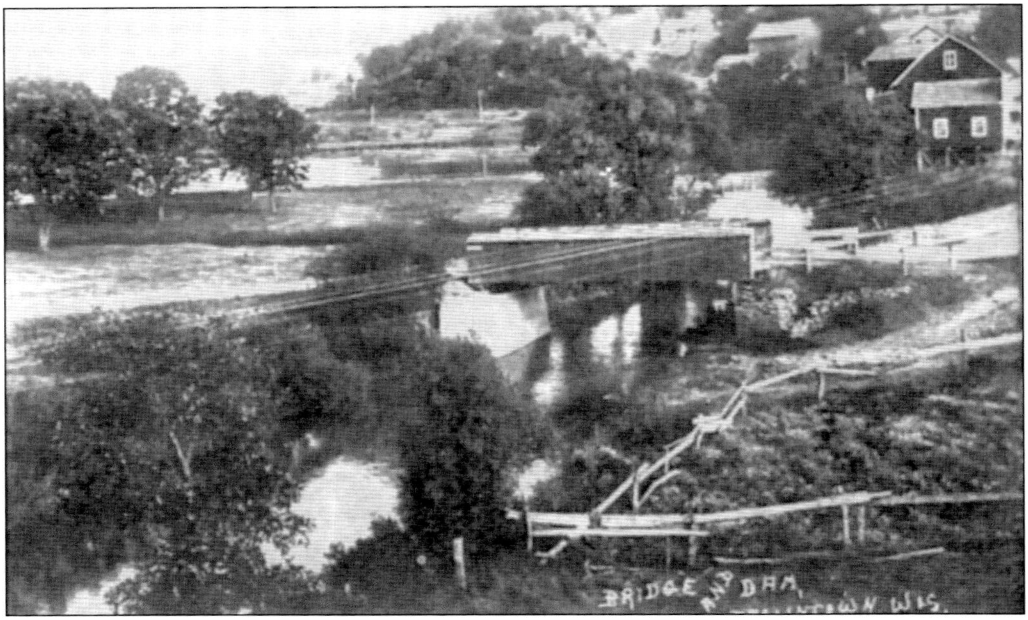

This photograph showing the covered bridge spanning Skinner Creek dates to the early 1900s. By this time, Browntown had electric power as is evidenced by the power poles and wires in the photograph. In the background are the mill, dam, and millpond, which provided a place for winter skating but also ice for the local icehouse. (Browntown Historical Society.)

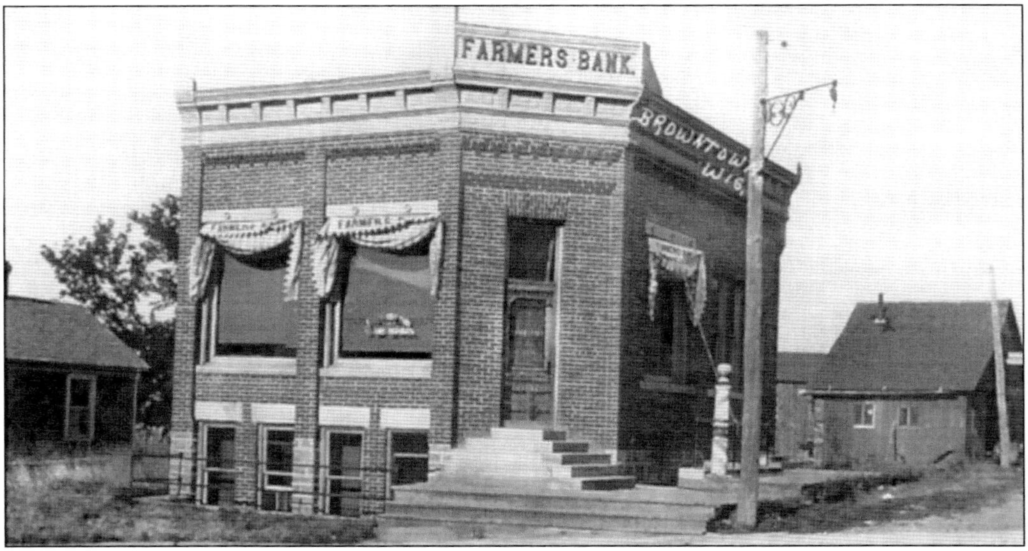

The Farmers and Merchants Bank located at the corner of South Mill Street and East Main Street was the first bank in Browntown. It closed during the Great Depression. During its lifetime, this building housed a number of businesses including a tavern and a pool hall. The building was torn down in the 1980s. For a number of years, the Commercial and Savings Bank of Monroe had a branch bank in Browntown. (Browntown Historical Society.)

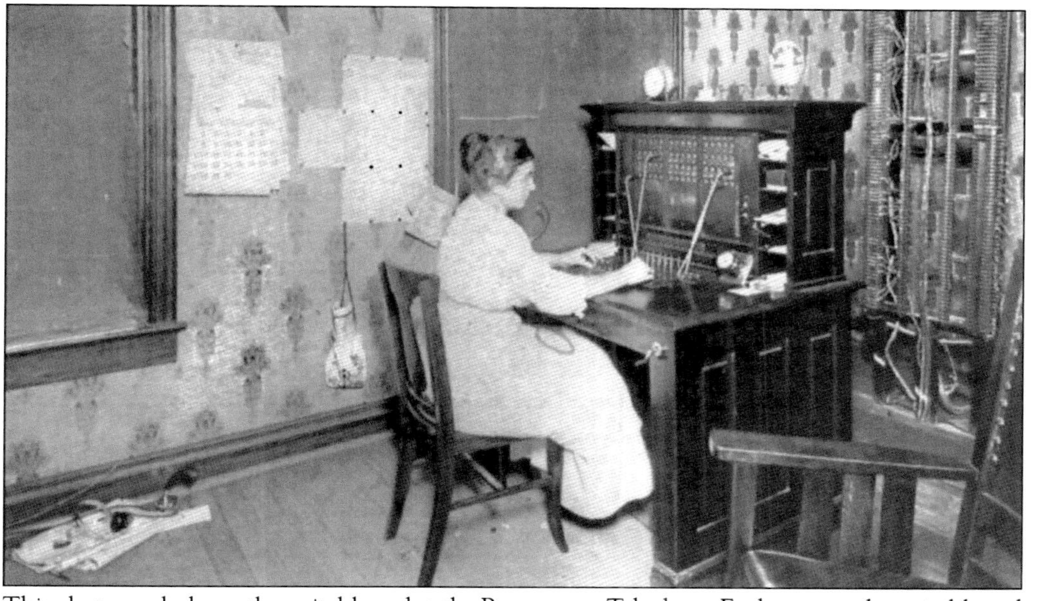

This photograph shows the switchboard at the Browntown Telephone Exchange; at the switchboard is Annie Binger. The local telephone operator was one of the most important people in any town. The telephone office ("central") was located above one of the local stores. (Browntown Historical Society.)

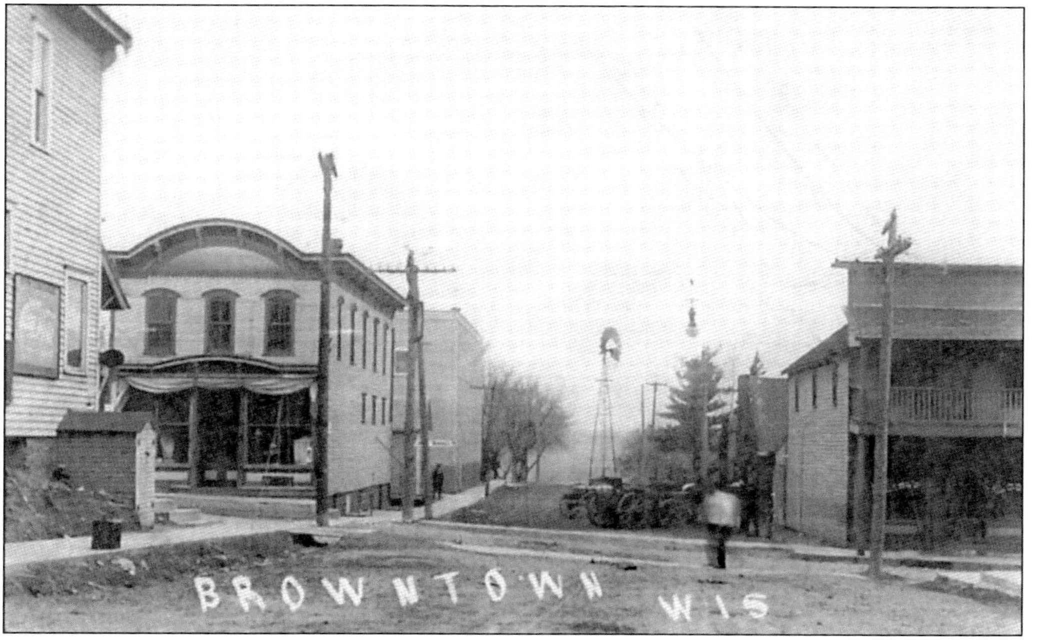

This 1939 photograph shows the Ben Maddrell store. The second story of the store housed a public hall used for roller skating, dances, and other public events that may well have included traveling theater companies, concerts by area bands, school plays, and numerous other events. (Browntown Historical Society.)

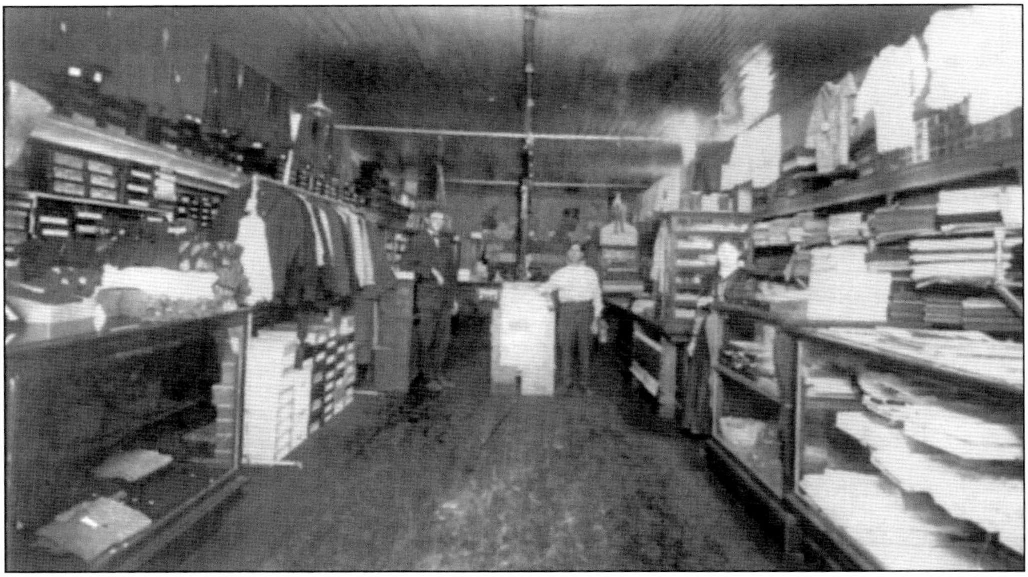

This photograph shows the interior of the Ben Maddrell store, which provided clothing for Browntown area residents. Several times each year, salesmen from distant cities rode the trains to small towns across America, bringing with them trunks loaded with samples of the newest fashions for the upcoming season. (Browntown Historical Society.)

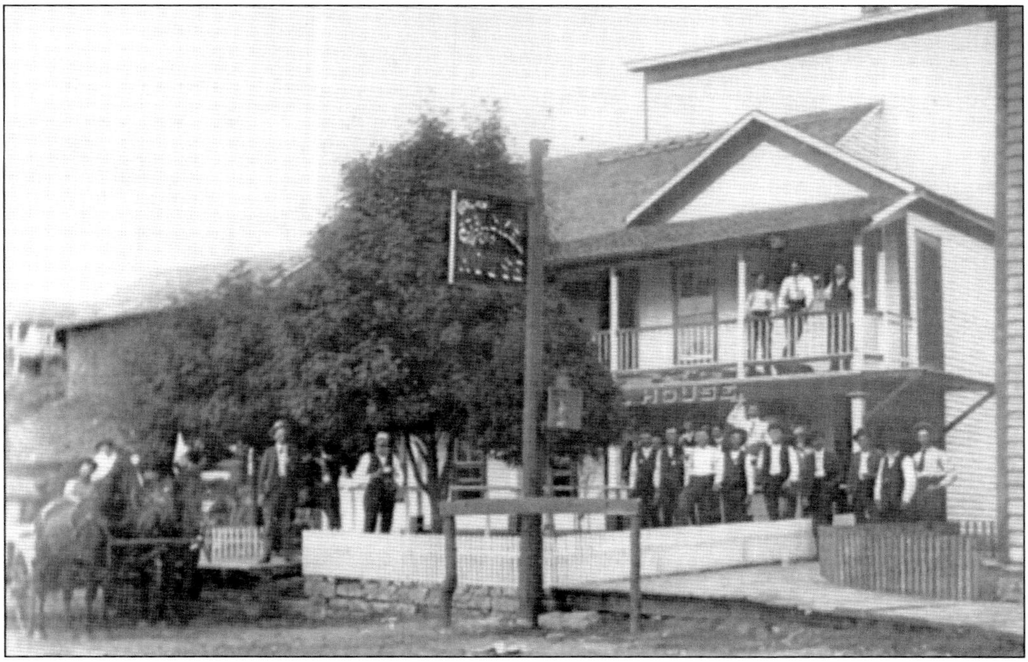

This photograph shows the first Trickle House Hotel, which burned on Sunday June 8, 1913. After this fire, owner Ned Trickle rebuilt the hotel east of this location and closer to Center Street. The third floor held a stage and show space where such acts as the Doc Carver Wild West Shows and Granddaddy White performed. In 1946, the second Trickle House was sold and torn down for the lumber, which was used to build two houses in Monroe. (Browntown Historical Society.)

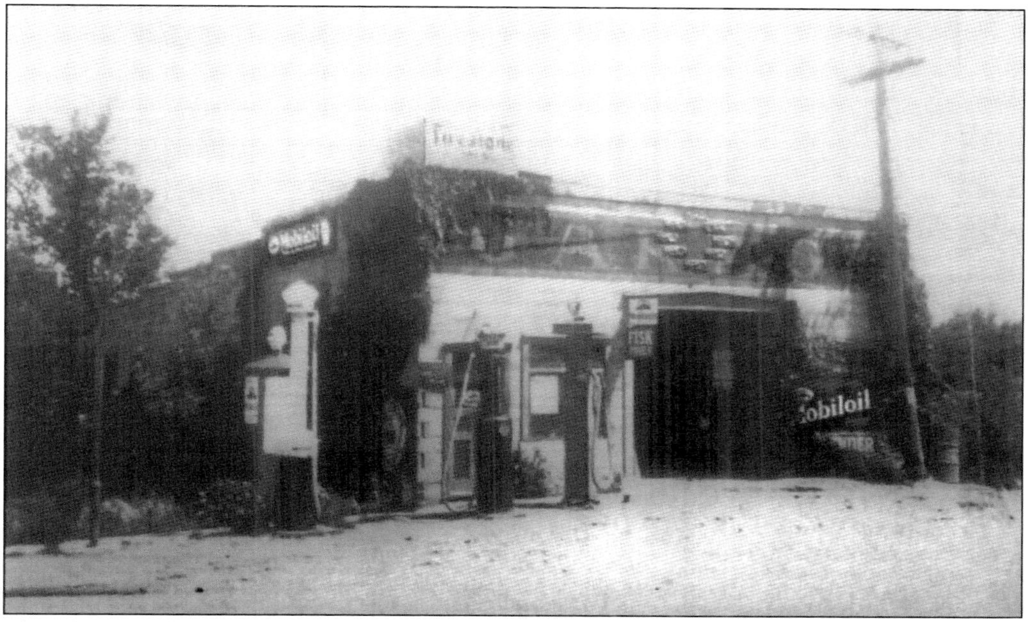

This photograph shows the Heine Sanders Garage on East Main Street. Sanders's business was a general repair shop that kept the residents' cars and trucks running. Like most small-town garages, each afternoon the waiting room probably became the gathering place for the town's characters to get together and swap yarns of days long gone. (Browntown Historical Society.)

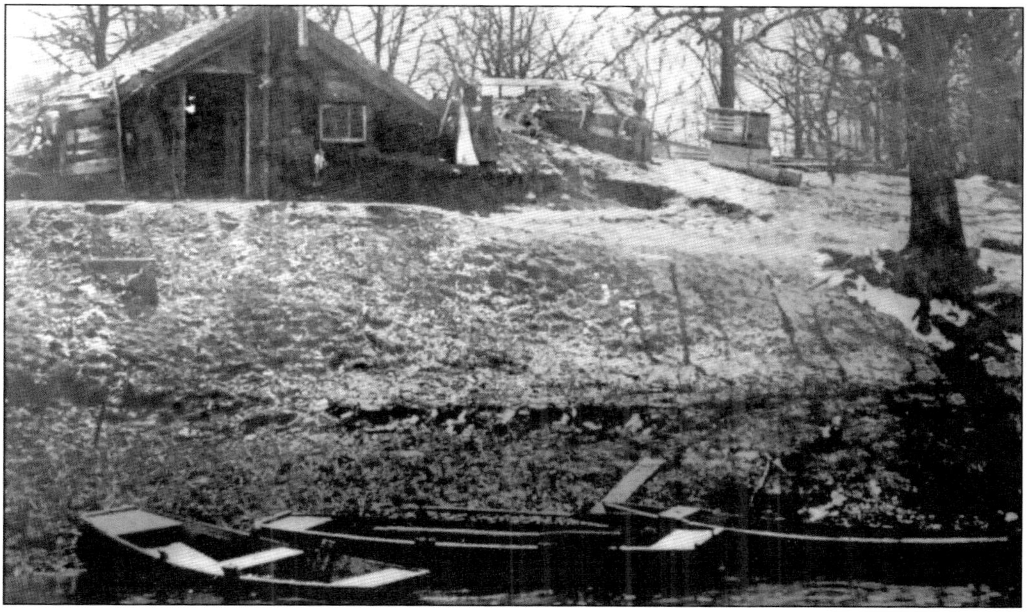

Cut-Nose, a Native American probably of the Winnebago or Sac tribe, lived for many years in this house on the Pecatonica River south of Browntown. Cut-Nose is seated just to the right of the front door of his humble home. The Browntown Historical Museum has several pieces of his handiwork on display. (Browntown Historical Society.)

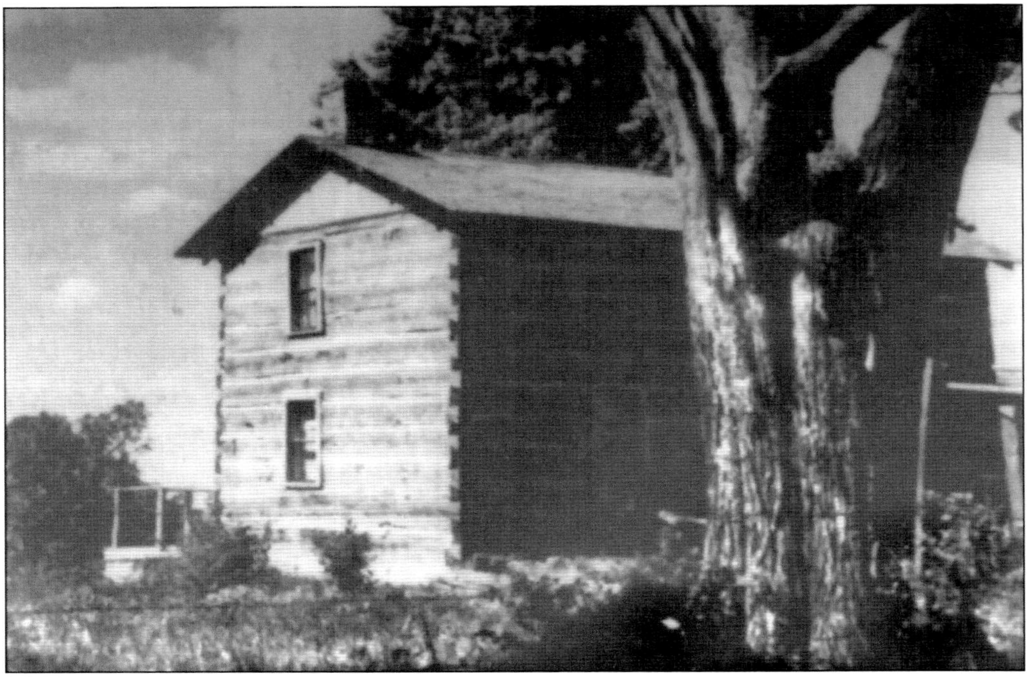

This palatial cabin belonging to the Mordecai Kelly family was built in 1845 on the former road that connected Beloit, Monroe, and Shullsburg. While it was constructed as a two-story home for the Kelly family, it also served as a stagecoach stop. It was not unusual to find as many as 12 travelers staying with the Kelly family. (Browntown Historical Society.)

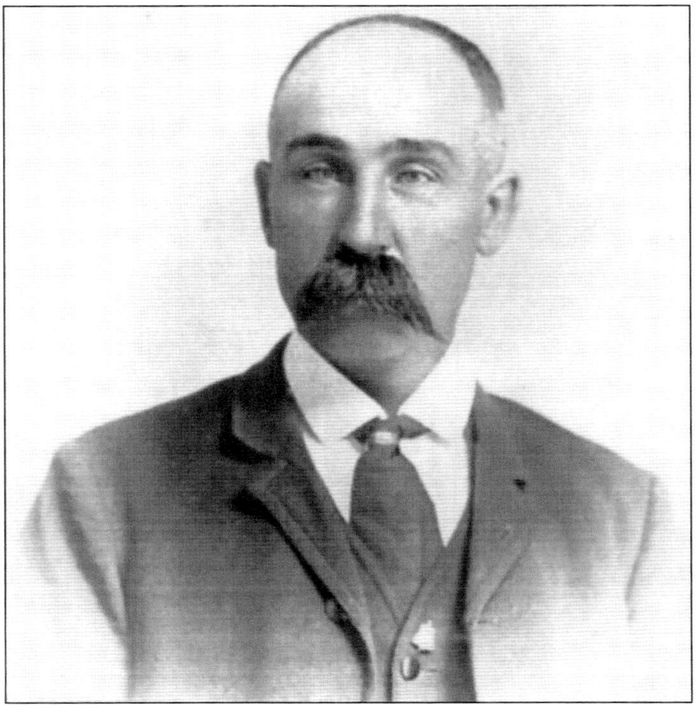

Most towns had a person charged with lighting the street lamps each night, and most often their names are lost to history. This is not so in the case of John Stover, who was the Browntown lamplighter. Stover was born in 1856 and passed away in 1931. In his earlier years, Stover and three of his brothers ran the family farm for their widowed mother. The farm was located just northeast of Browntown. Stover also served as the village marshal. (Browntown Historical Society.)

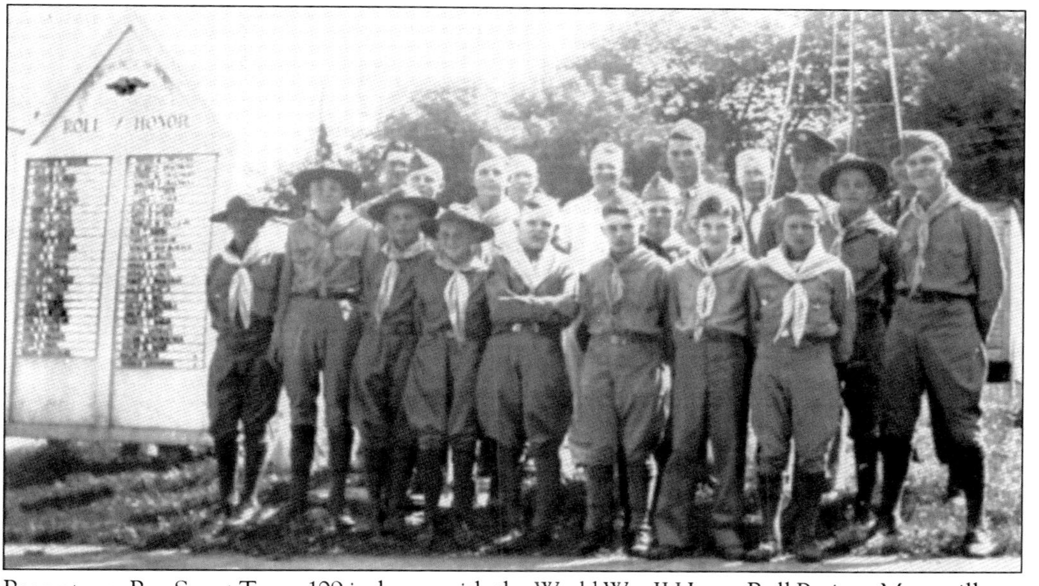

Browntown Boy Scout Troop 109 is shown with the World War II Honor Roll Project. Many villages in Green County had similar signs with the names of each of the town's sons and daughters who have gone off to war. The Green County commitment to service to country reaches as far back as the Civil War, when well over 2,000 county residents served. (Browntown Historical Society.)

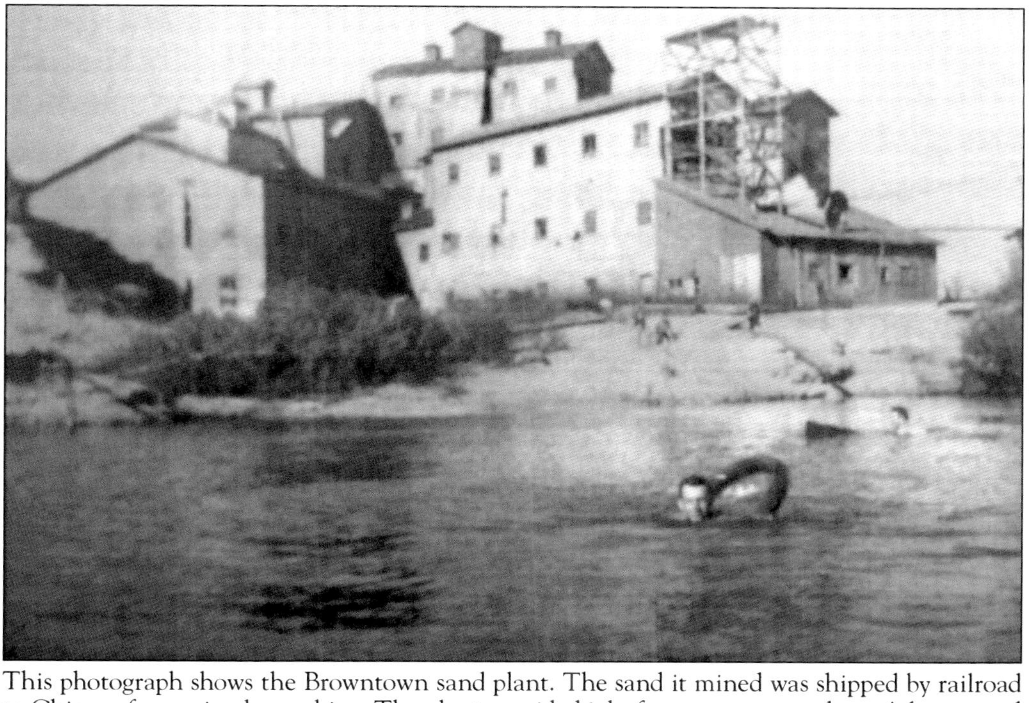

This photograph shows the Browntown sand plant. The sand it mined was shipped by railroad to Chicago for use in glassmaking. The plant provided jobs for many area workers. A large pond in front of the sand plant was used by area children as the local swimming hole. (Browntown Historical Society.)

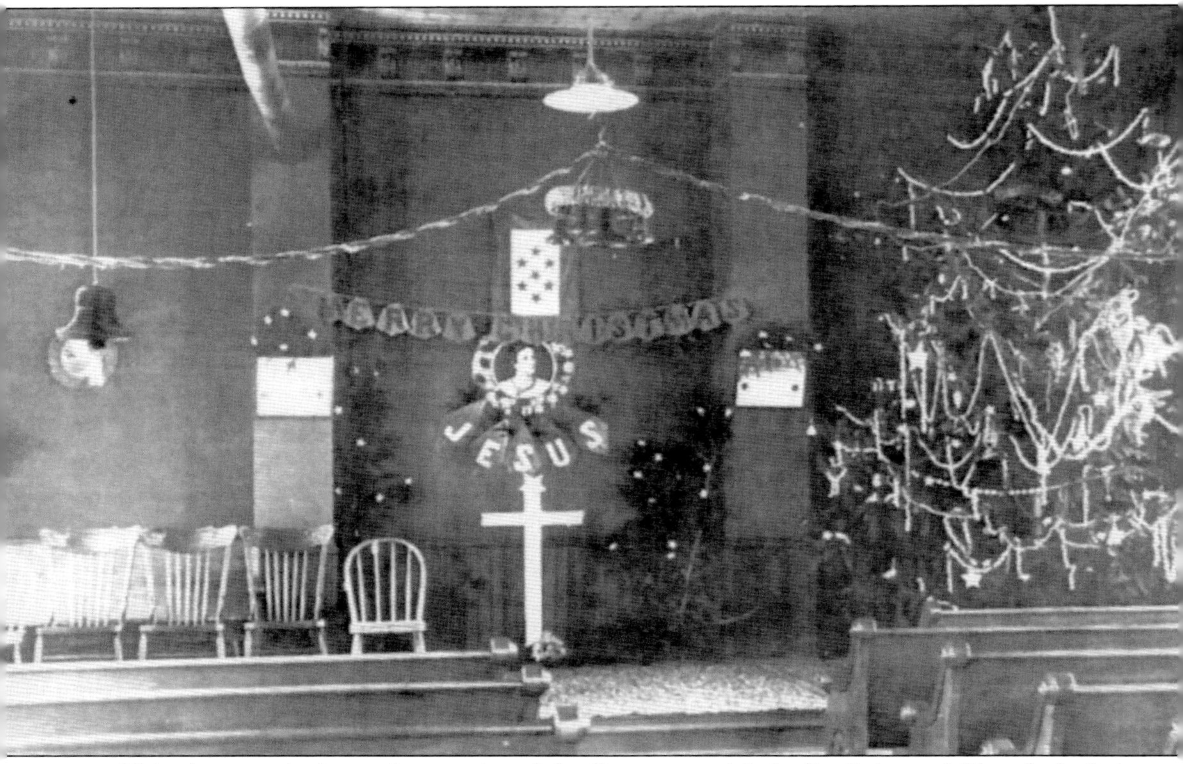

This photograph shows the exterior of the Browntown Methodist Episcopal Church, built in the late 1800s. The design of this church is typical of the vernacular architecture used on many churches in southern Wisconsin. Each Christmas, the interior of this church was decorated for the season, and the children in Sunday school presented their annual Christmas program for eager parents and friends. (Browntown Historical Society.)

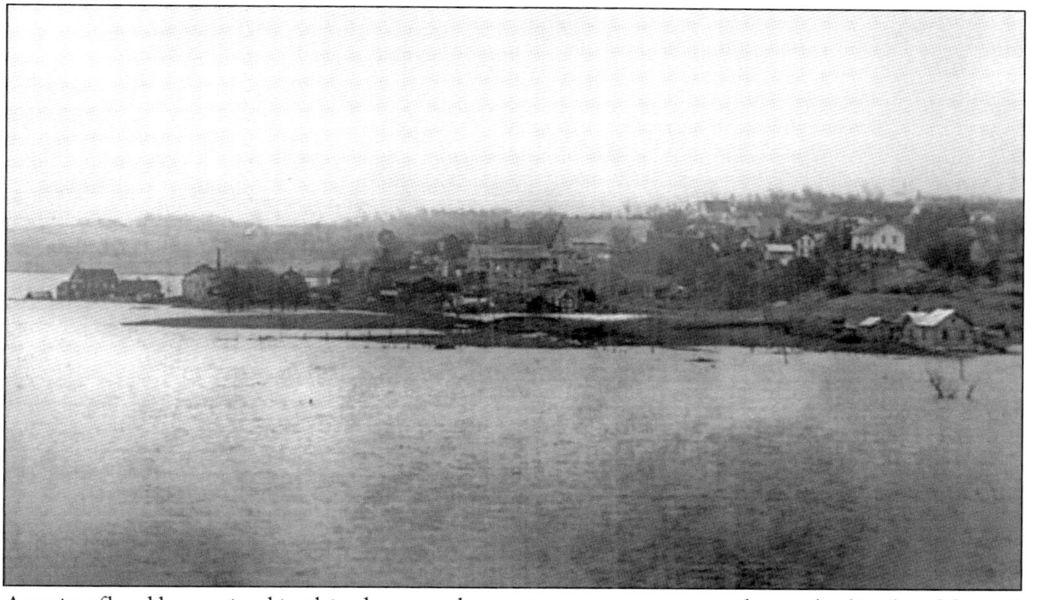

A spring flood has arrived in this photograph, causing concern among those who lived and farmed in the floodplain of Skinner Creek and the nearby Pecatonica River. Both rivers are prone to early spring flooding. Notice in the center of the image how the fence posts are beginning to disappear in the rising waters. (Browntown Historical Society.)

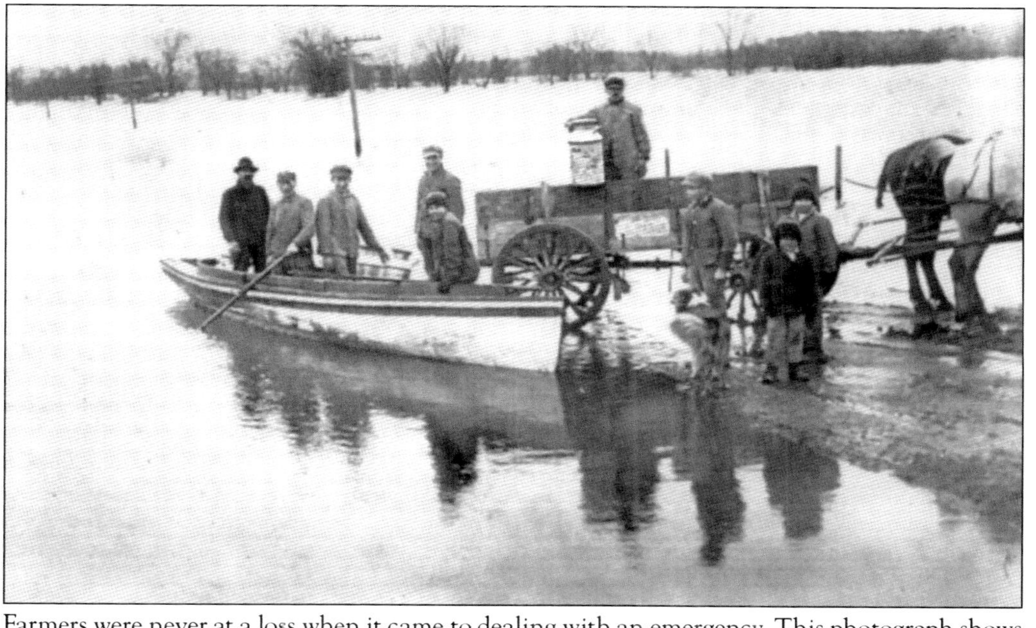

Farmers were never at a loss when it came to dealing with an emergency. This photograph shows a number of farmers loading their 10-gallon cans of cream into a boat in order to get them to the local creamery for processing into butter. The man standing in the wagon is Edmon McGuire. (Browntown Historical Society.)

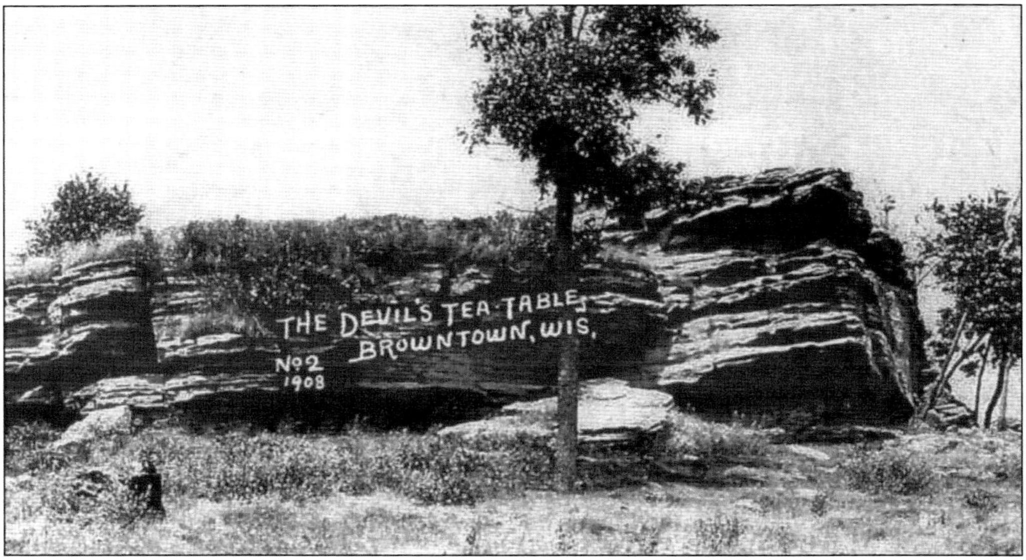

The Devil's Tea Table is an unusual rock formation found near Browntown. There are one or two other similar rock formations found in Green County. For many years, area residents used the Devil's Tea Table as a picnic grounds. The Browntown Boy Scouts also used the area for their annual camping trips. (Browntown Historical Society.)

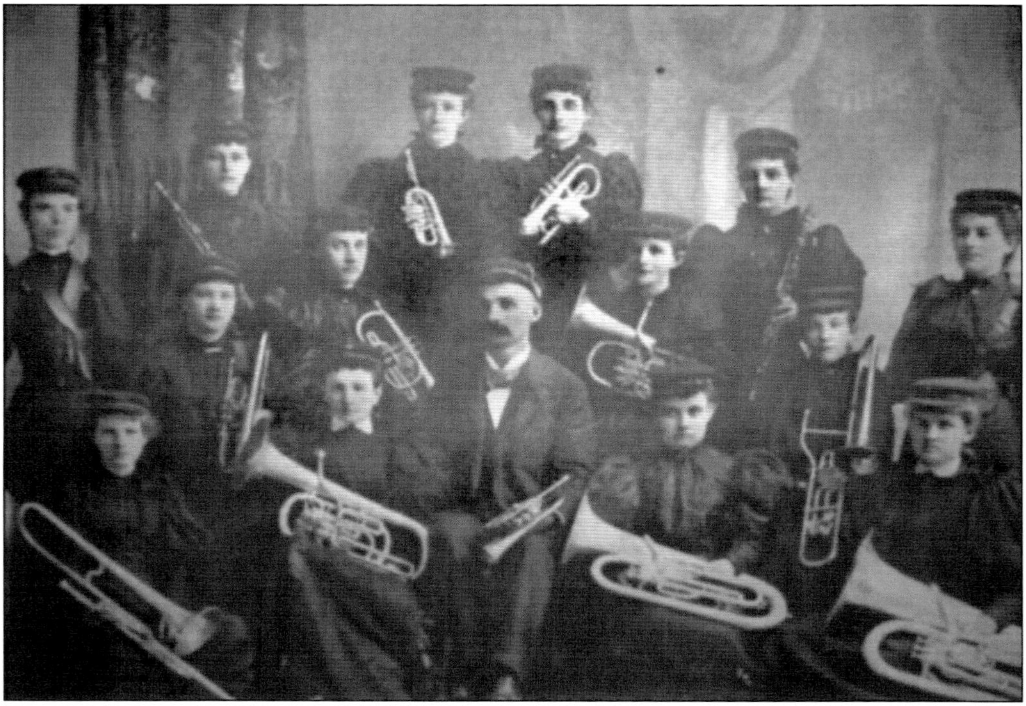

Most small towns could boast a local band or two, and Browntown was no different. As small as Browntown was, its residents were able to field three bands to represent the community at band competitions. This 1890s photograph shows the Browntown All-Women's Band, one of very few female bands of the era. (Browntown Historical Society.)

Four

JUDA

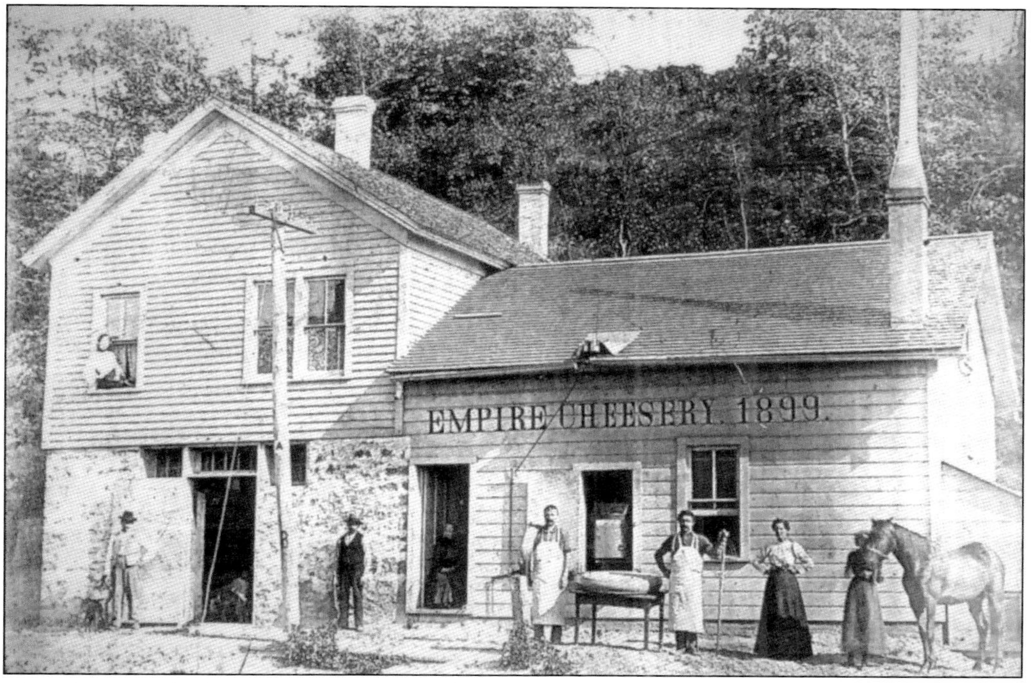

This photograph of the Empire Cheesery located at the east end of Juda was probably taken in the first years of operation. The cheese-making operations were carried out in the one-story portion of the building. After the day's work was completed, the wheels of cheese were moved to the cheese storage cellar located in the stone portion of the building. Today all that remains of this building is the stone foundation. (Paul Matzke.)

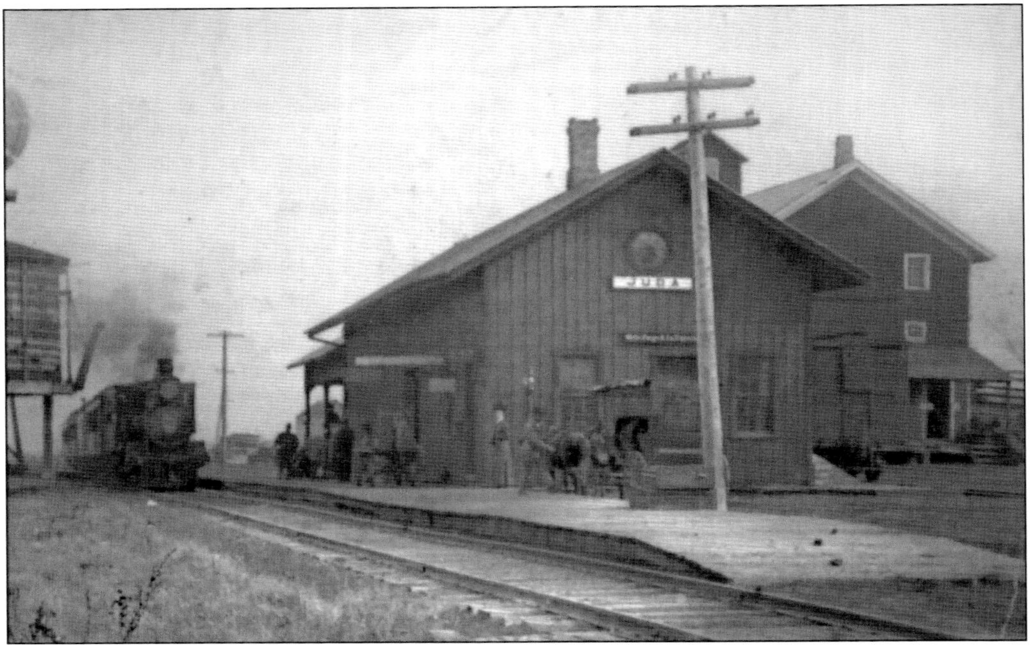

Juda was served by the Milwaukee Road Railroad beginning in 1857. It has had three railroad depots: the first two were lost to fires, which was common in the days of steam power; the third depot remains, but is no longer in use. A sign on the building indicates that this depot is also a Wells Fargo Express agency. (Paul Matzke.)

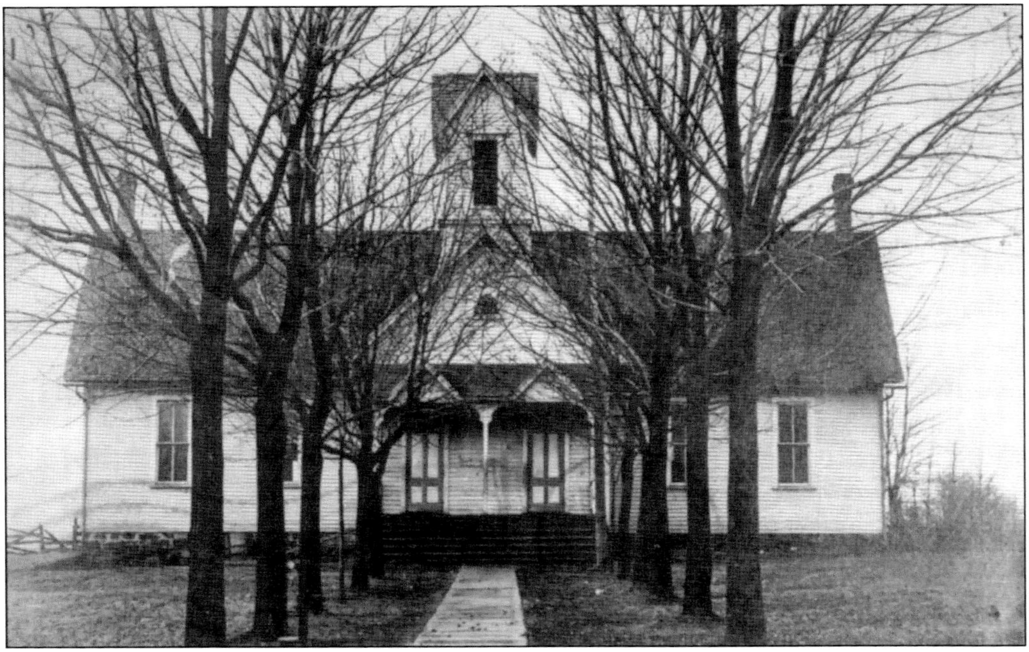

Juda, Green County's smallest community, has always put a high value on education, and despite its small population it still operates its own school district. This photograph shows the first Juda school, which probably taught grades 1–8, as did most small-town schools. (Paul Matzke.)

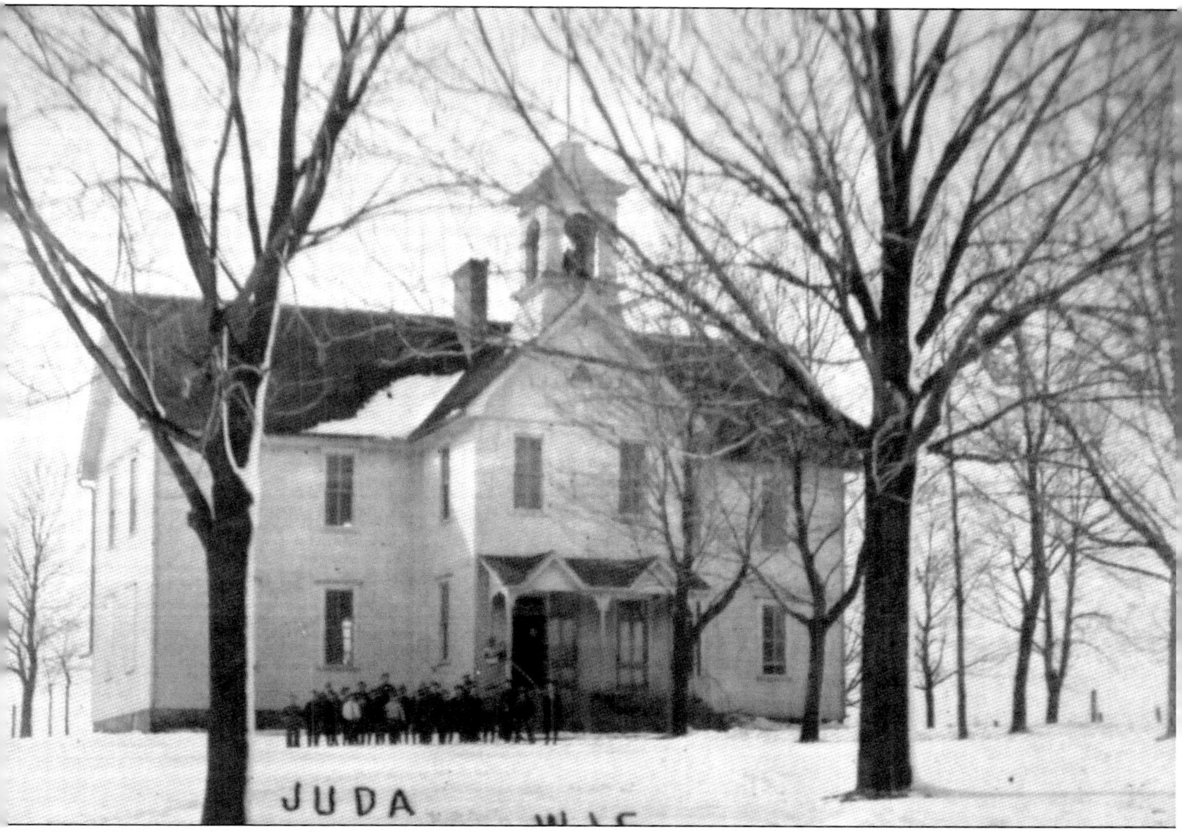

This photograph shows the same school on the previous page but with the addition of a second floor to accommodate a rapidly rising number of schoolchildren. The school was modern by the standards of the time and boasted a central heating system instead of a potbelly coal stove in each classroom. (Paul Matzke.)

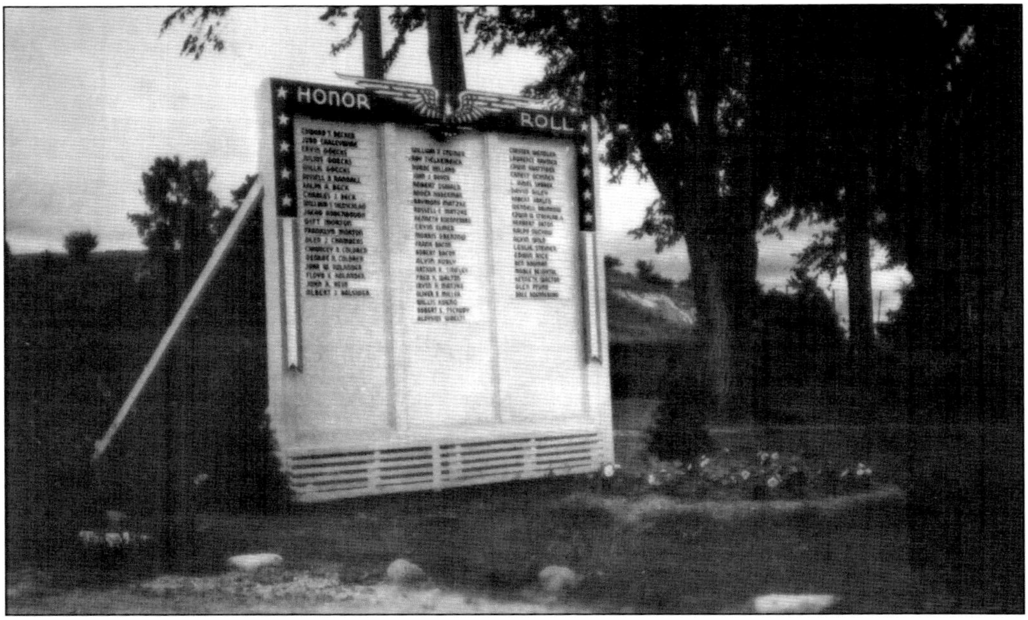

Here is the Juda World War II Honor Roll. World War II affected every household in America. The small towns in the country willingly sent their sons and daughters off to war in Europe and the South Pacific. Often numerous siblings and first cousins served at the same time, made evident here by the number of veterans on the Honor Roll who share the same last name. (Paul Matzke.)

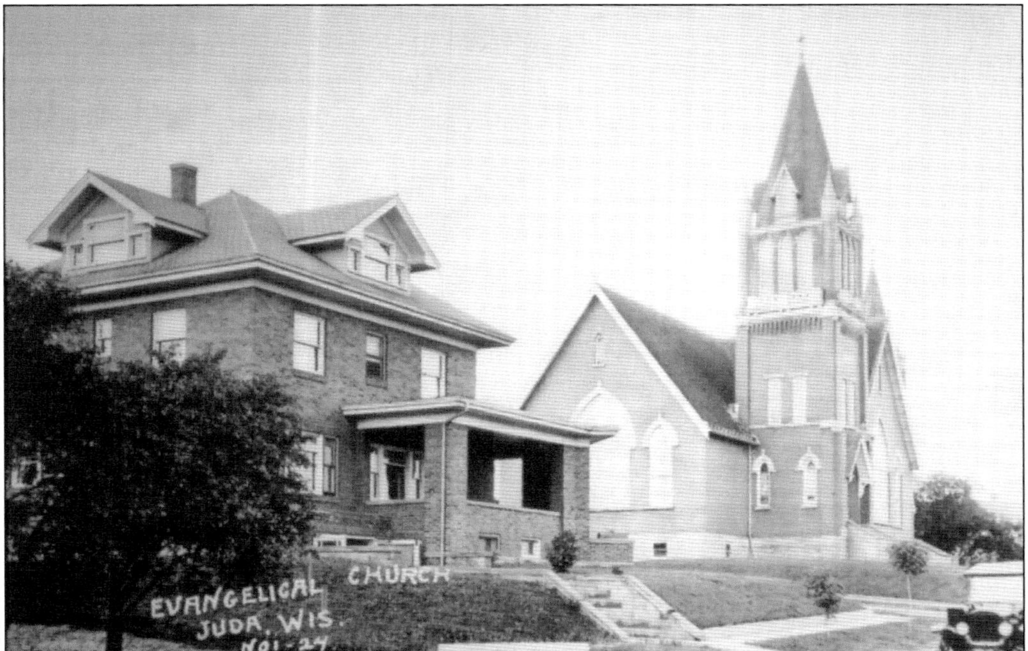

This photograph shows the Juda Evangelical Church and parsonage in the early 1920s. The architecture of this church is typical of that era. This church was razed to construct a more modern church building, which is still home to an active congregation. (Paul Matzke.)

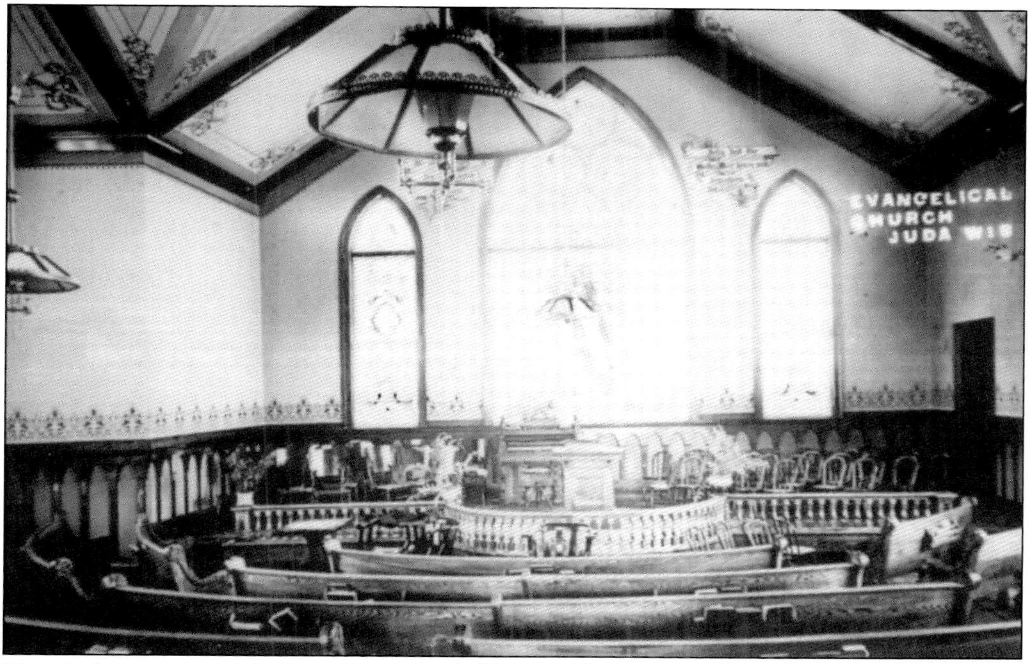

Here is the interior of the Juda Evangelical Church. The artistry of this beautiful old church is something of the past. The woodwork represents the finest of old-time craftsmanship. Notice the artwork at the ceiling and also the beautiful gas lamp. (Paul Matzke.)

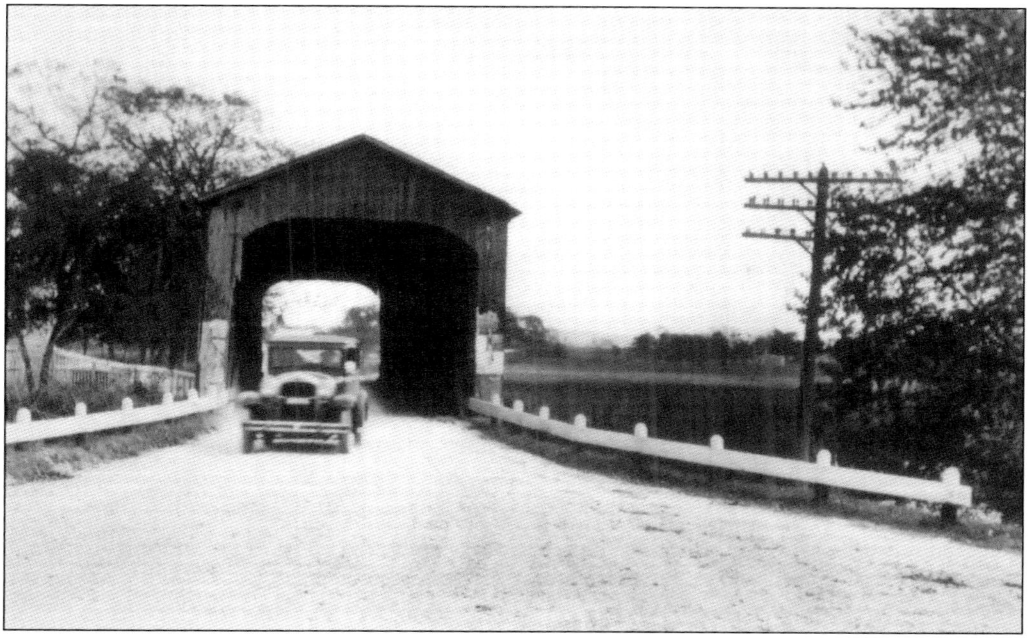

The bridges of Madison County have nothing on Green County. This pre-1927 covered bridge was on old Wisconsin Highway 20, which is now County KS. This bridge was one of at least three known covered bridges in Green County. The road followed the railroad tracks from Juda toward Monroe. (Paul Matzke.)

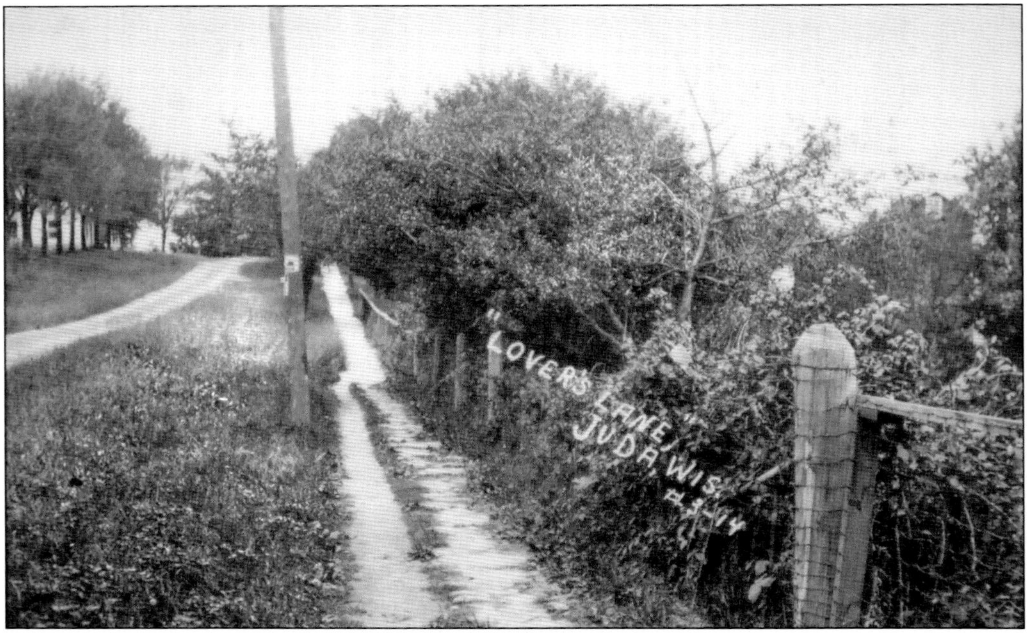

Anyone over 60 years of age has heard stories of the local Lovers Lane, but did Lover's Lane really exist? Indeed it did, as this photograph shows. If the well-worn footpath is any indication, Juda's Lovers Lane was not too far from the village itself. (Paul Matzke.)

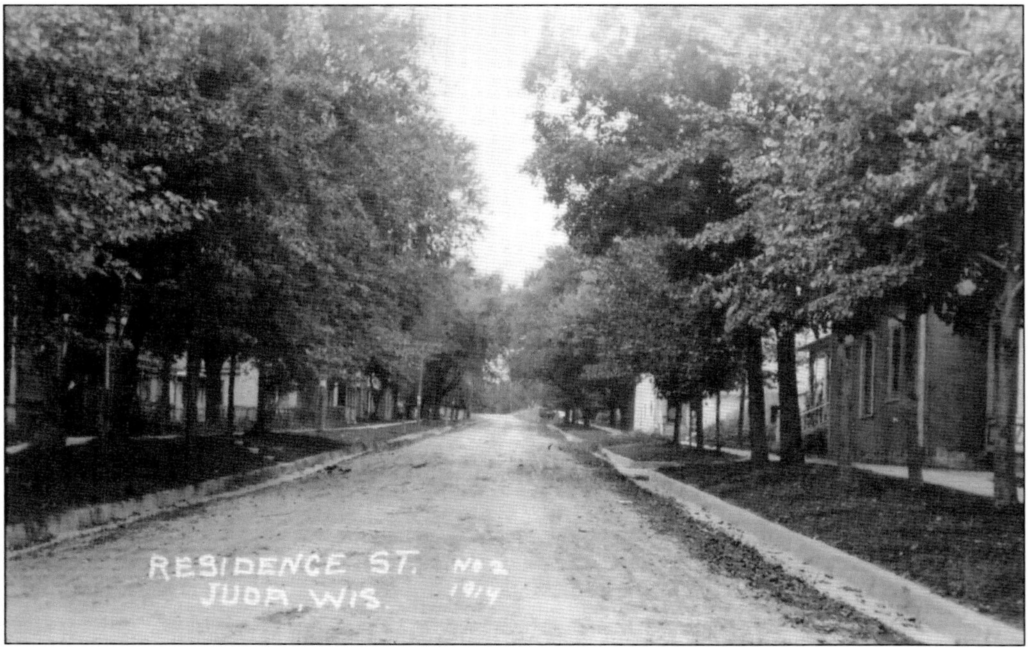

This fall scene took place on a residential street in Juda in 1914. Summer has ended, and the trees are beginning to shed their leaves. Soon the air will be filled with the fragrance of fall leaves being burned in backyards, and woodpiles will quickly expand for the coming winter. (Paul Matzke.)

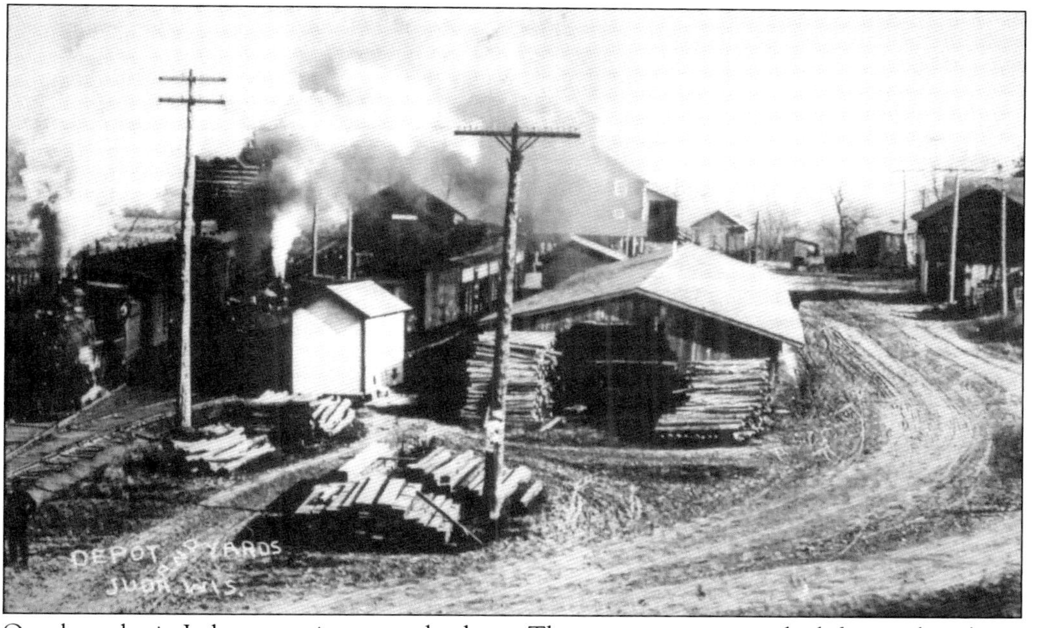

On a busy day in Juda, two trains are at the depot. The passenger train on the left is ready to leave for the daily westbound trip to Monroe. The train on the right has a number of cars loaded with lumber, coal, and the other staples needed by Juda homes and businesses. (Paul Matzke.)

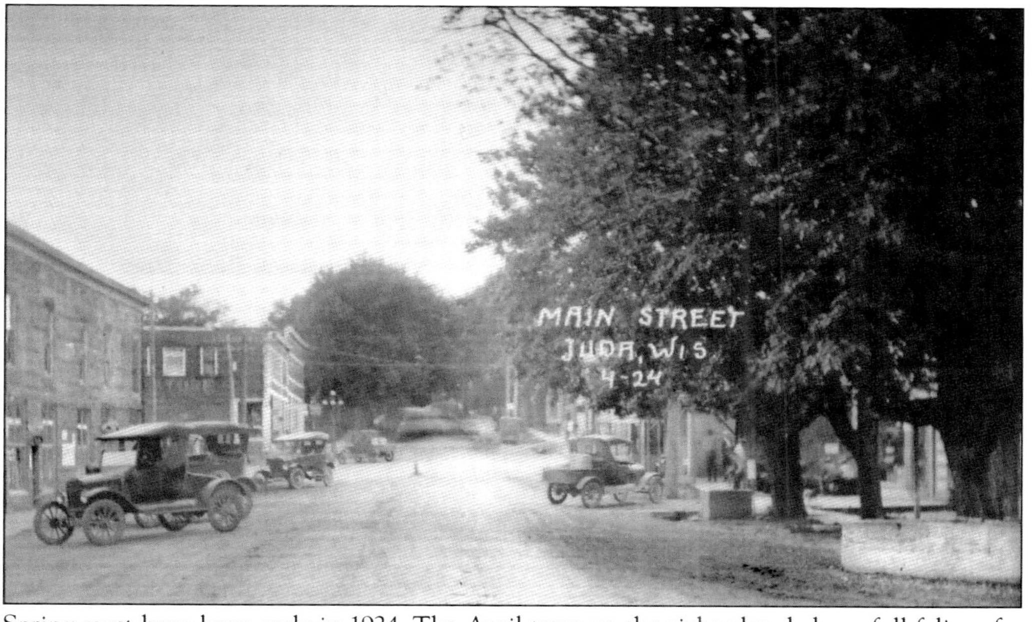

Spring must have been early in 1924. The April trees on the right already have full foliage for the year. This Main Street scene shows downtown Juda coming alive for the day's commerce. Several people have already arrived to head to the markets for the day. Between the first and second tree, several of the town's folk are sitting down either for a good card game or a great story. (Paul Matzke.)

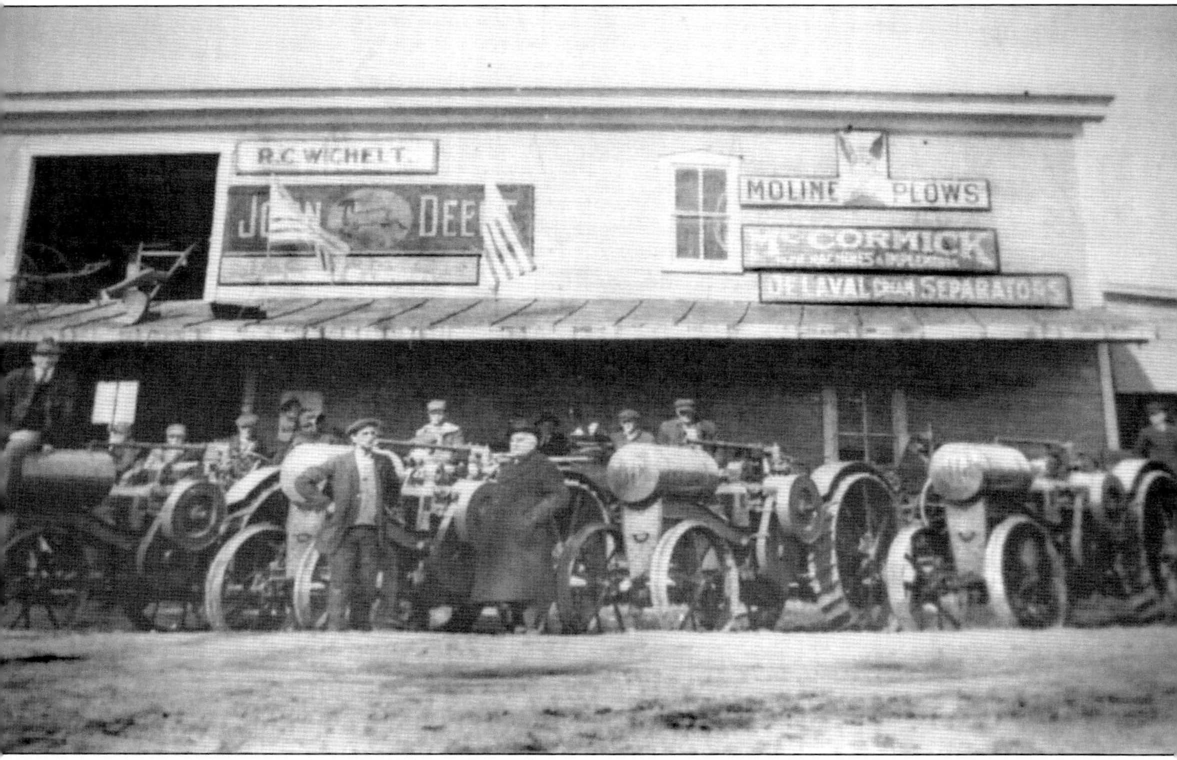

A load of new tractors has arrived at the R. C. Wichelt Implement Company. Wichelt sold John Deere tractors, Moline plows, McCormick reapers, and DeLaval cream separators. The man wearing the topcoat in the center of the photograph is the tractor company field man who is on hand for this delivery of new tractors. (Paul Matzke.)

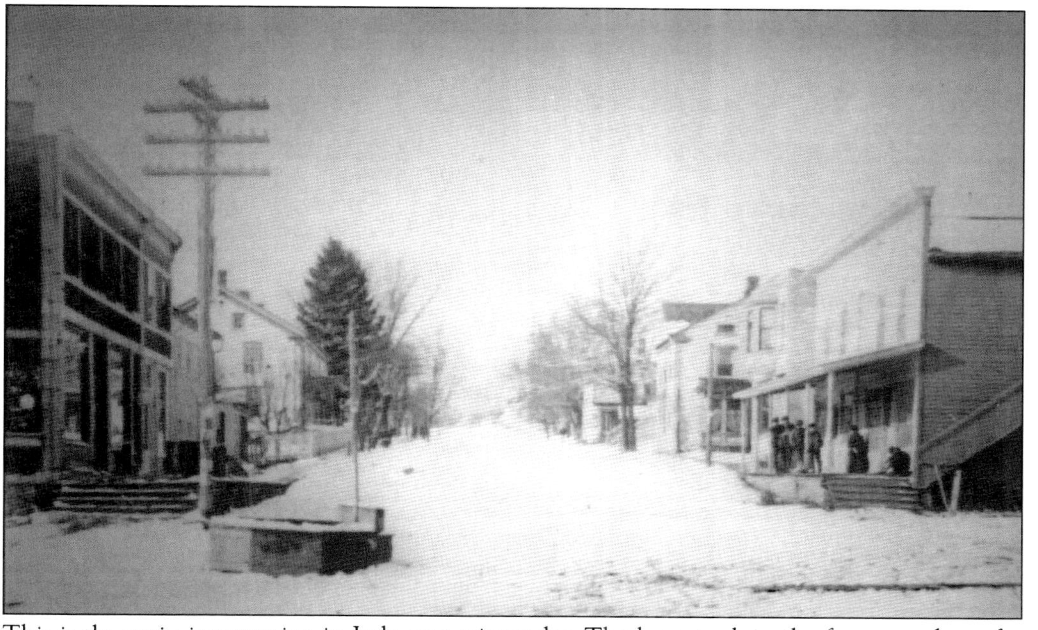

This is the main intersection in Juda on a winter day. The large tank in the foreground was for watering horses when they were driven into town. It also served farmers driving their cattle to the stockyard. The stockyard owners disliked this tank because the thirsty cattle would drink water just before being weighed for sale, increasing the price the farmer received for his livestock. (Paul Matzke.)

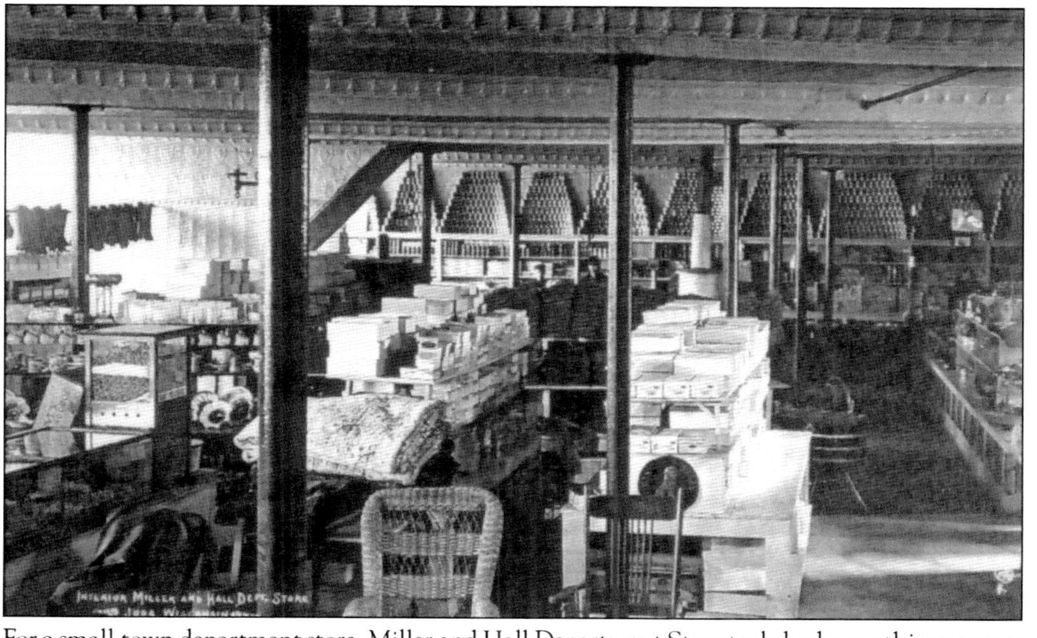

For a small-town department store, Miller and Hall Department Store truly had everything anyone needed. Stores like Miller and Hall carried groceries, clothing, furniture, school supplies, and various other necessities. Notice the canned goods stacked high on the back wall. This store was truly modern with its pressed-metal ceiling, the mark of a successful business. (Paul Matzke.)

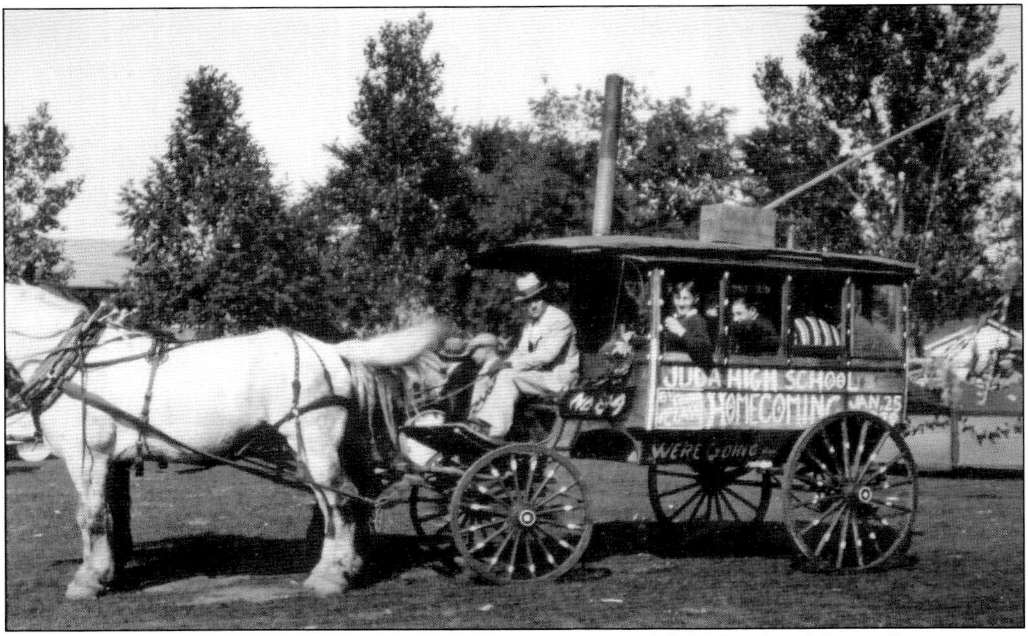

Area high schools held their homecomings either during a fall high school football game or in winter. Juda held their homecoming in January. (Paul Matzke.)

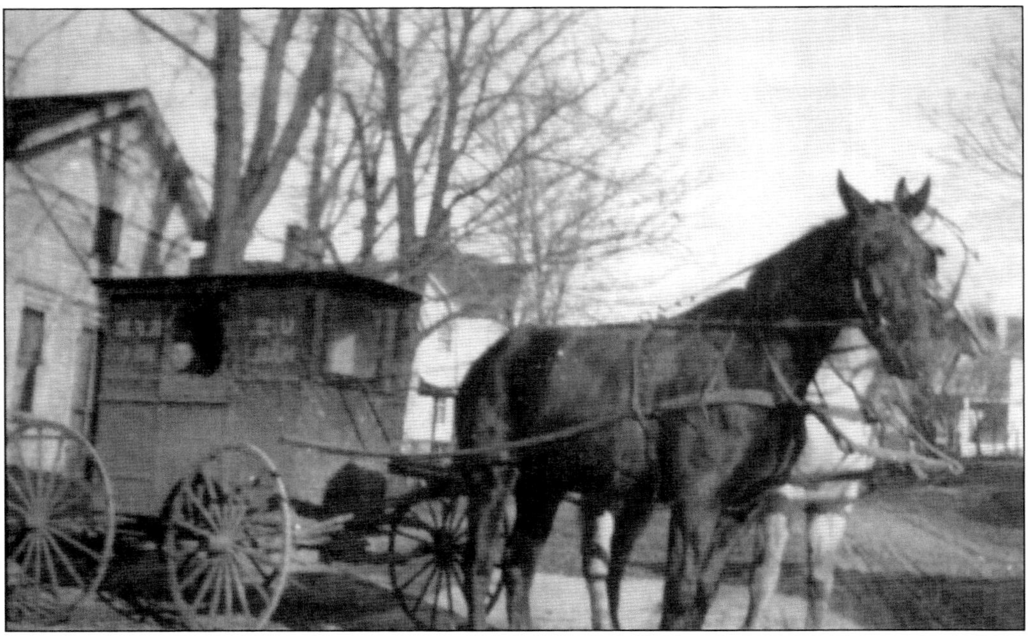

Roy Fries, the Rural Free Delivery mailman is driving his mail buggy. Fries was Juda's rural mailman for many years. He had three horses that he could hitch to his mail buggy and changed horses as one tired. His horses all knew the route, and he never had to guide the horses to each stop. This photograph was printed backward when made. (Paul Matzke.)

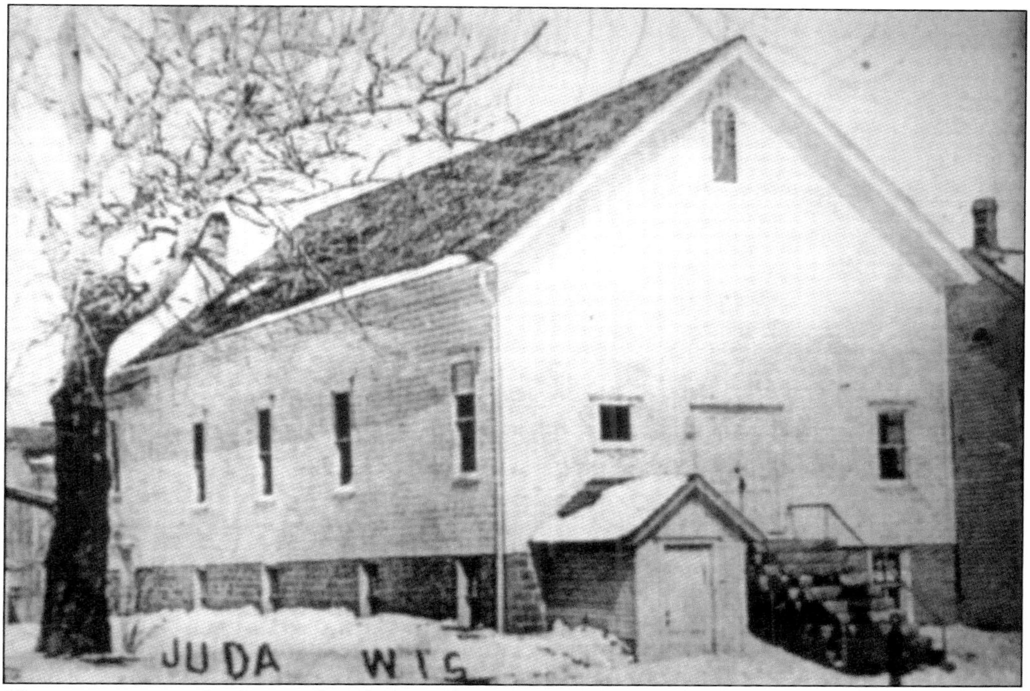

This structure was built as a church, but when the church disbanded the building was purchased to be used as a community center. Over the years, it served as a community center and saw family reunions, fund-raising suppers, traveling shows, plays, and Chautauquas. In the 1960s, the building was torn down and the material used to construct a house. (Paul Matzke.)

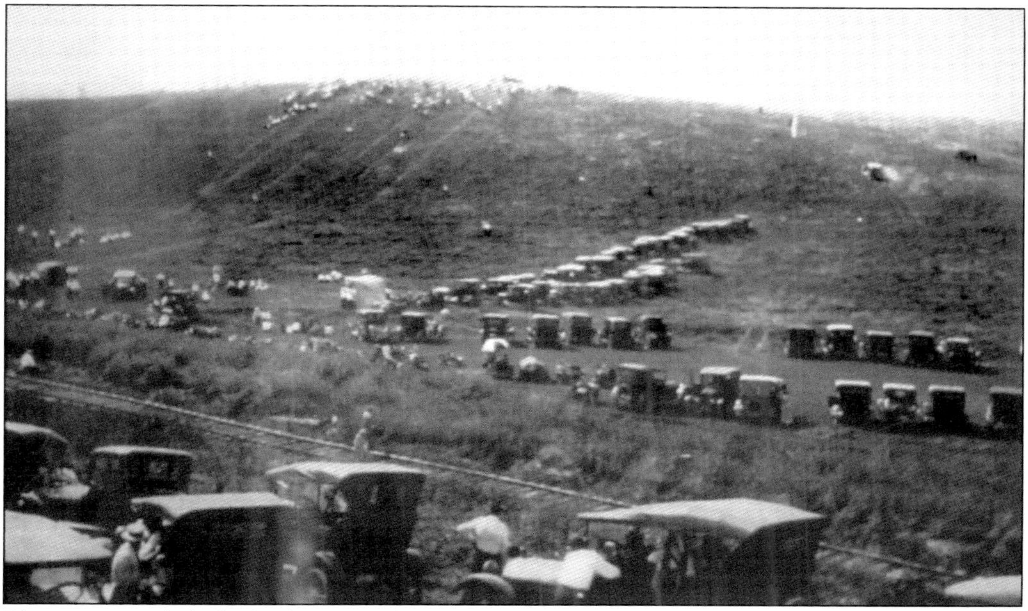

This motorcycle hill climb near Juda drew quite a large crowd. Children were excited to see motorcycles climbing what were, to them, very steep hills. Family events such as this led to a picnic and a day in the countryside. (Paul Matzke.)

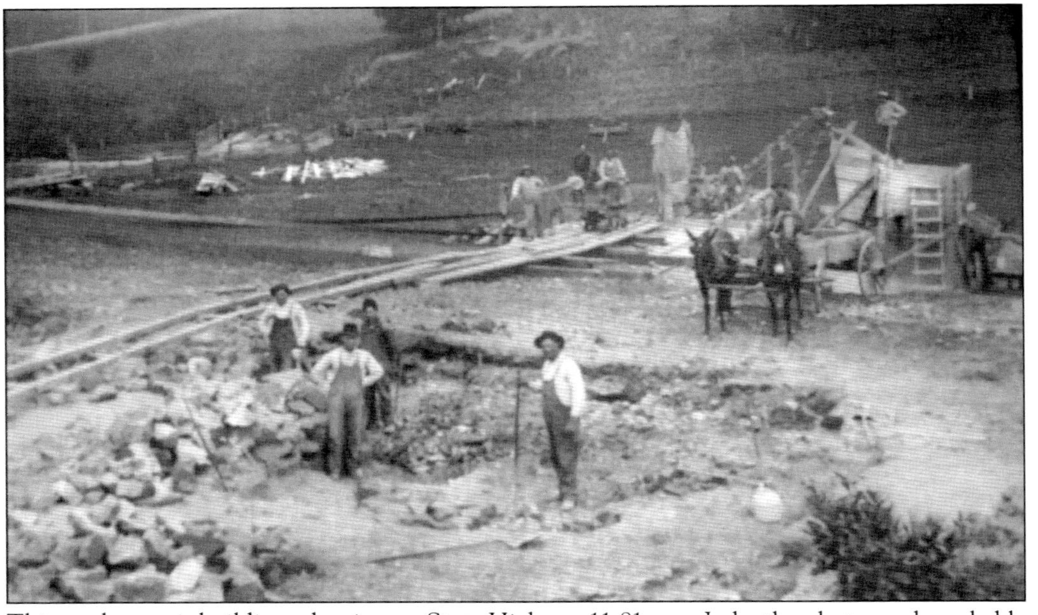

This work crew is building what is now State Highway 11-81 near Juda; the photograph probably dates to before 1927. The work crew was probably more than happy to pose, because it meant a break in their strenuous work. Notice the set of tracks on the left; it was likely used to move small amounts of heavy material at a time. Much of the work was done by mules. (Paul Matzke.)

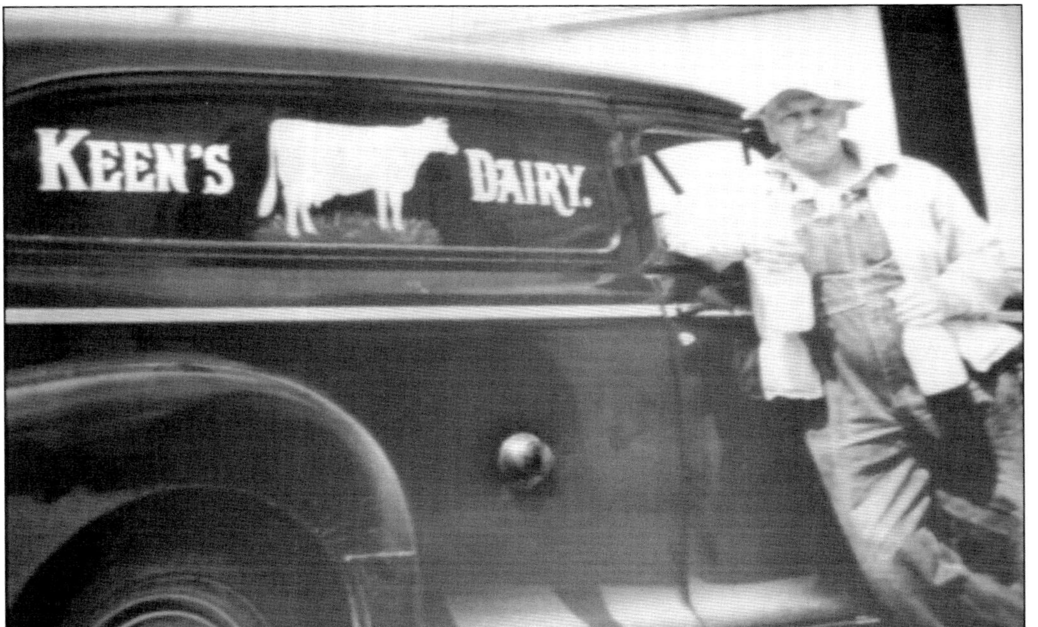

This early-1950s photograph features Keen's Dairy, which operated out of a Mill Street location in Juda. Shown here is Art Keen, owner of the business that produced and delivered milk door to door each day. The business operated into the 1960s. (Paul Matzke.)

Five

Monroe

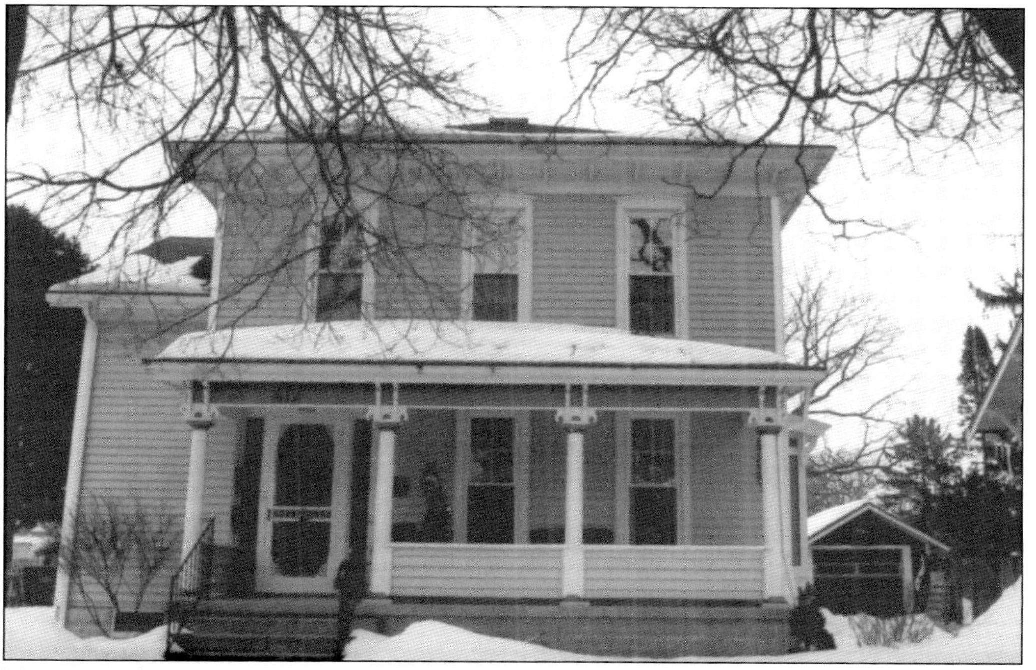

Monroe was home to Janet Jennings, the "Forgotten Angel." Jennings was a contract nurse during the Civil War. She had no nursing training when she went to Washington D.C. to take care of her wounded brother, but within weeks, she was placed in charge of several hospital tents. She also worked directly with Clara Barton to establish the American Red Cross. The Janet Jennings home is on the National Register of Historic Places.

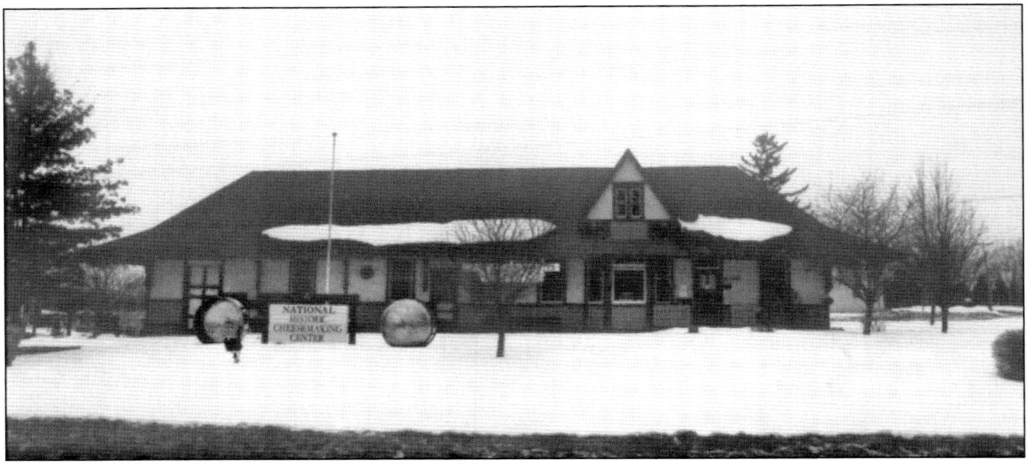

Monroe's former Milwaukee Road Railroad depot today serves as the Historic Cheesemaking Center and the Green County Welcome Center. This depot was threatened with demolition but was moved to its present site, restored, and serves as a great place to begin a visit to Green County.

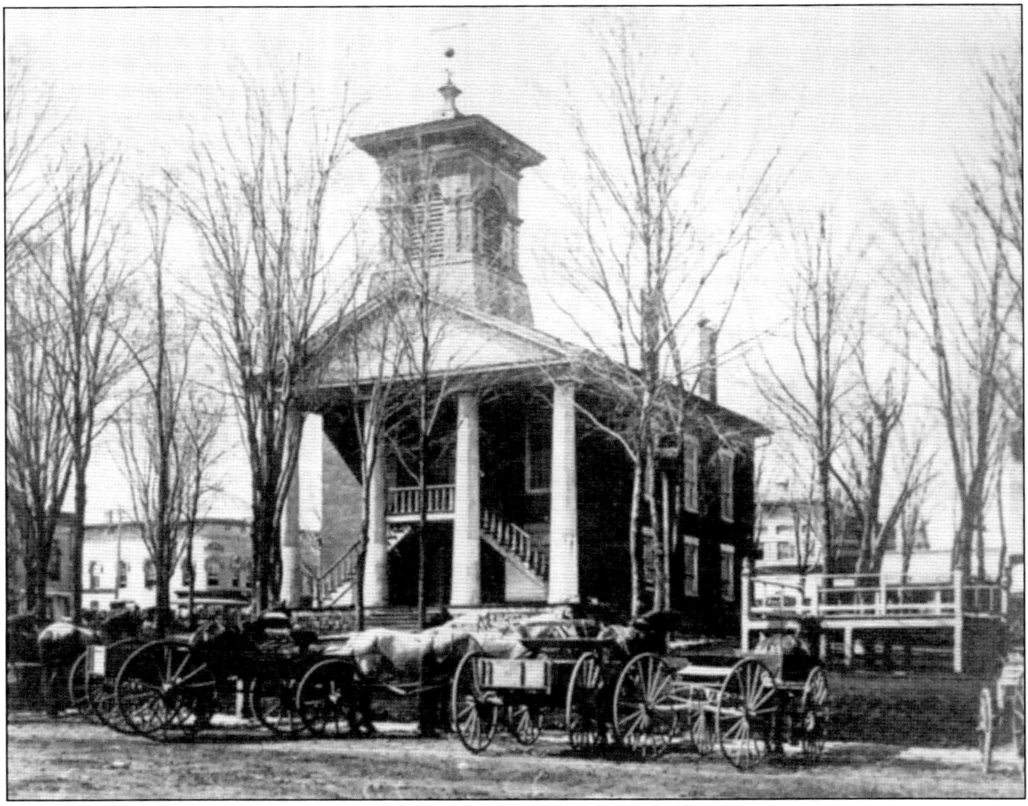

Green County has had three courthouses to serve the needs of the residents. This is the second courthouse; the photograph probably dates to the mid-1880s. This building was torn down and replaced with the current Green County Courthouse. This beautiful structure at one time had a dome on the roof.

This photograph shows the current Green County Courthouse, which is still being used for many of the county offices. The courthouse is built in Richardsonian-Romanesque architecture popular between 1890 and 1910. This building designed by G. Stanley Mansfield is on the National Register of Historic Places.

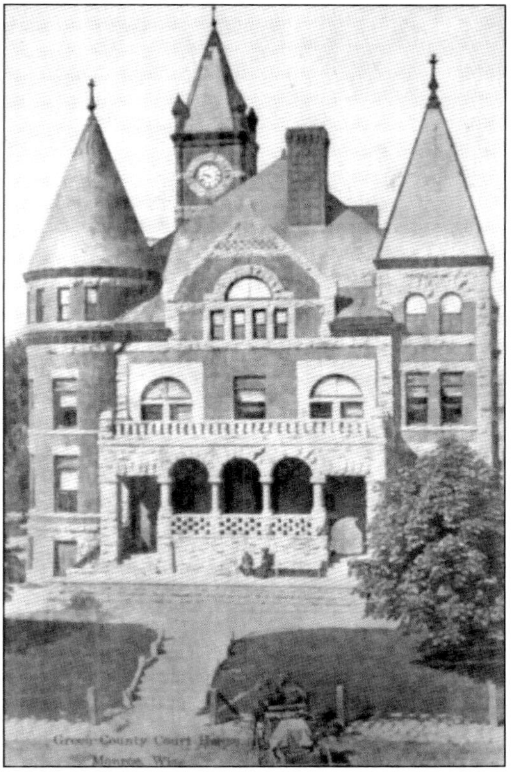

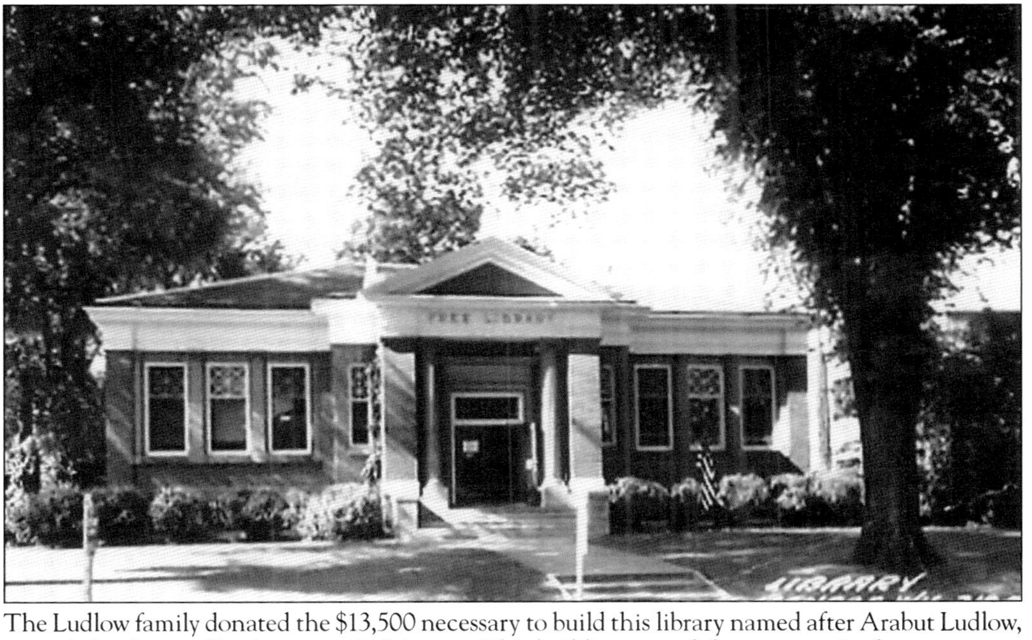

The Ludlow family donated the $13,500 necessary to build this library named after Arabut Ludlow, an early banker and businessman in Monroe. This building served the community for many years until the Lee Geiger family purchased the former Monroe Clinic building and donated it to the City of Monroe to be used for library purposes.

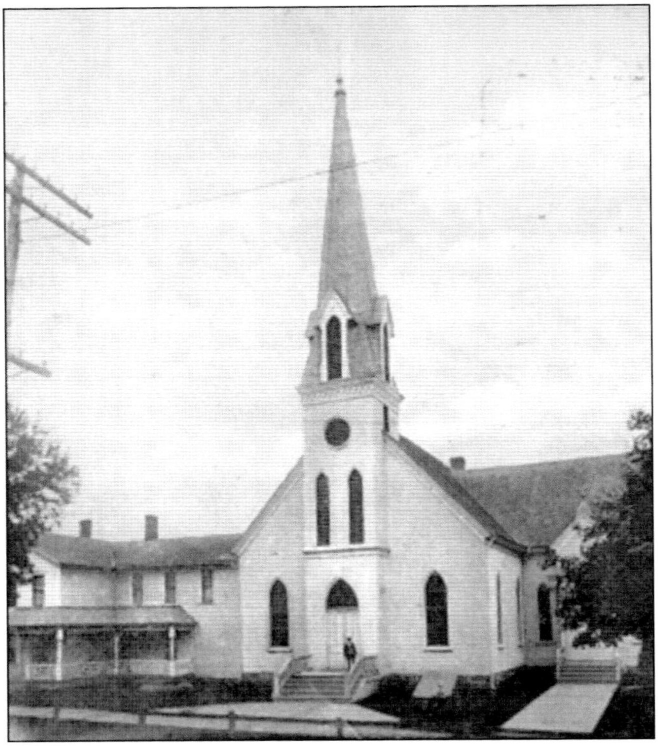

The congregation of St. John's Church was formed in 1862 by Andreas Lanz, harness-maker Samuel Schneider, tailors John Kaderly and Peter Spahr, and J. J. Tschudy, the county registrar of deeds. The church was dedicated on August 31, 1862, with Reverend Kroehnke of Rock Run, Illinois, officiating. The church's first communion was held that day, as was the first baptism—that of Samuel Schuler, who became a lifelong church member.

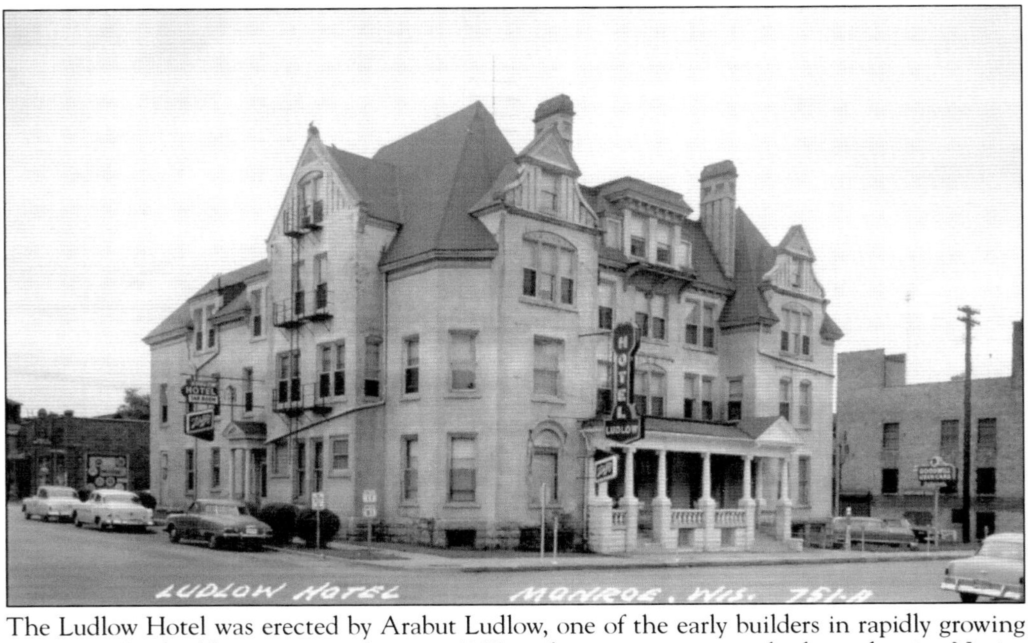

The Ludlow Hotel was erected by Arabut Ludlow, one of the early builders in rapidly growing Monroe. This building was torn down in 1955, and a variety store was built on the site. Notice the sign on the left side of the building advertising the Tap Room, a polite name for a tavern catering to gentlemen of business and commerce. The second sign advertises Schlitz beer, which was reintroduced in 2008 using the century-old formula.

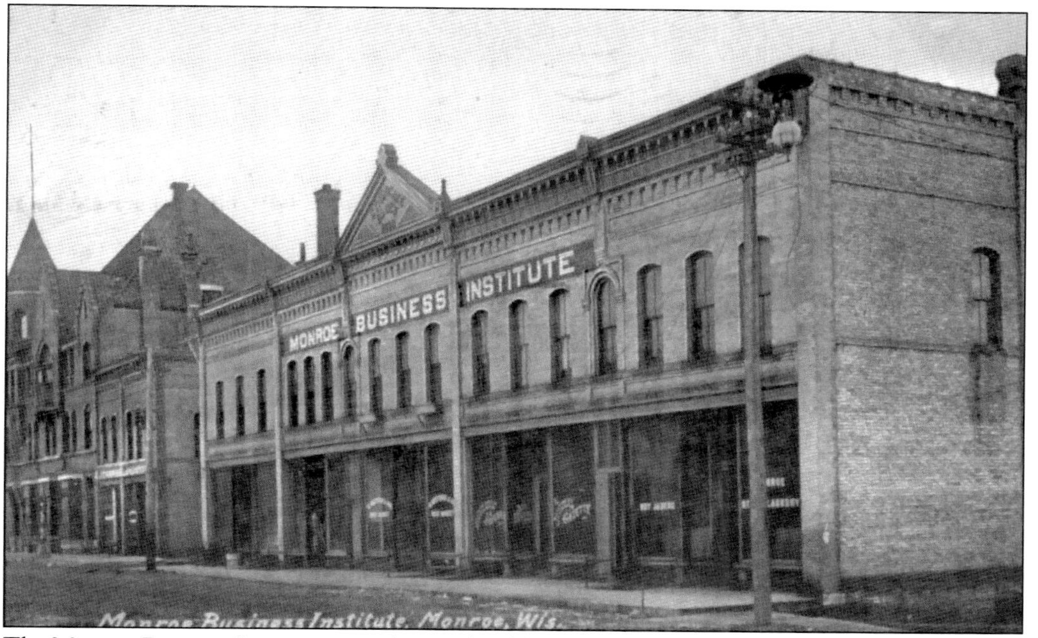

The Monroe Business Institute served as a school for young people seeking training in the world of commerce. Many of its students came to Monroe for a one-year course of studies. Upon completion of classes, many of the students went back to their hometowns to work in a small business.

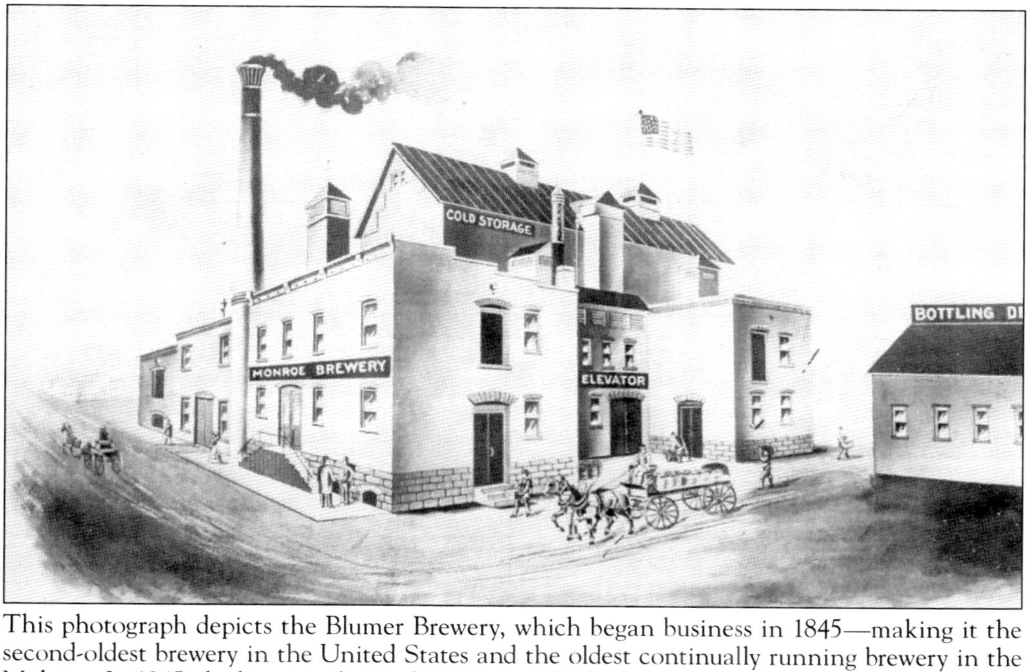

This photograph depicts the Blumer Brewery, which began business in 1845—making it the second-oldest brewery in the United States and the oldest continually running brewery in the Midwest. In 1945, the brewery changed its name to the Huber Brewery. The brewery offers tours, a museum, and a gift shop.

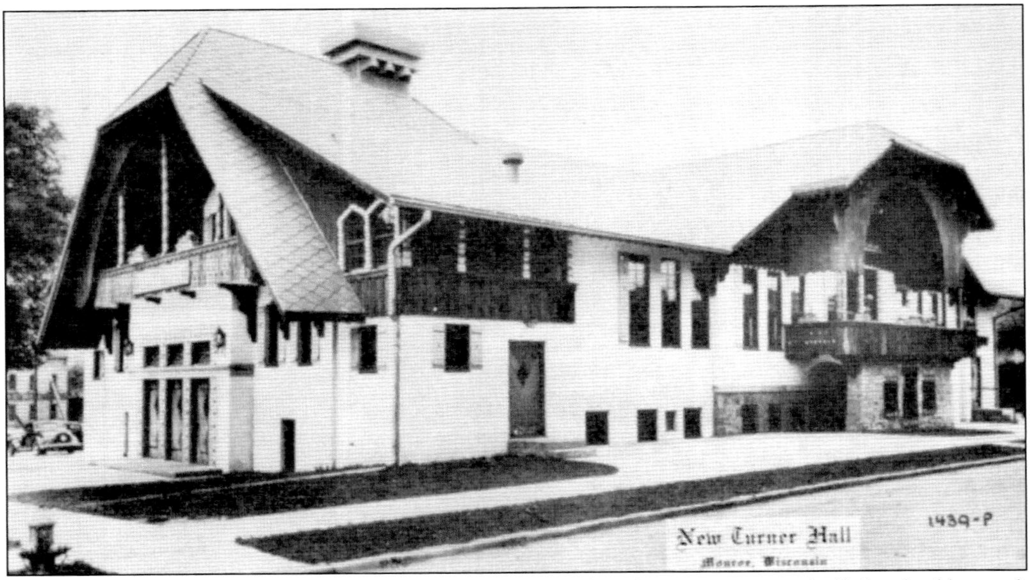

This photograph shows the newly completed Turner Hall replacing a previous hall that had burned. Turner Hall still serves as the gathering place for the Swiss of southern Wisconsin and northern Illinois. Turner Hall conducts Swiss cultural events and brings in groups from Switzerland to entertain area residents many times each year.

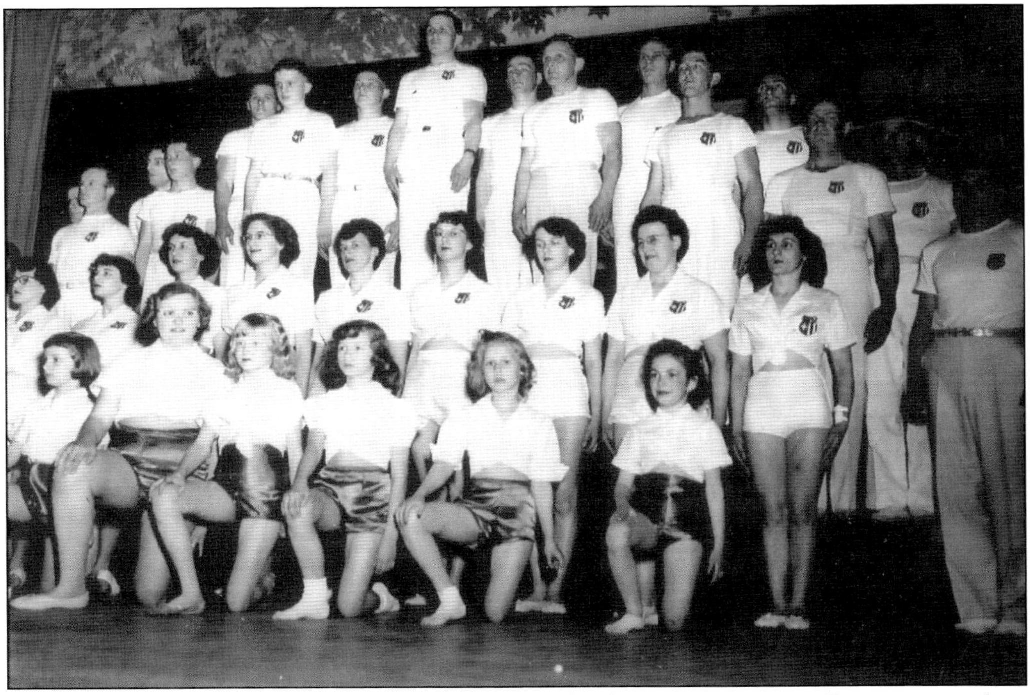

This is the finale of another great program presented by the Monroe Turners. Featuring members from most towns in Green County, the Monroe Turners participated in these local programs and in nationwide competitions. One member, Marie Blumer-Herbert, was a member of the 1952 United States Olympic gymnastics team that competed in Helsinki, Finland. (Turner Hall.)

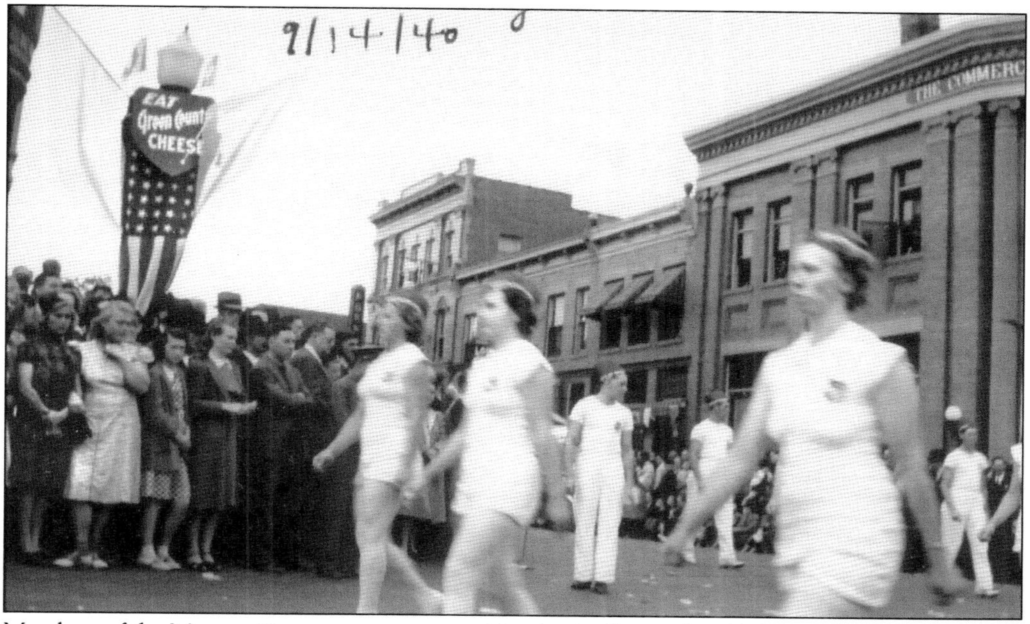

Members of the Monroe Turners are seen marching in the September 14, 1940, Cheese Day parade. They are shown on the northeast corner of the Courthouse Square. Shown in the background is the former Commercial and Savings Bank, which was torn down to create a small downtown park. (Turner Hall.)

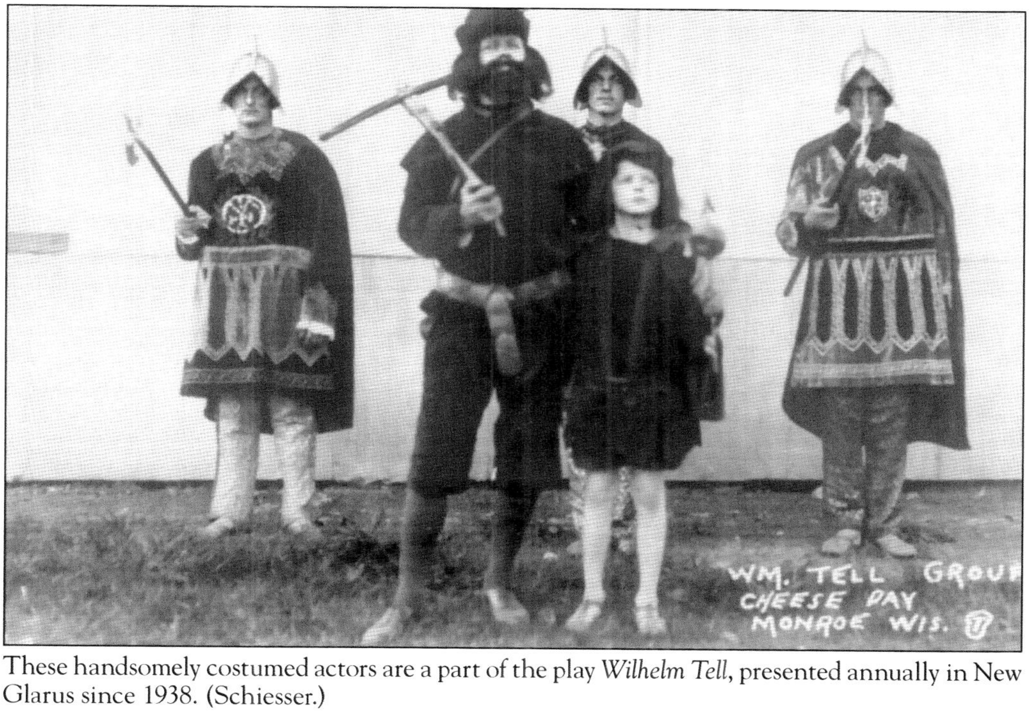

These handsomely costumed actors are a part of the play *Wilhelm Tell*, presented annually in New Glarus since 1938. (Schiesser.)

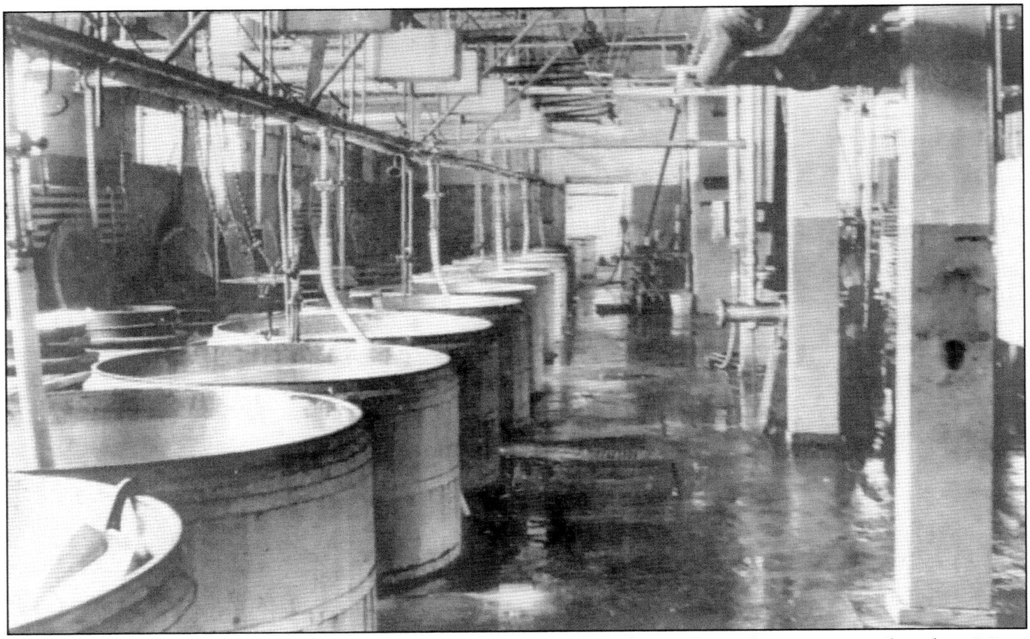

The Swiss cheese that Green County is famous for is made in these large copper kettles. Most cheese factories had several kettles filled each morning with milk to be turned into the finest Swiss cheese in America. Cheese factories' capacity was often measured by the number of kettles they made each day. (Schiesser.)

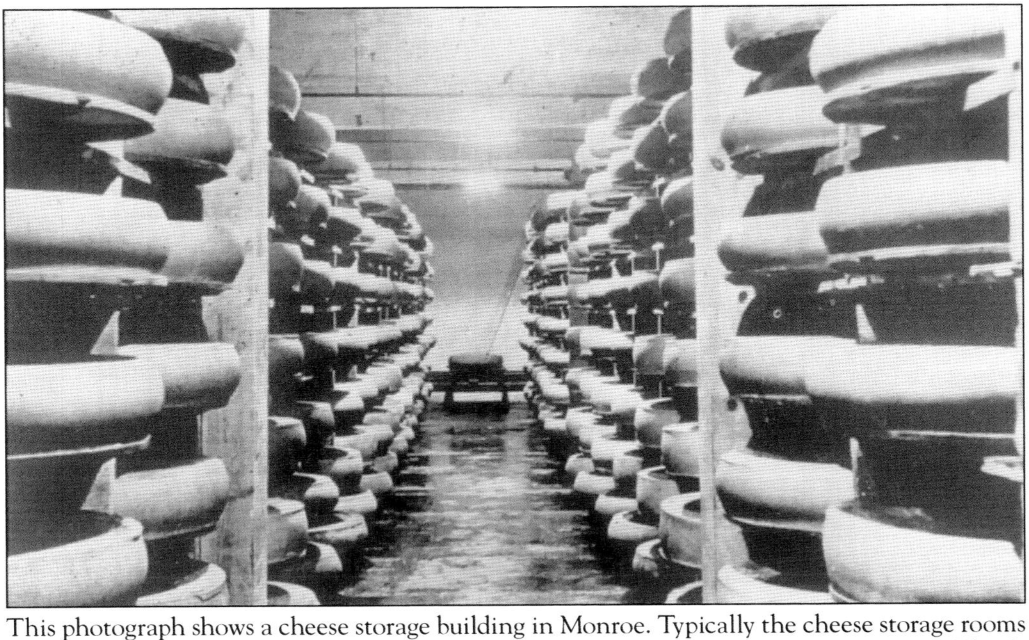

This photograph shows a cheese storage building in Monroe. Typically the cheese storage rooms were built into the ground to take advantage of naturally cool underground temperatures. Wheels of Swiss cheese like these take a minimum of six months to properly age. (Schiesser.)

These men at Marty Swiss Cheese Company in Monroe are shown rotating the wheels of Swiss cheese to ensure proper aging. Cheese makers had to be very strong and in excellent health to rotate these wheels of cheese—each weighing over 200 pounds. Marty Swiss Cheese was a well-known brand across the country. (Schiesser.)

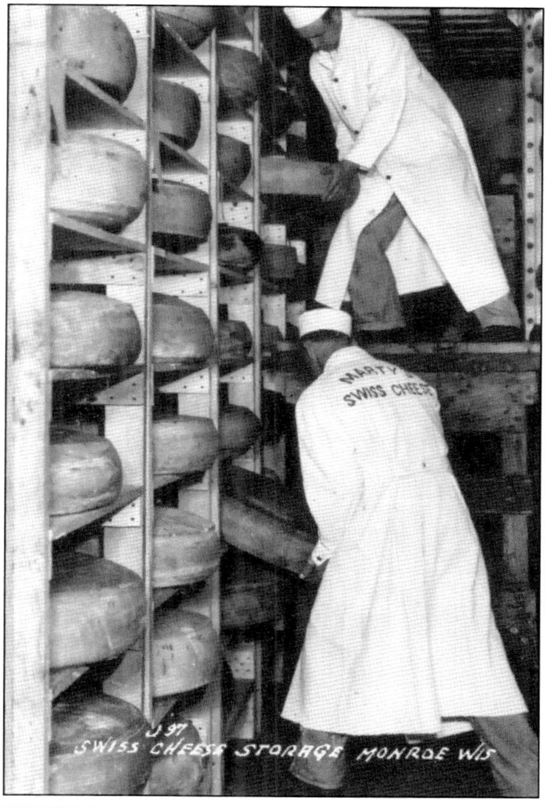

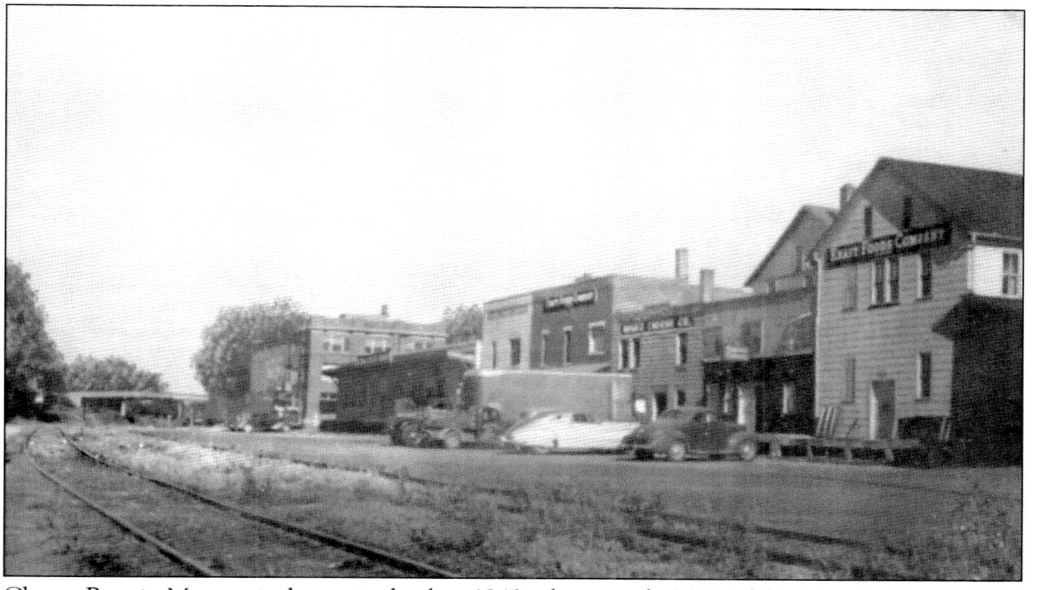

Cheese Row in Monroe is shown in this late-1940s photograph. Most of the many Monroe cheese companies were located here in great part because of easy access to the Milwaukee Road Railroad. The Milwaukee Road train depot is just to the left side in this photograph. Today the depot serves as the site of the Historic Cheesemaking Center, a fitting new purpose for the old depot.

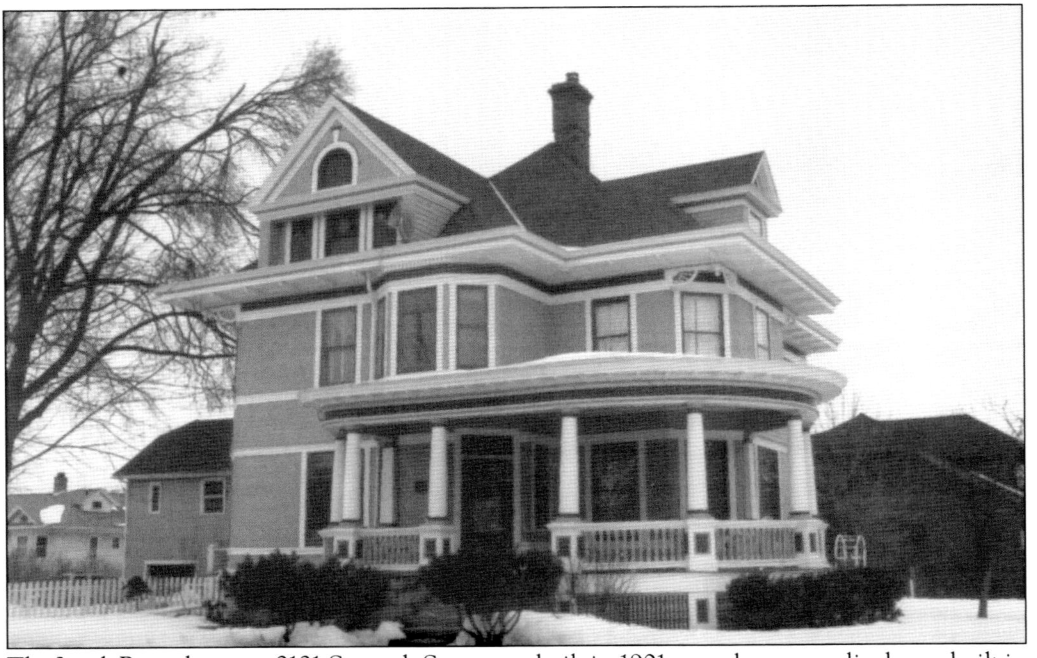

The Jacob Regez home at 2121 Seventh Street was built in 1901 to replace an earlier home built in 1884 but destroyed during a lightning storm. This Queen Anne home was designed by architect Fridolin J. Heer and Son. Regez was one of the early marketers of Green County–produced cheese. The home is on the National Register of Historic Places.

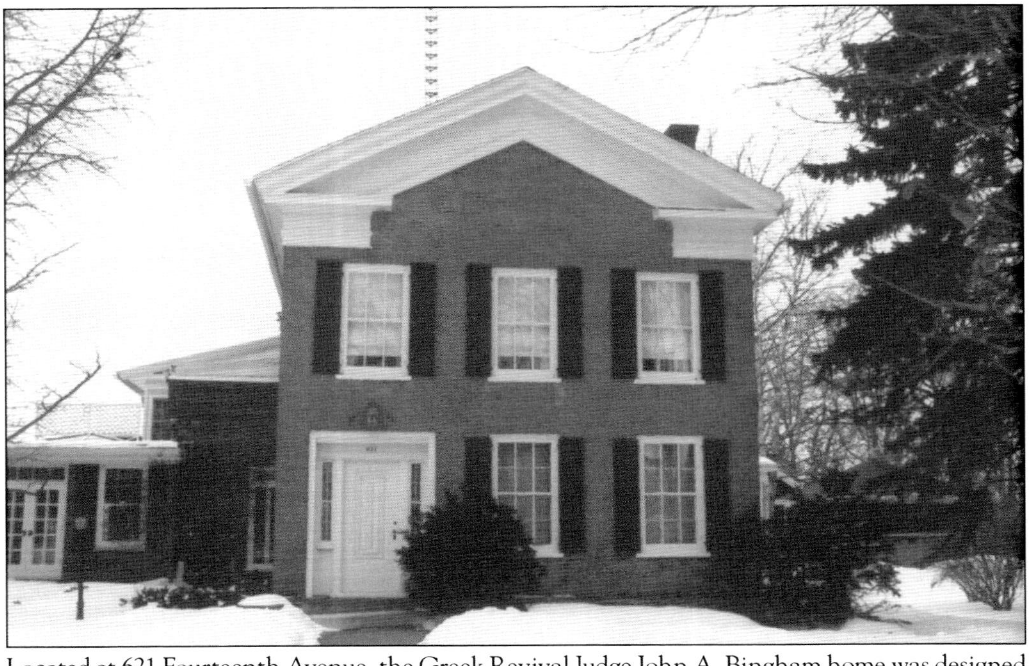

Located at 621 Fourteenth Avenue, the Greek Revival Judge John A. Bingham home was designed by Norman Churchill. Bingham was the first attorney in Monroe, and he also served as the first elected judge in Green County. This home is listed on the National Register of Historic Places.

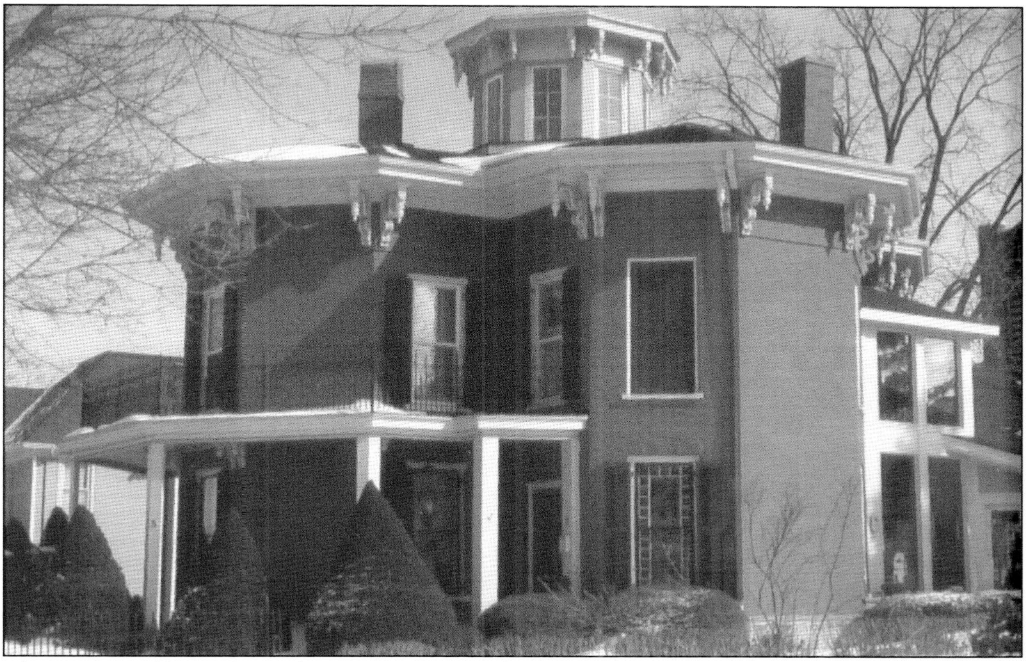

This octagonal home located at 1410 Seventeenth Avenue was designed by architect Orson Fowler. The interior features inlaid parquetry, three grand winding staircases, natural air-conditioning, and an enclosed cupola. This house is listed on the National Register of Historic Places.

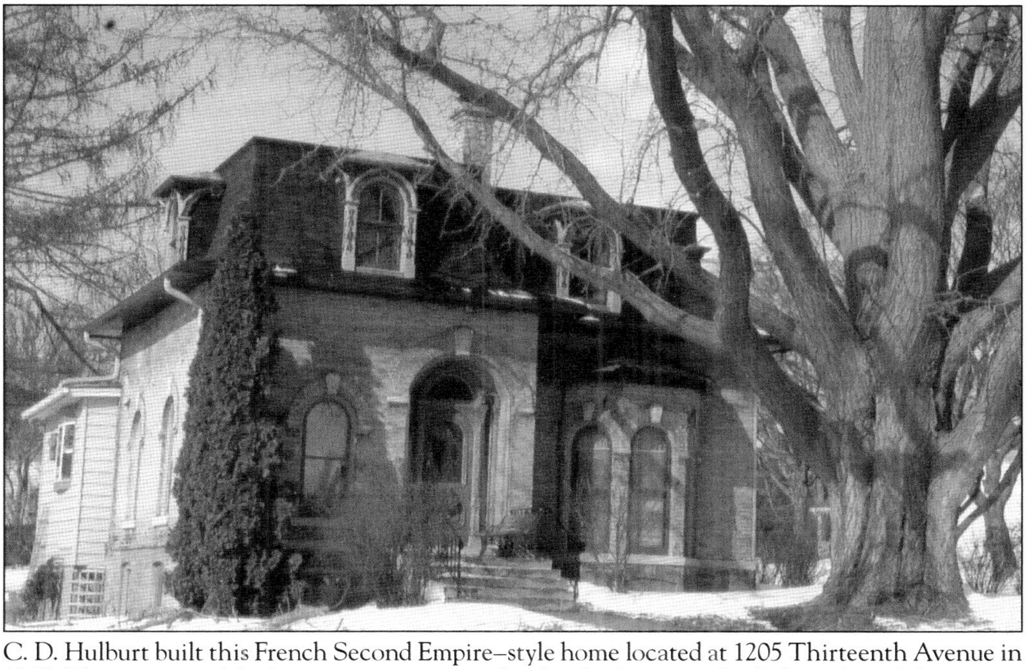

C. D. Hulburt built this French Second Empire–style home located at 1205 Thirteenth Avenue in 1860. The exterior of the home uses cream city brick, which was no doubt brought to Monroe via railroad from brick factories in the Milwaukee area. The large tree in the front yard is the Wisconsin champion ginkgo tree. The home is listed on the National Register of Historic Places.

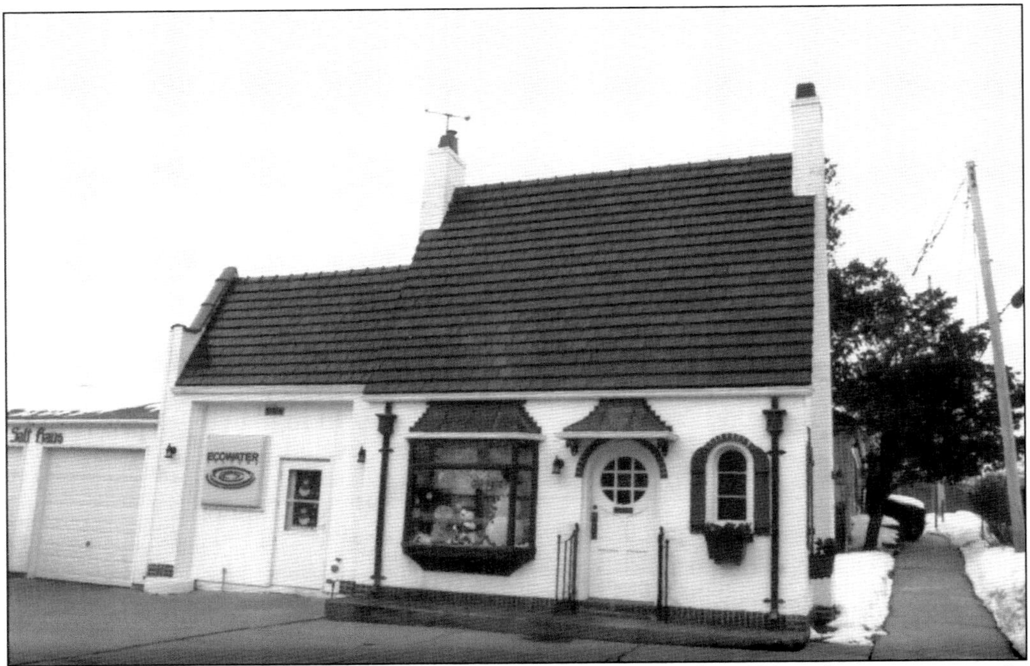

In the 1930s, oil companies tried various methods of making their gas stations stand out from the crowd. The Freitag Pure Oil Station at 1323 Ninth Street, shown here, is an outstanding example of the architecture used toward that end. This station was built in the cottage style of architecture. It was designed by Carl A. Peterson and constructed in 1935. It is listed on the National Register of Historic Places.

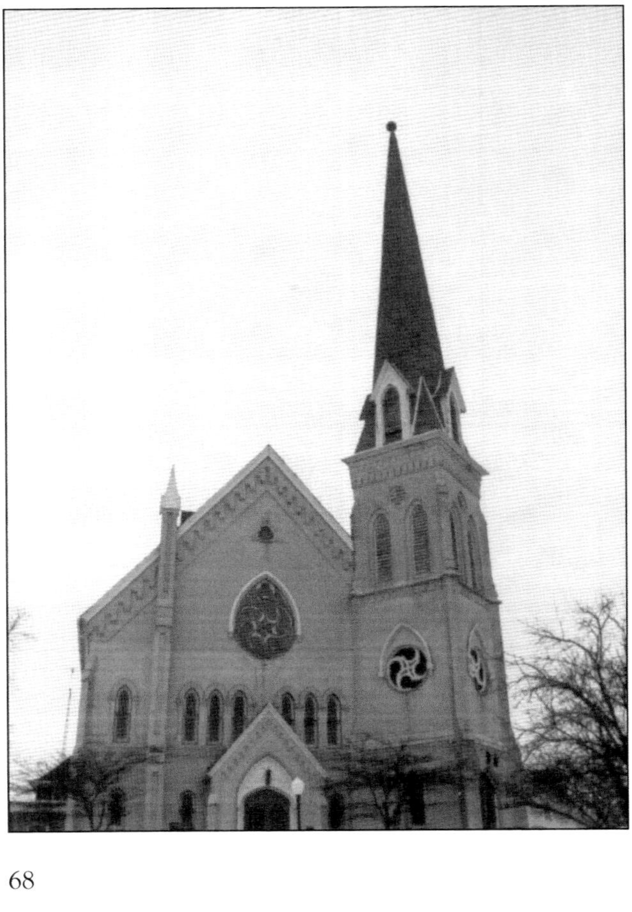

Located at Eleventh Street and Fourteenth Avenue, the First Methodist Church was designed by famed Milwaukee architect Edward Townsend Mix using late Gothic revival–style architecture. This beautiful church has been serving as the Monroe Arts and Activities Center since the 1970s and provides an excellent venue for arts events of all types. The church is listed on the National Register of Historic Places.

Six

MONTICELLO

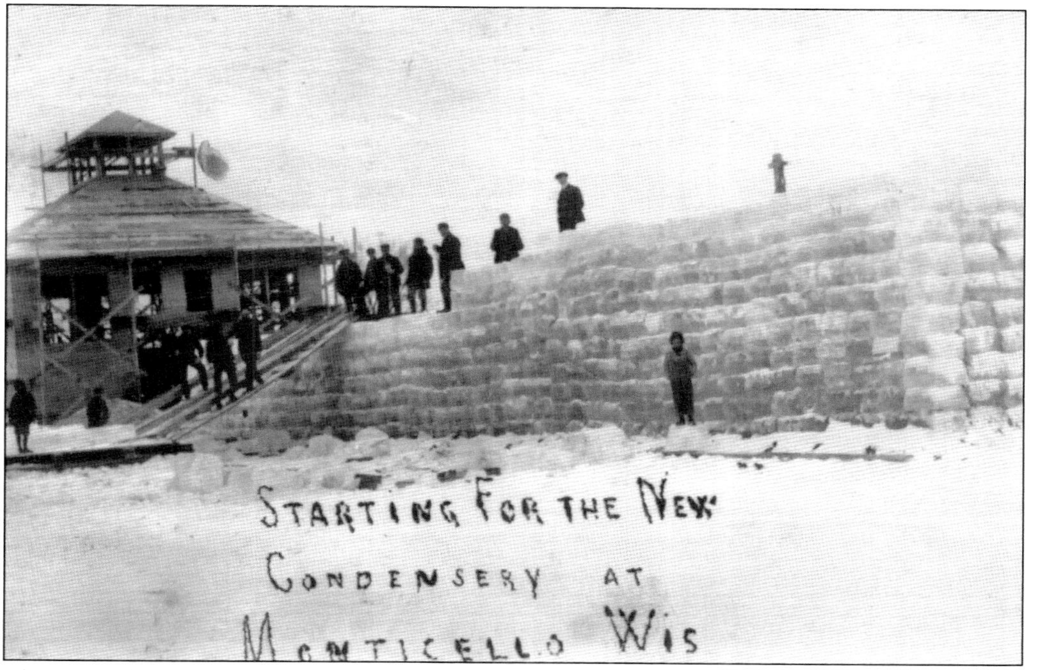

This unusual photograph shows a large shipment of ice that was needed for the new milk condensery that was being built in Monticello. Unfortunately the ice arrived before the building was constructed. Workers built the structure around this mountain of ice. The condensery was in the Jim Town section of Monticello. (Monticello Area Historical Society.)

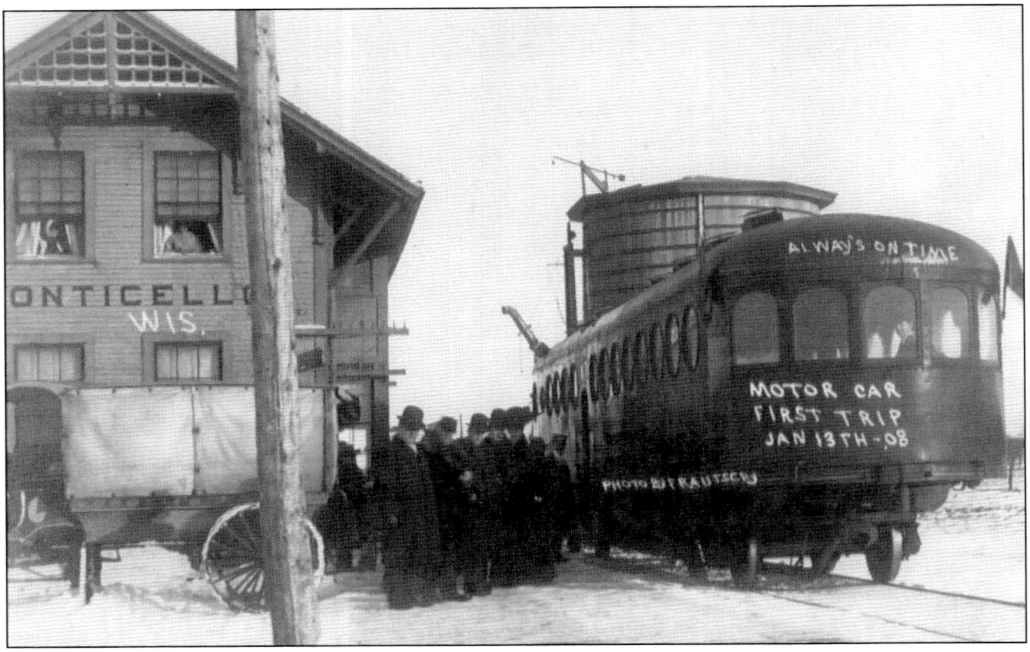

The first run of the Illinois Central Railroad Motor Car occurred on January 13, 1908. This McKeen Motor Car was thought to be a revolutionary new way of transporting passengers, but design problems quickly proved that Wisconsin winters were an unexpected challenge. To see this strange new train, hundreds of people traveled to the stations along this line, which reached from Freeport, Illinois, to Madison, Wisconsin. Notice the people in the second-floor windows of the depot. (Monticello Area Historical Society.)

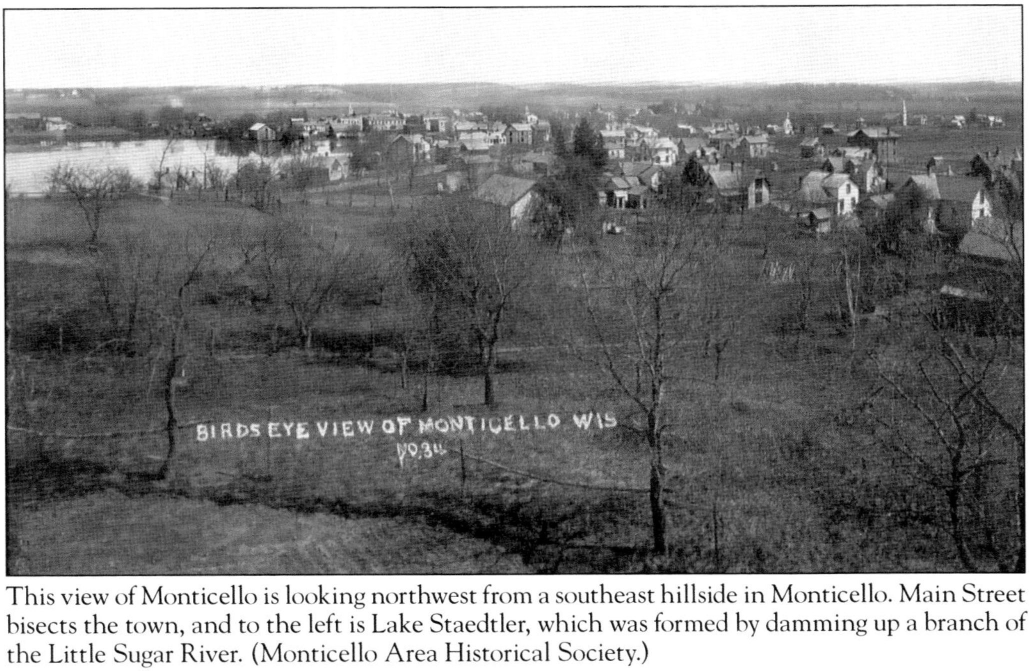

This view of Monticello is looking northwest from a southeast hillside in Monticello. Main Street bisects the town, and to the left is Lake Staedtler, which was formed by damming up a branch of the Little Sugar River. (Monticello Area Historical Society.)

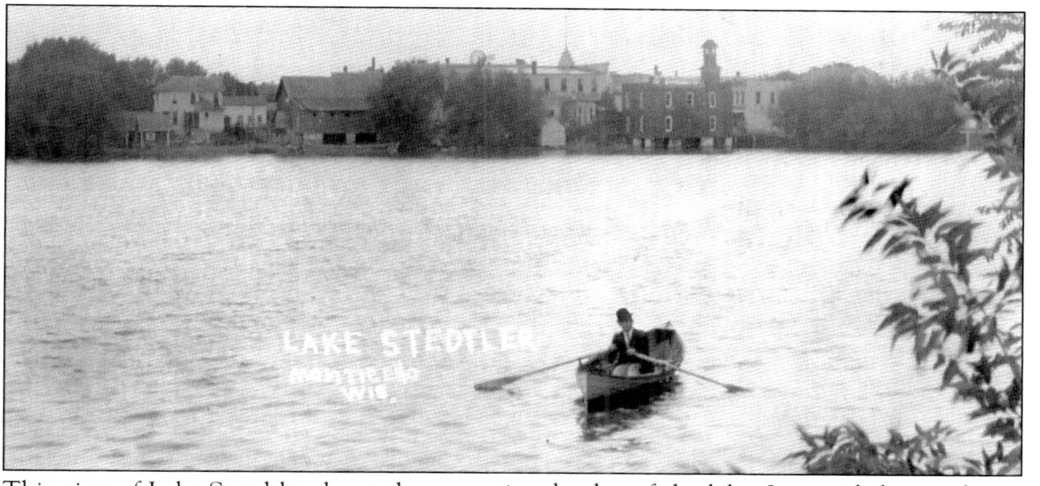

This view of Lake Staedtler shows the recreational value of the lake. It provided many hours of boating and fishing and a swimming hole for local children. The lake was drained when waterpower was no longer needed. In the 1960s, forward-thinking local citizens embarked on a project to create a new lake. (Monticello Area Historical Society.)

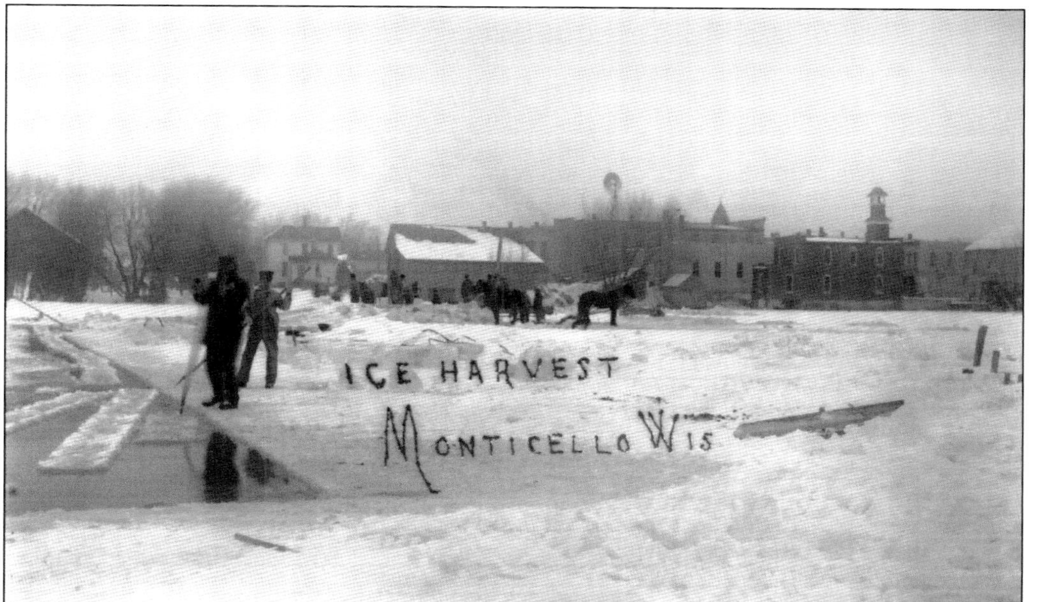

In the days before refrigeration, natural ice was used to keep food cold. Once the ice was thick enough, men from town would gather with horses, wagons, sleighs, and saws to cut the ice into blocks. Once cut, the blocks were hauled to the icehouse for summer use. (Monticello Area Historical Society.)

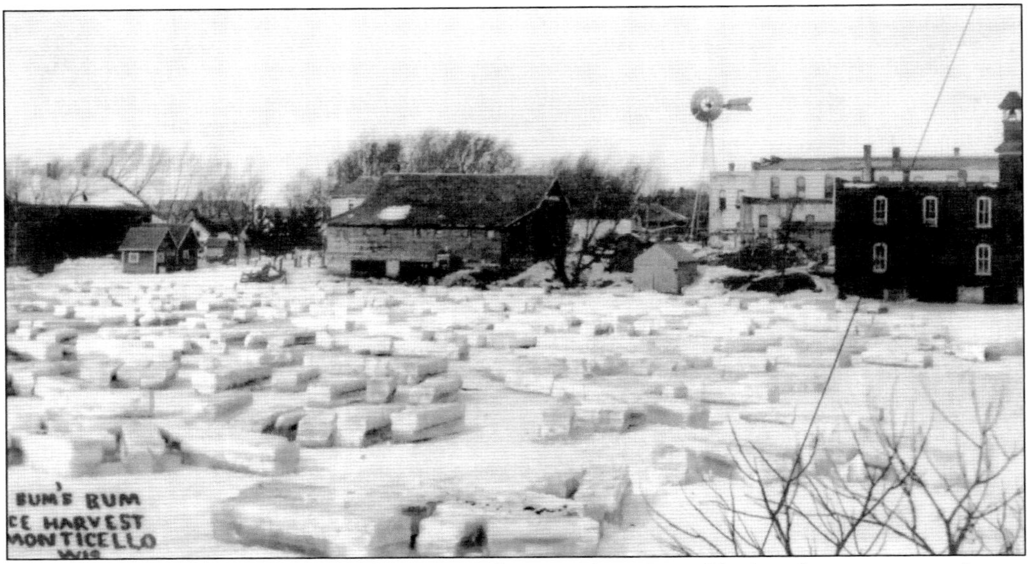

The ice harvest is seen here in full swing. Icehouses where large blocks of ice were stored were insulated with sawdust. Each layer was separated with sawdust so the blocks did not freeze together. Ice on the millpond was often harvested several times each winter to ensure an ample supply of ice to last until the following year's harvest. (Monticello Area Historical Society.)

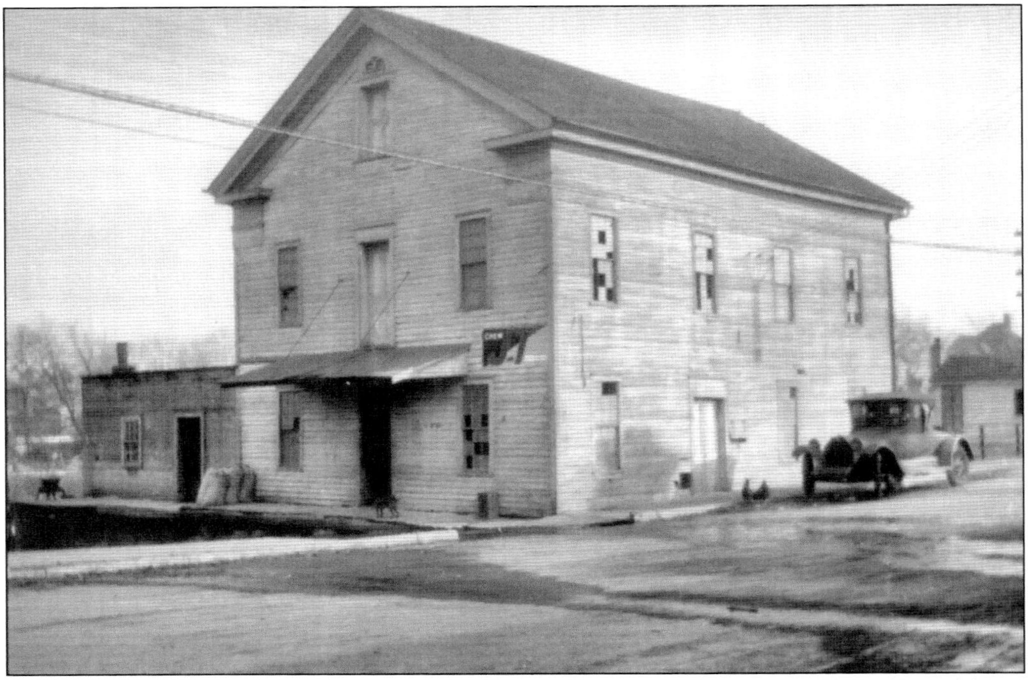

In 1895, Orin Bacon sold this mill to J. Henry Staedtler, who operated the mill until he sold it to his son Henry Staedtler Jr. He operated the mill and sold it to Ben Disch in 1920. By this time, the mill was no longer producing flour but did continue grinding livestock feed for area farmers. This building stood where the current Monticello Village Hall is now located. (Monticello Area Historical Society.)

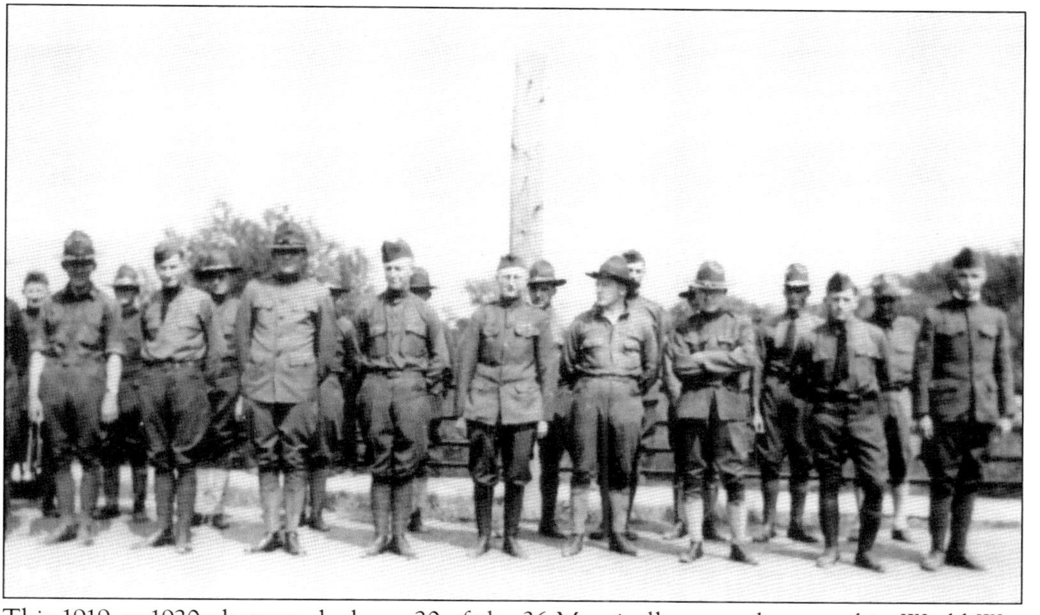

This 1919 or 1920 photograph shows 20 of the 36 Monticello men who served in World War I. Monticello has an outstanding history of its men and women serving in the military during wartime. Monticello and the surrounding towns of Washington and Mount Pleasant sent nearly 200 of its sons to the Civil War. Many of these men did not speak English nor were they yet citizens when they went off to war. (Monticello Area Historical Society.)

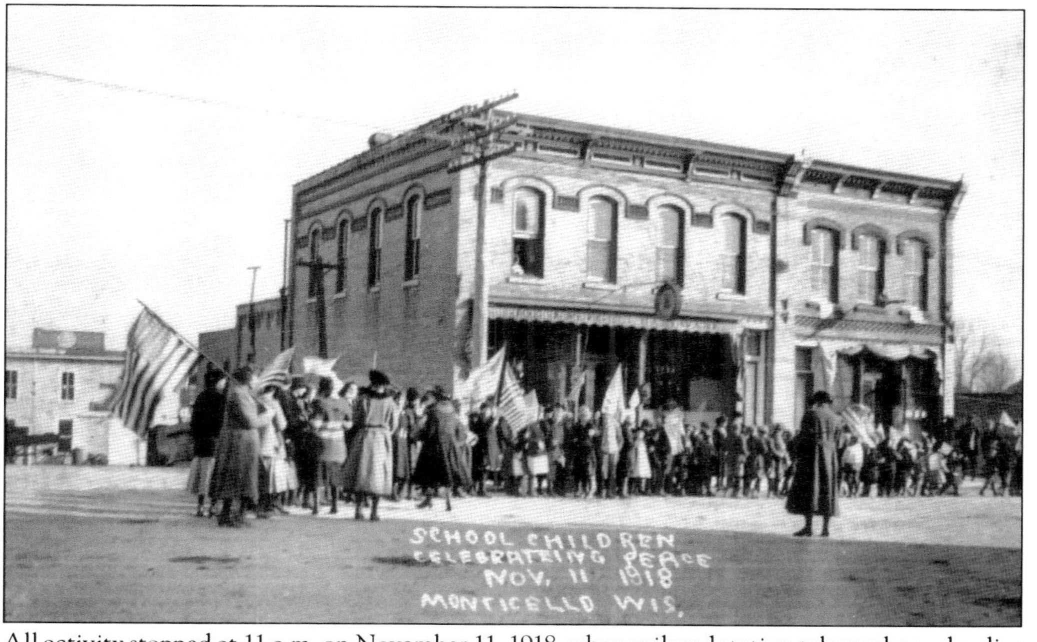

All activity stopped at 11 a.m. on November 11, 1918, when railroad station telegraphs and radios across the country announced that World War I had come to an end. The sons and daughters of Monticello were soon coming back home. Monticello school students walked downtown to celebrate the armistice. (Monticello Area Historical Society.)

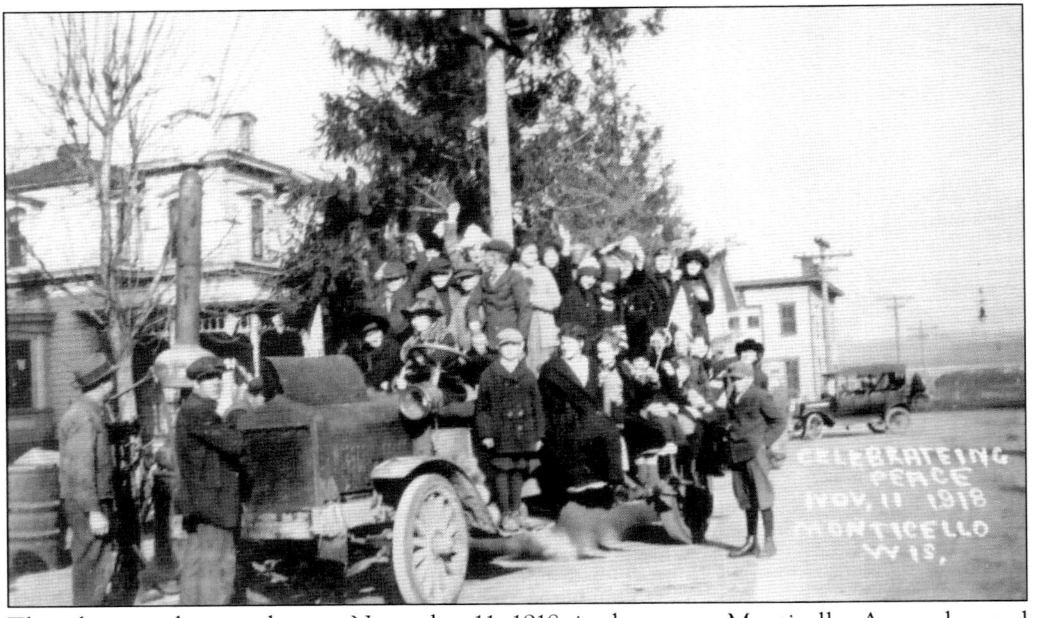

This photograph was taken on November 11, 1918, in downtown Monticello. As word spread to the countryside that World War I had ended, people stopped what they were doing, changed clothes, and quickly came into Monticello to share the good news with friends and family who may not yet have heard the news. (Monticello Area Historical Society.)

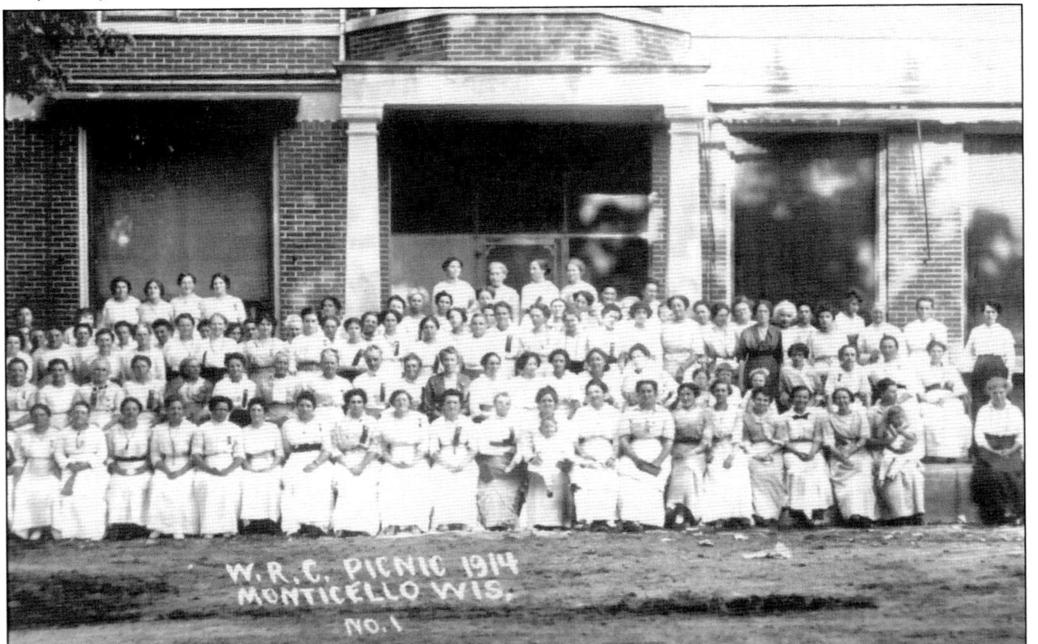

Members of the John Ross chapter of the Women's Relief Corps (WRC) pose in front of the Grand Central Hotel in Monticello during the group's 1914 picnic. The John Ross chapter was formed on January 23, 1904, and was active until well into the 1960s. (Monticello Area Historical Society.)

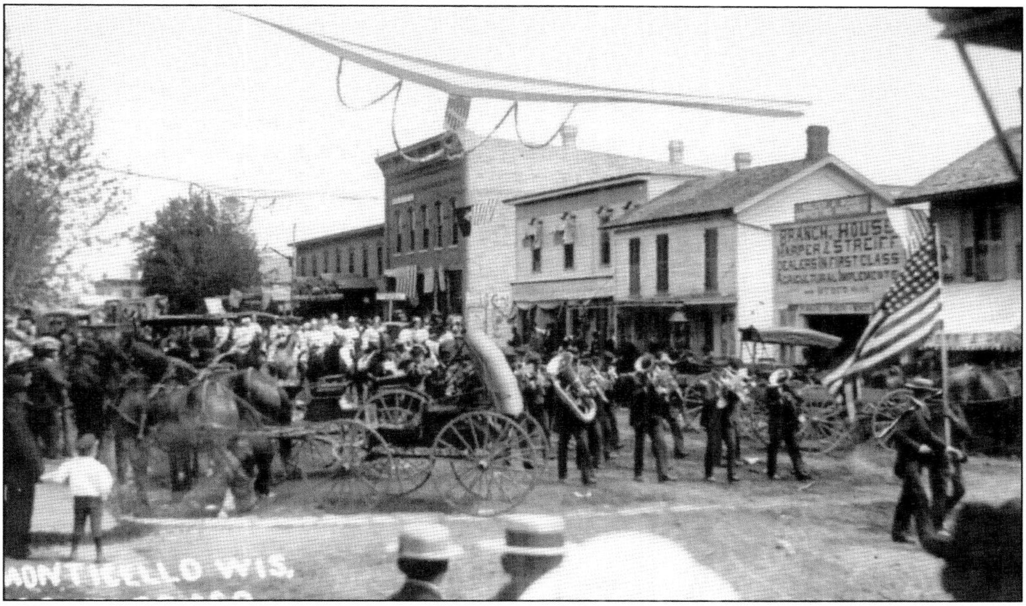

A big parade makes its way down Main Street Monticello. The date and occasion are unknown, but judging from the dress of the spectators, it probably is a Fourth of July parade. The flag bearer on the right appears to be a Civil War veteran. It was a tradition for Civil War veterans to carry the flag in parades. (Monticello Area Historical Society.)

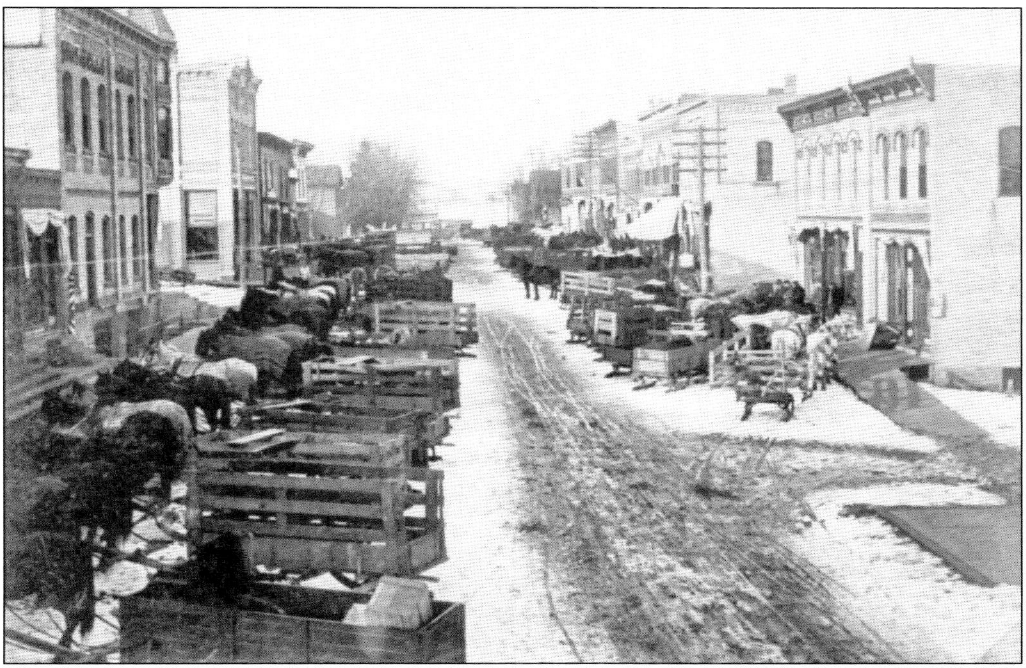

This view of Monticello's Main Street on market day looks north. Judging from the number of wagons with tall side racks, it is stock day at the two stockyards served by the Illinois Central and Milwaukee Road Railroads. The tall building on the left is the Monticello House Hotel. (Monticello Area Historical Society.)

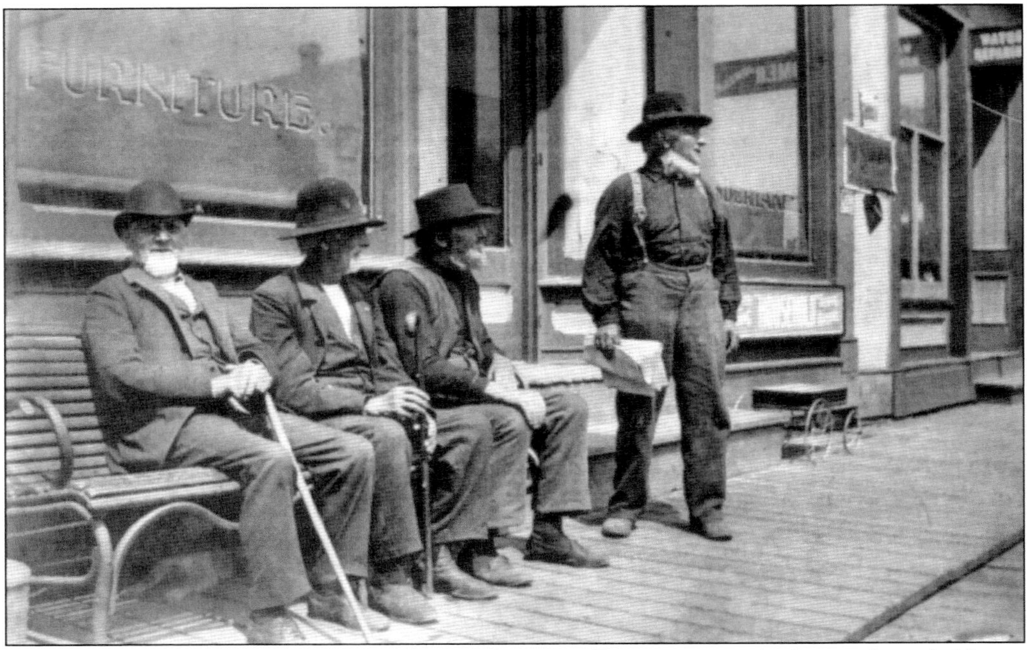

Life is good for these wise elderly gentlemen of Monticello. Every town had a number of old men who enjoyed sitting downtown passing the day away. Their working years had ended long ago, but their stories lived on. Many was the young boy who was entertained by these great storytellers. (Monticello Area Historical Society.)

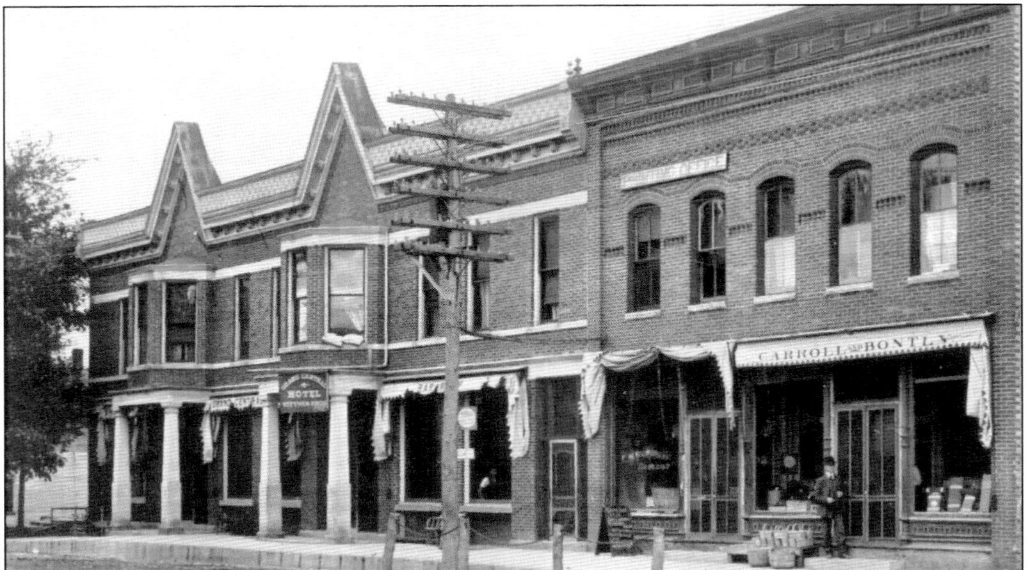

The first hotel on this site began in 1877 and in 1902 was replaced with the Grand Central Hotel built by brothers Gottfried and Albert Wittwer. The Grand Central Hotel boasted a large dining room, well-appointed rooms, and a bar. A large dance hall hosted traveling shows, high school plays, weddings, wedding dances, and other civic events. The Louis Wyss family ran the hotel until it burned in December 1981. (Monticello Area Historical Society.)

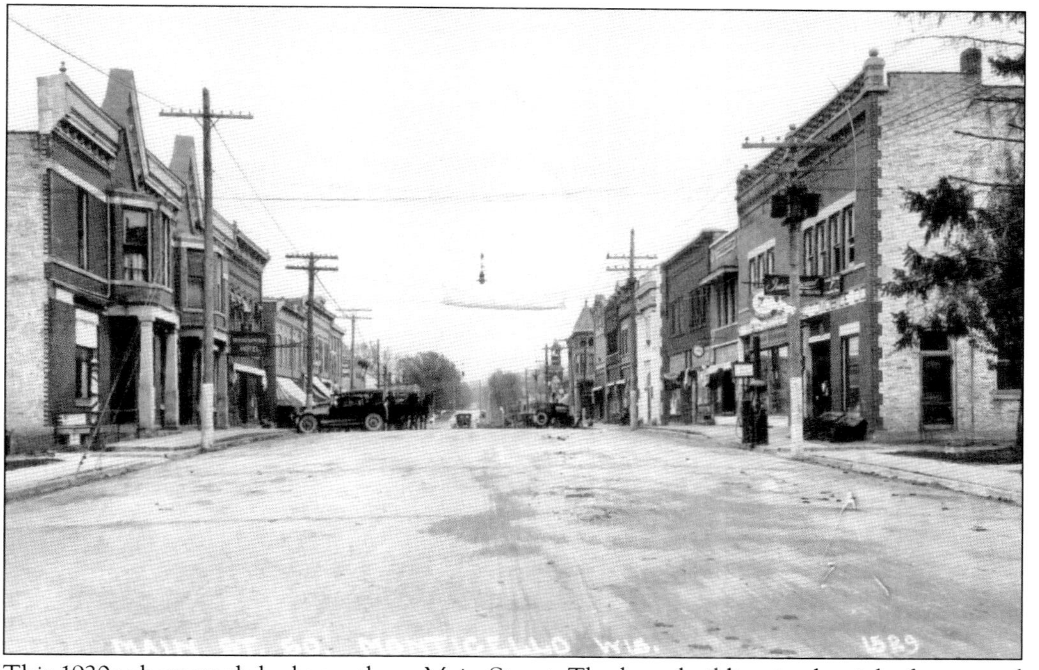

This 1920s photograph looks south on Main Street. The large building in the right foreground is the Monticello Auto Company. There was a wooden ramp at the back of the building used for driving cars upstairs for storage. The next buildings on that side of the street were a tavern, Streiff's Grocery, and the Bank of Monticello. The Monticello Auto building was torn down in the 1970s to make way for an enlarged grocery store. (Monticello Area Historical Society.)

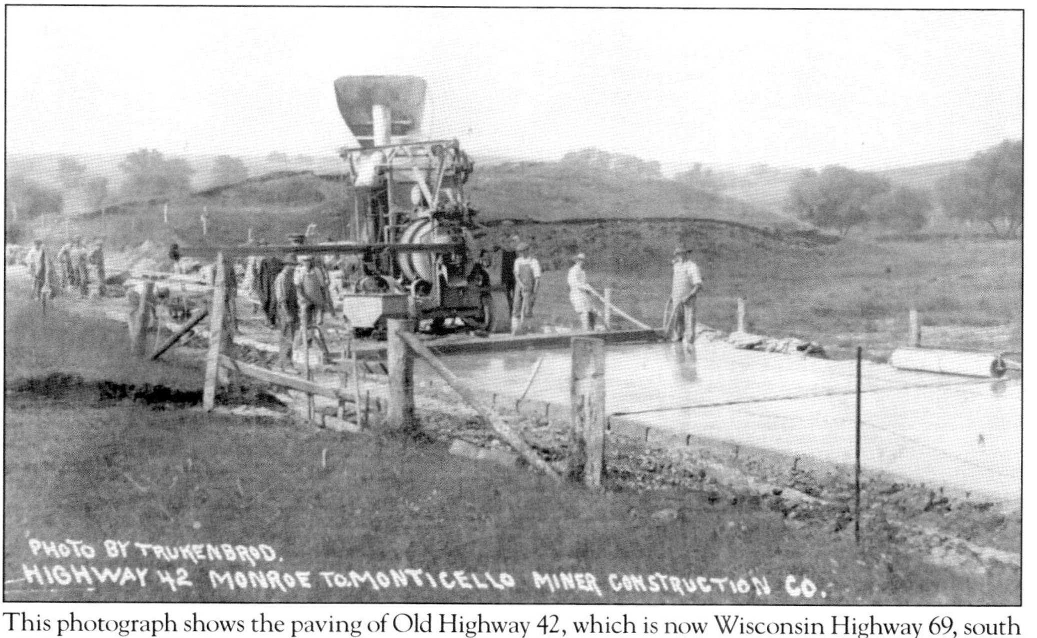

This photograph shows the paving of Old Highway 42, which is now Wisconsin Highway 69, south of Monticello. Work began on this project at Spring Valley (north of New Glarus) in March 1921, and it was completed in October 1923. This improvement made travel to Monroe much easier.

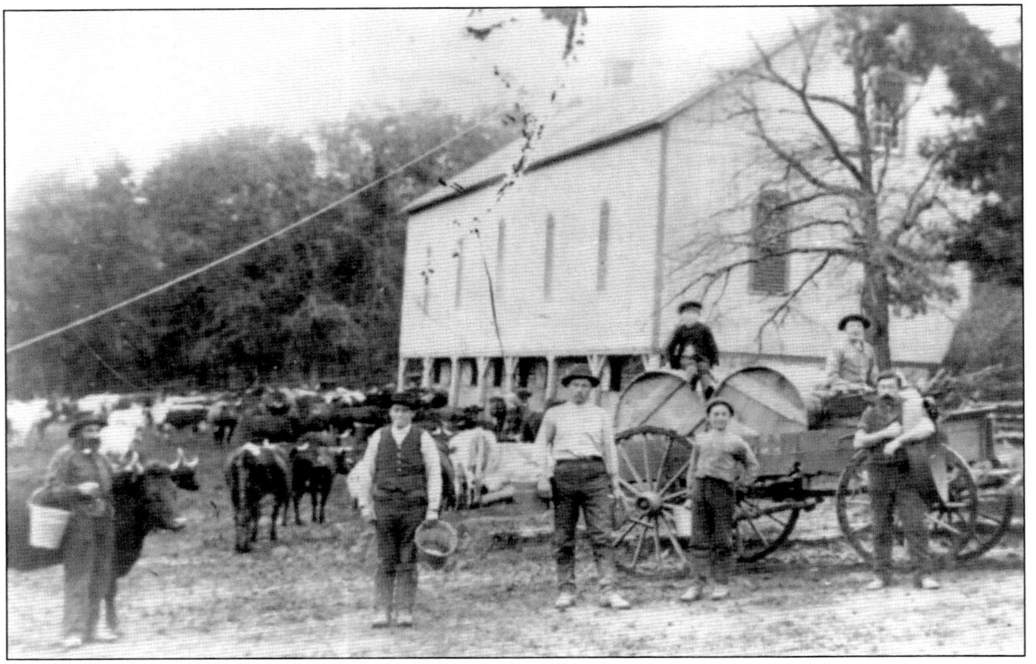

It was on Nic Freitag's farm, seen here, where the Swiss cheese enterprise in America began in 1869. Nikolas Gerber began making cheese in a factory located in a small building on the farm. Gerber's cheese-making equipment is on display at the Swiss Historical Village in New Glarus.

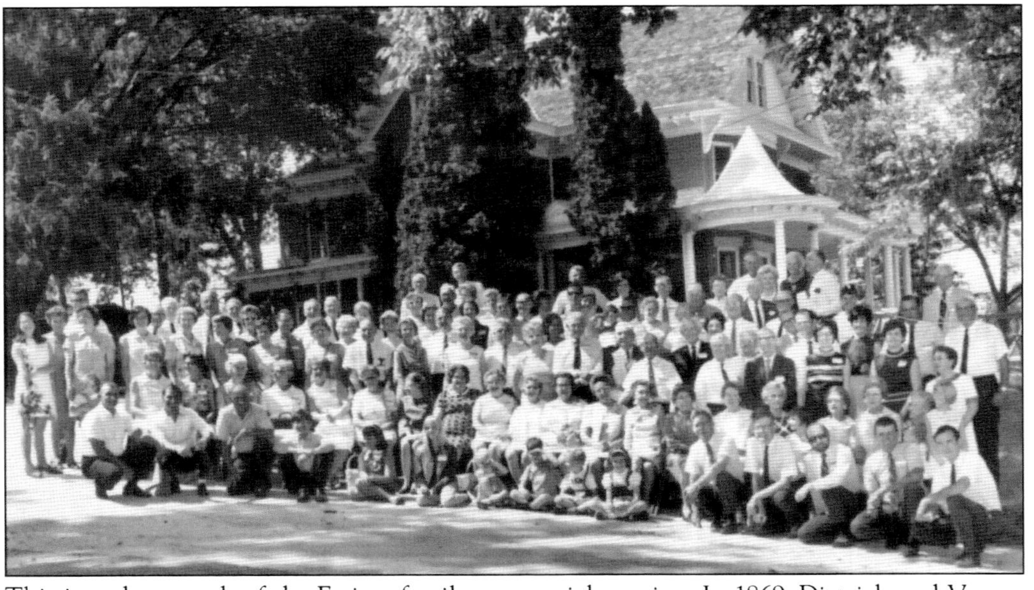

This is a photograph of the Freitag family centennial reunion. In 1869, Dietrich and Verena Freitag, natives of Switzerland, purchased the farm from Fridolin Streiff, one of the two founders of nearby New Glarus. In 1906, the brick house shown here was built by the Freitag family. The house was designed by a local architect. It is listed on the National Register of Historic Places. (Monticello Area Historical Society.)

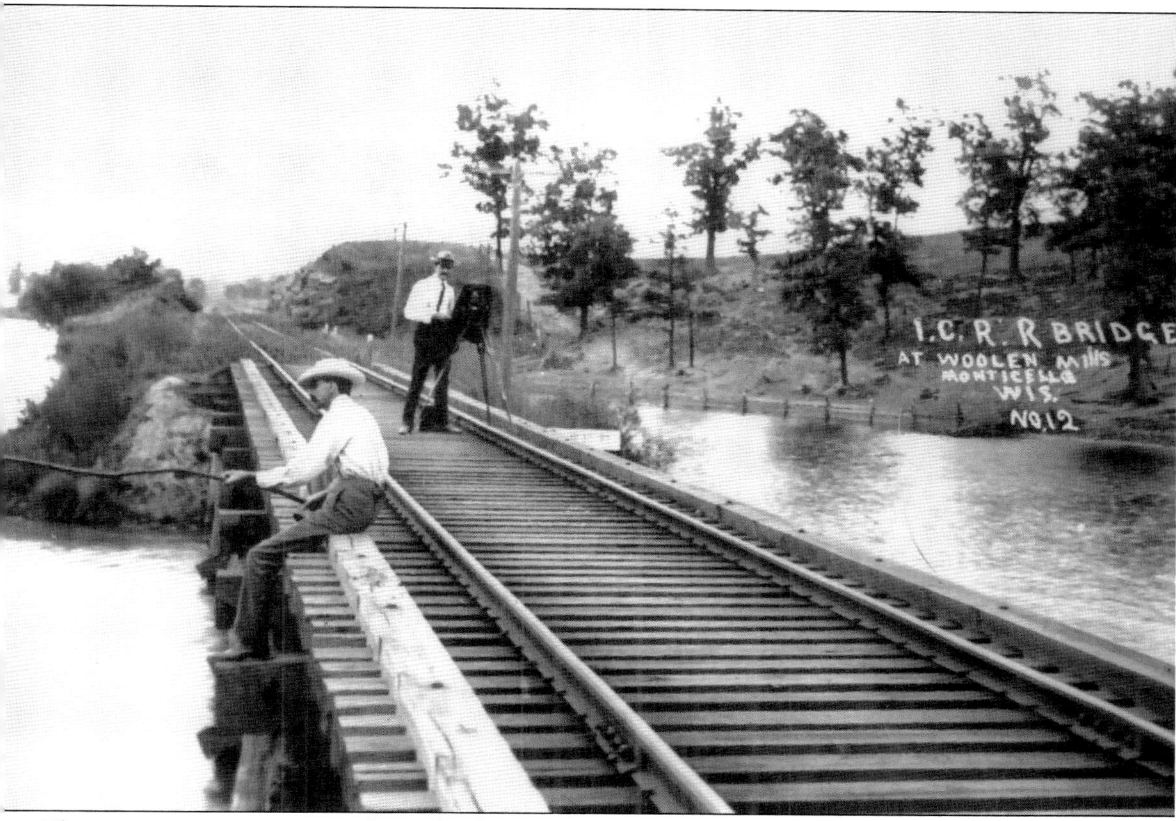

These two men are enjoying a leisurely afternoon fishing off the Illinois Central Railroad bridge just north of Monticello. The body of water they are fishing in is the Monticello Woolen Mill pond, which was created by a dam on the Little Sugar River designed to provide the power needed to operate the nearby woolen mill. Notice how well dressed the fishermen are. (Monticello Area Historical Society.)

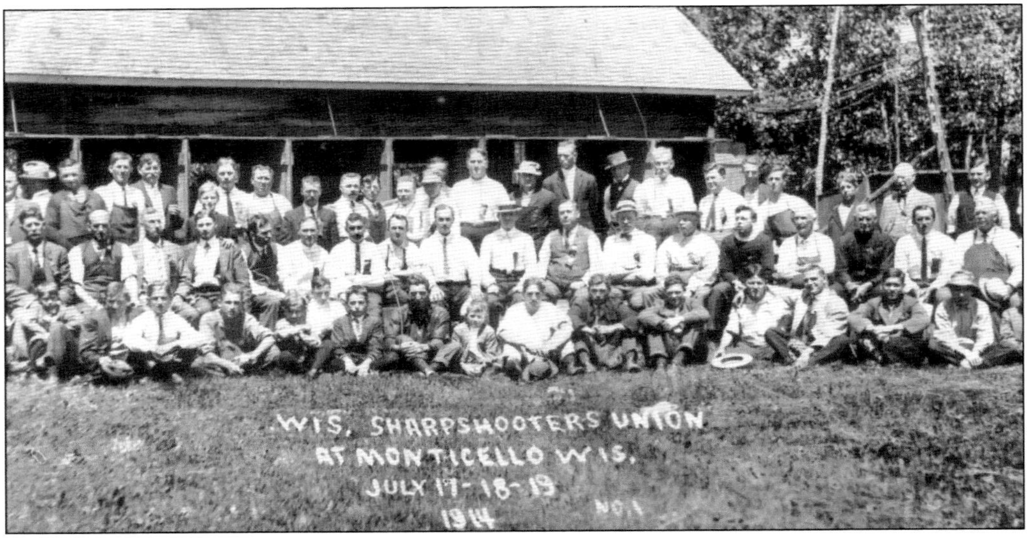

The Wisconsin Sharp Shooters Union held a statewide shooting competition at the Monticello Shooting Park located just west of Monticello on July 17–19, 1914. Competitions such as this were family events complete with picnics and entertainment with people coming from many miles away. The shooting house is long gone. (Monticello Area Historical Society.)

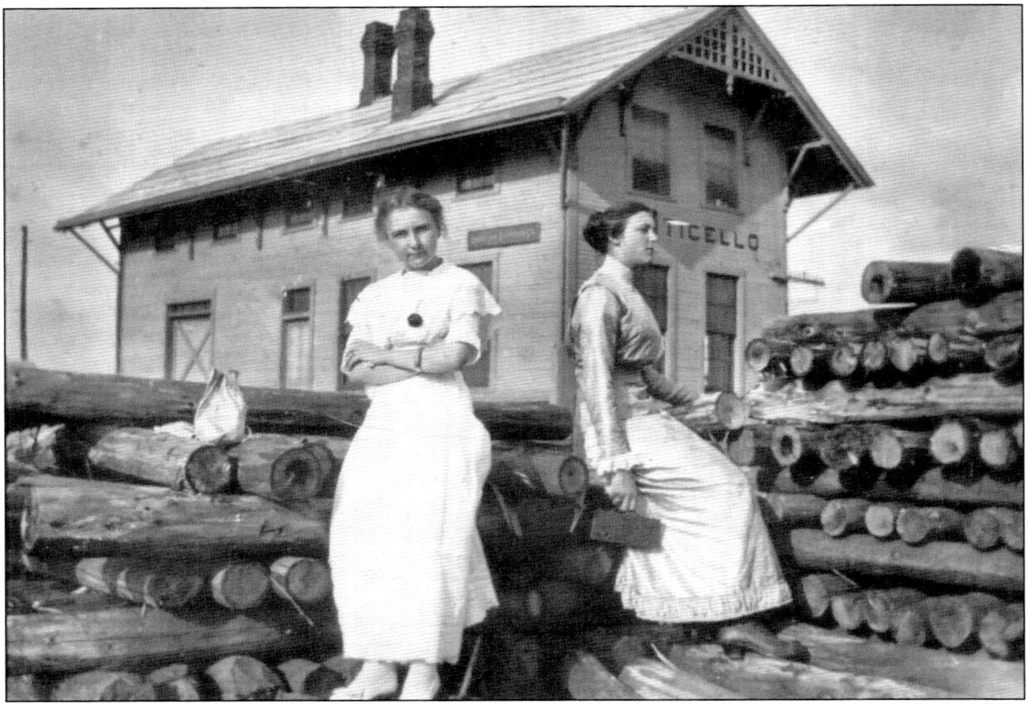

These two young women are posing on what appears to be a pile of telegraph or telephone poles soon to be used in the Monticello area. In the background is the Illinois Central Railroad depot. Many of the train depots the railroad built along this line were of the two-story style, which provided living quarters on the upper floor for the depot agent and his family. (Monticello Area Historical Society.)

Seven

NEW GLARUS

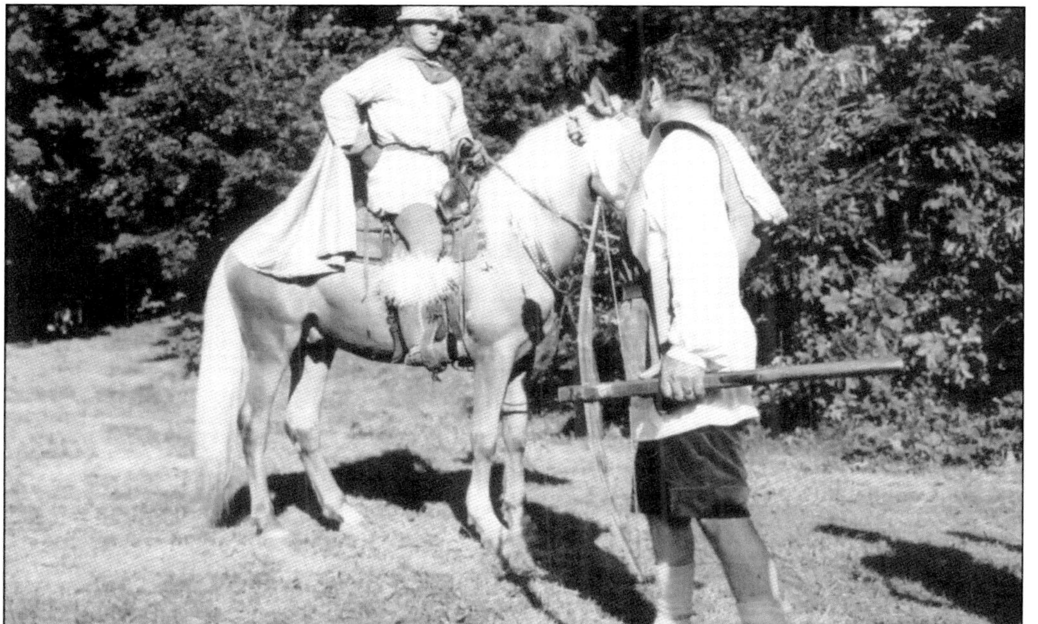

Each year on Labor Day weekend since 1938, the Swiss of New Glarus have presented the Wilhelm Tell Pageant, depicting the Swiss struggle for independence from the Austrian tyrant Herman Gessler. The pageant's production of *Wilhelm Tell* has the distinction of being the longest-running foreign-language play presented in the United States. (Tell Guild.)

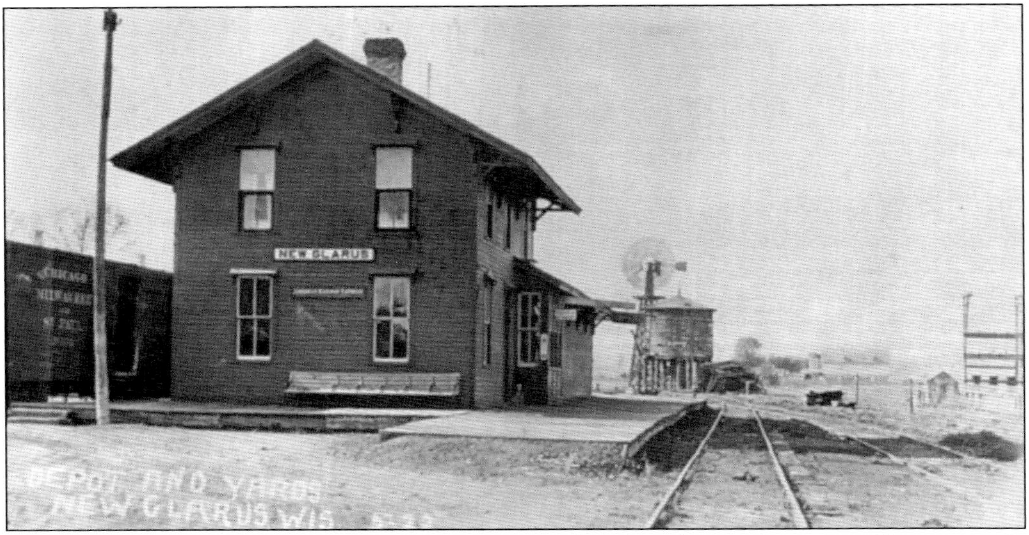

This is the New Glarus depot. The Milwaukee Road Railroad arrived in New Glarus in early August 1887, just four months after the railroad began extending from Albany, which was 16 miles southeast of New Glarus. The depot agent and his family lived in the two-bedroom apartment above the depot. This depot has been restored, and is now listed on the National Register of Historic Places.

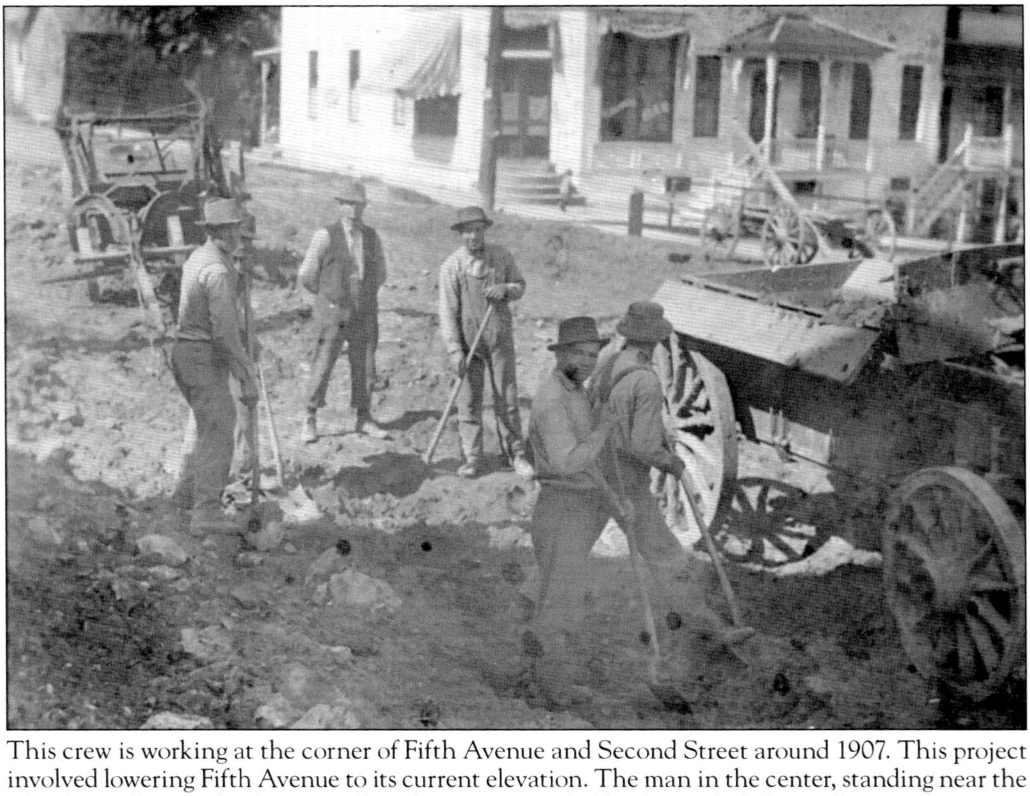

This crew is working at the corner of Fifth Avenue and Second Street around 1907. This project involved lowering Fifth Avenue to its current elevation. The man in the center, standing near the wheel, is Bill Voegeli of Monticello. This project probably also included installing water mains.

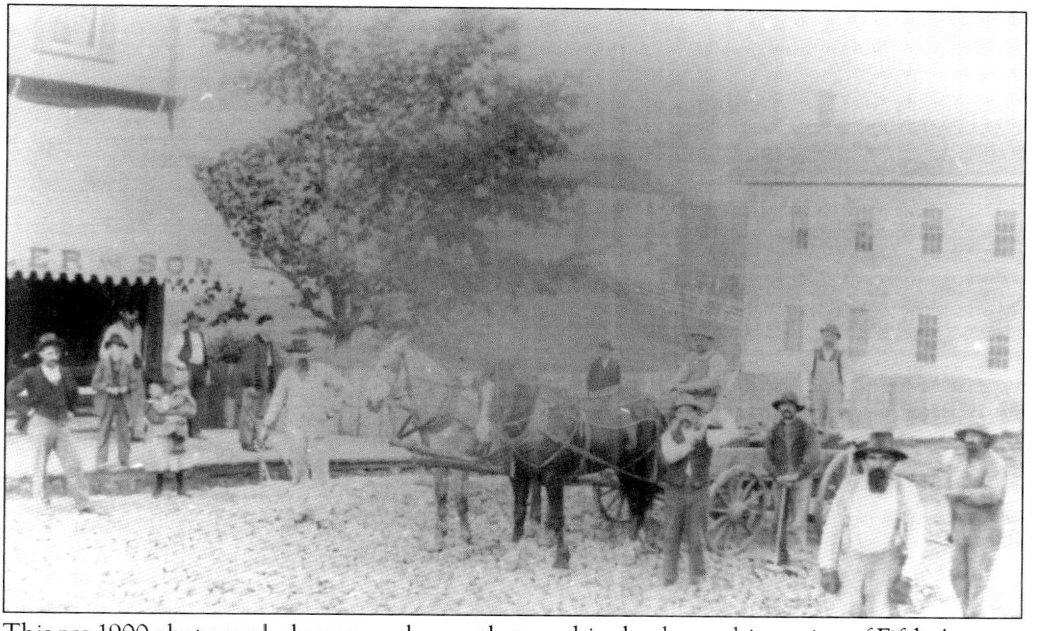

This pre-1900 photograph shows a work crew that was hired to lower this section of Fifth Avenue. The store on the left is the S. A Schindler store, which now houses a tavern. The building on the far right is the first schoolhouse, which today houses a gift shop. In the background is the second church to stand on that site.

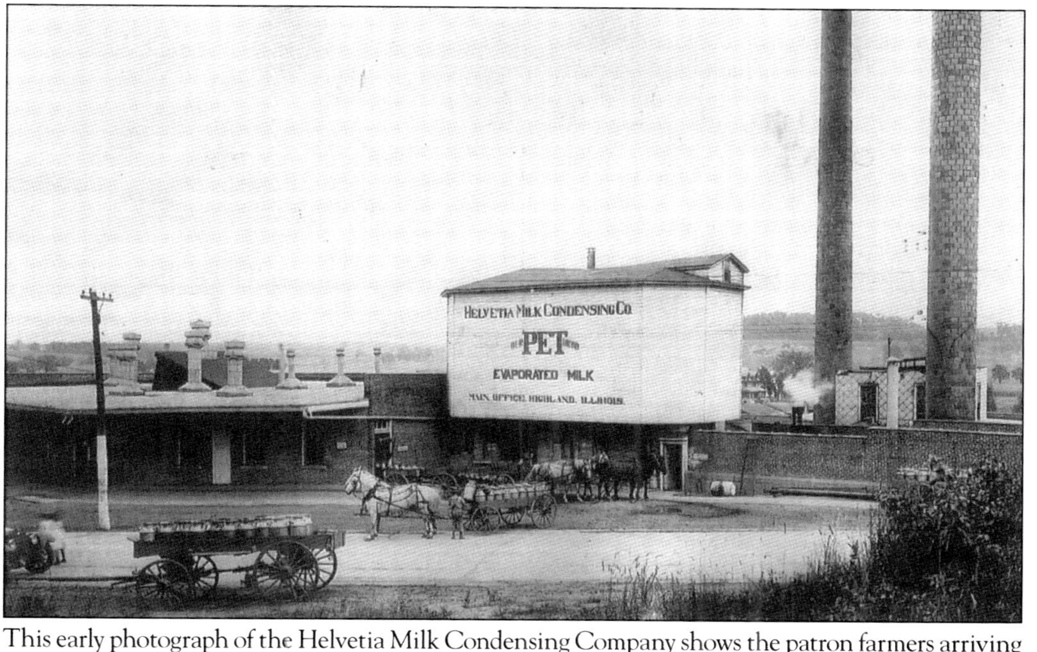

This early photograph of the Helvetia Milk Condensing Company shows the patron farmers arriving with their daily loads of milk, which will quickly be turned into cans of PET brand condensed milk. During World War II, this factory provided much of the condensed milk purchased by the government to feed American soldiers around the world. To these men and women, a cup of coffee with a dash of PET condensed milk was a much-welcomed gift from home.

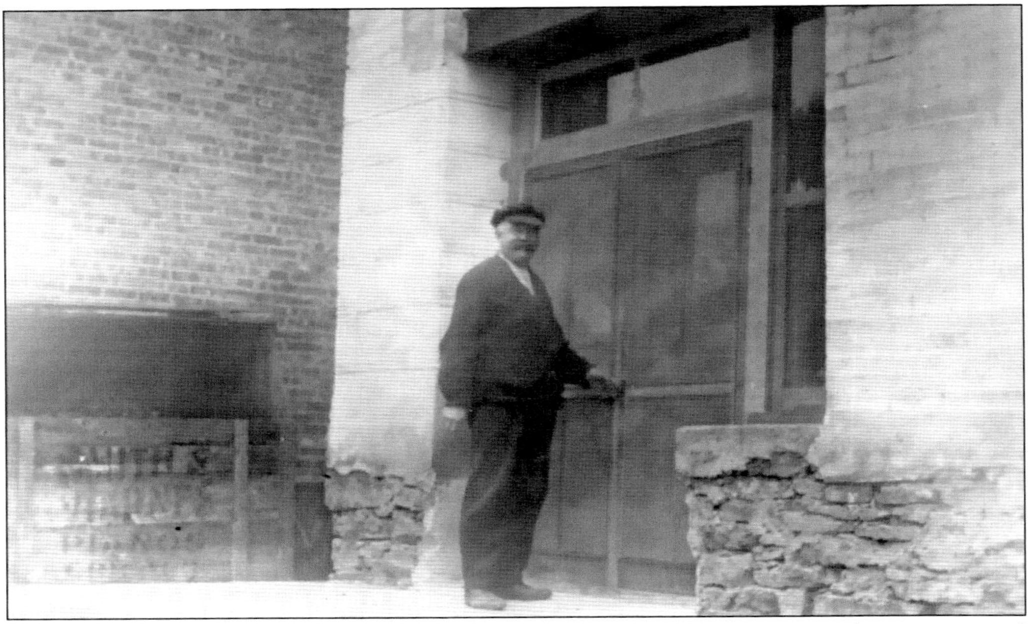

John Theiler was the founder of the *New Glarus Post* newspaper. For many years, the paper printed a Swiss edition. In this photograph, what was the basement has become the first floor. Here is where the huge printing press was located. John's son Arthur Theiler owned and operated the *Post* until he retired in the early 1960s. (Schiesser.)

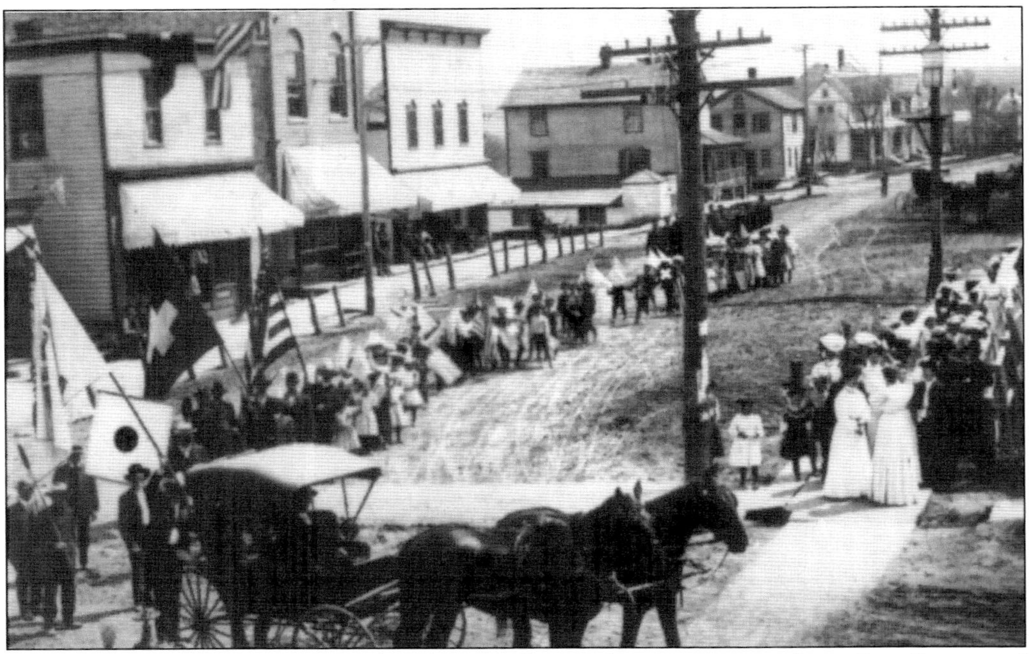

Any good event called for a parade. This parade is making its way north on First Street and onto Fifth Avenue to the back area of the village. This is a parade leading up to an event at the Shooting Park. The white flag with the large dark circle was flown at shooting events. The men directly behind the buggy are carrying the tools needed to pack, clean, and load a cannon.

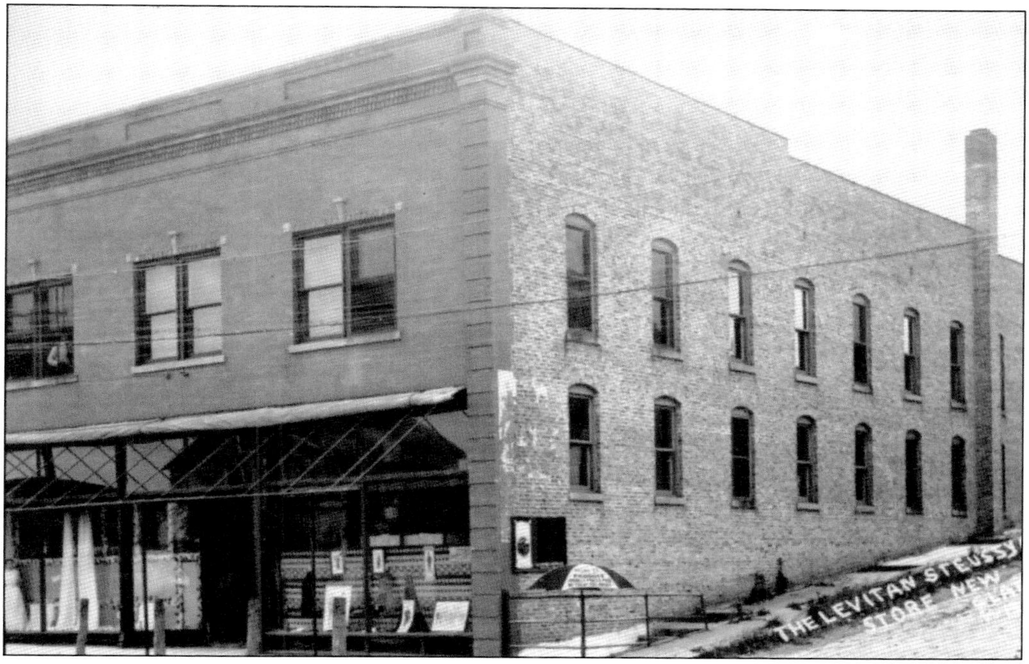

This photograph shows the newly constructed building that housed the Levitan and Steussy general merchandise store. Sol Levitan was a Jewish traveling salesman from Russia who settled in New Glarus. After leaving New Glarus, "Uncle Sol " (as he was lovingly called) was elected to numerous terms as the Wisconsin state treasurer. The store building seen here later housed a bowling alley on the second floor. It burned in the late 1950s. (Monticello Historical Society.)

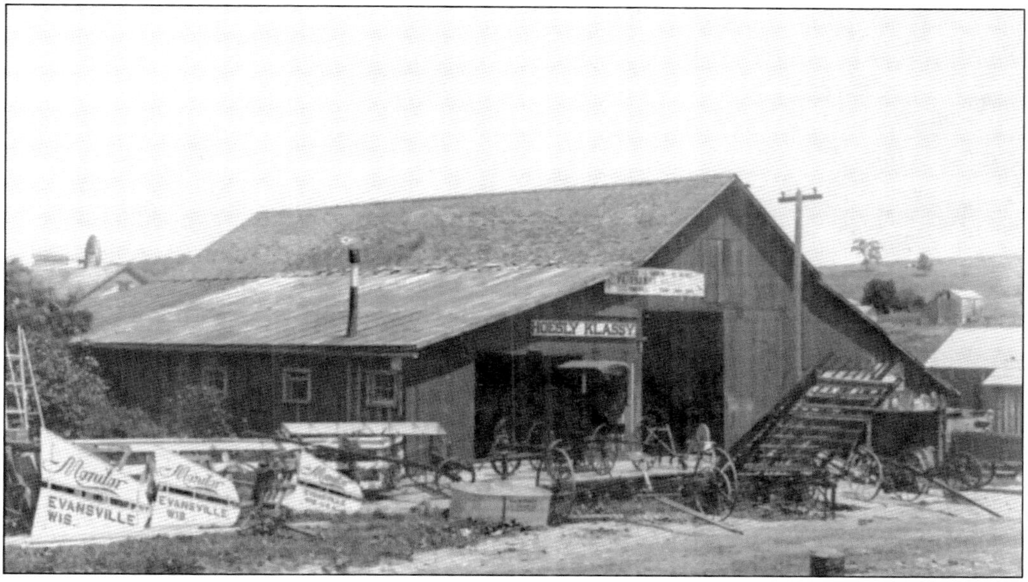

This undated photograph shows the Hoesly and Klassy Implement Company located at 26 Fifth Avenue. This company sold both farm equipment and water systems. Among the equipment shown here are a hay elevator, dump rake wagons, and buggies. On the left are several vanes for Monitor well pumps and windmills, which were made in Evansville, Wisconsin.

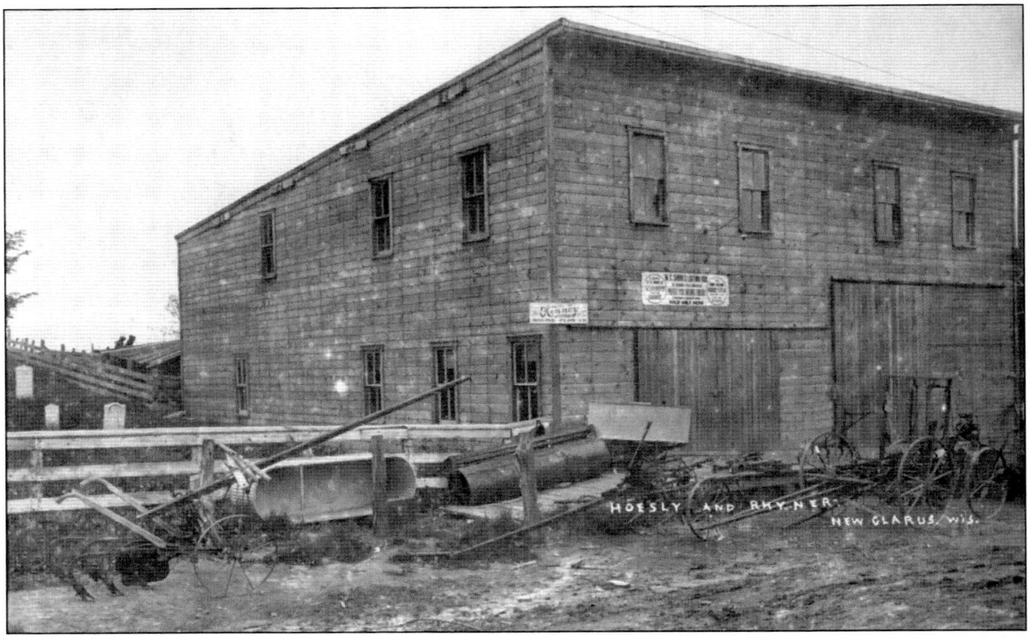

This photograph is the same building seen in the previous photograph. The ownership of the business has changed, and Klassy's name has been replaced with the last name of Rhyner. Buildings were seldom torn down; instead, they were expanded. In the case of this building, carpenters took off the roof and added a full second story to the building. Notice the gravestones in the background.

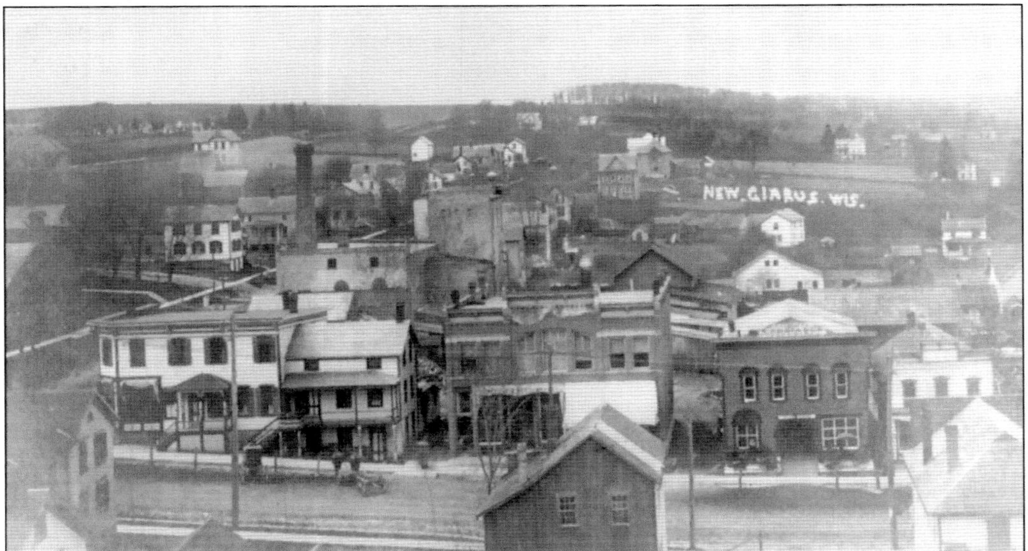

This photograph looks west from the church steeple. The large building in the center left is the Four Corners Bar. The basement of this building housed a bowling alley. The next building to the right served as Stricklers Market for many years, and the far right portion of the building served as the local post office with a bar in the basement. The next building is the Streiff Blacksmith shop. The blacksmith shop equipment is now at the Swiss Historical Village in New Glarus.

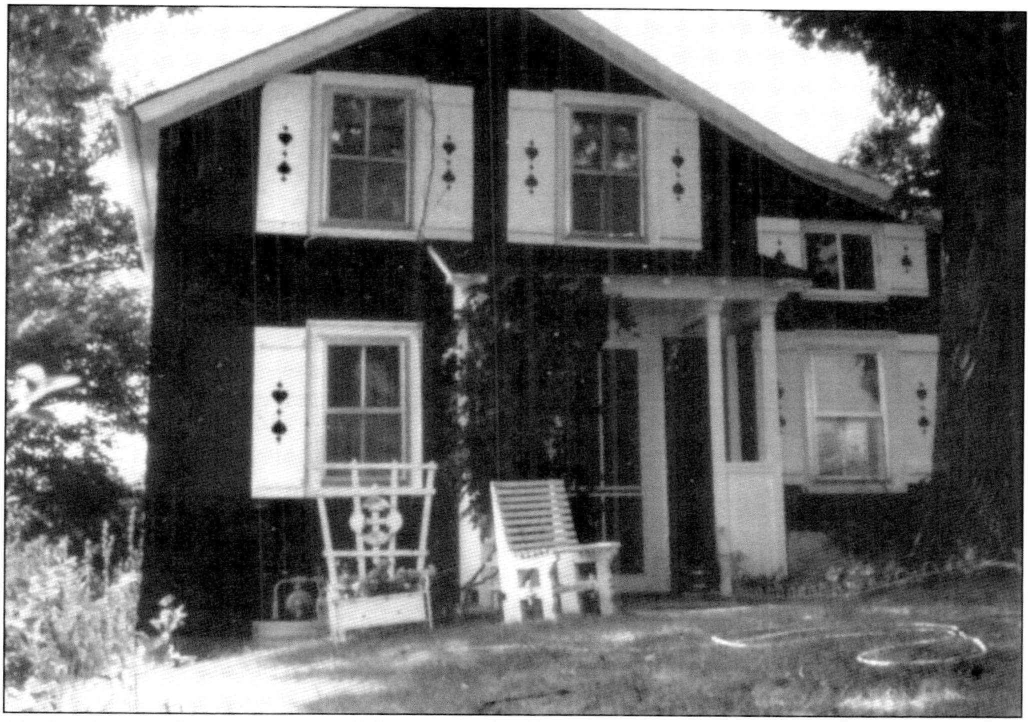

The Luchsinger house was one of the earliest buildings in New Glarus. Part of the building was a log cabin covered over with siding. The balance of the building was constructed using the post-and-beam method of construction. This building was demolished in the late 1980s to make way for a new house.

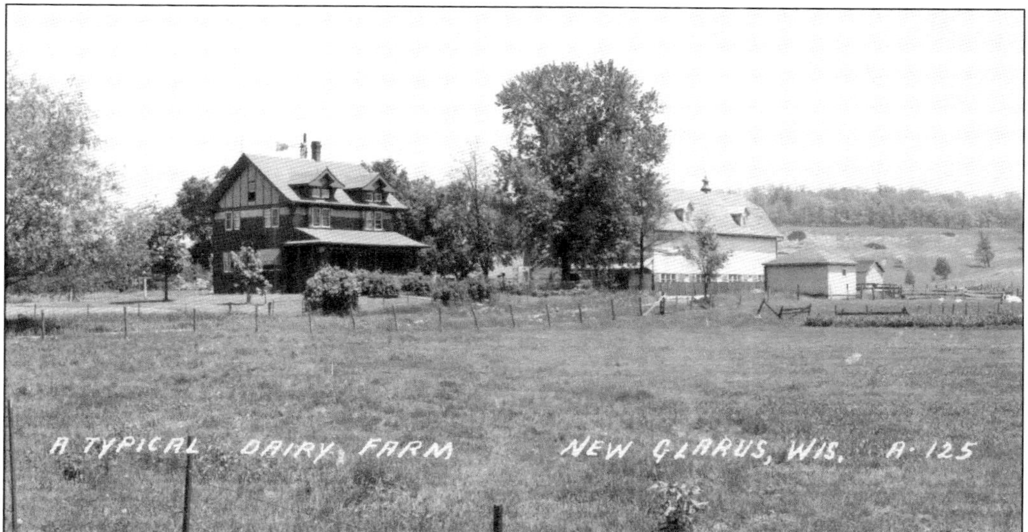

This photograph of the Werner and Esther Streiff-Stauffacher farm at the north edge of New Glarus shows a fairly typical farm scene. Today all that remains of the farm is the house. Werner Stauffacher was noted for the fine rare chickens he raised as a hobby. For many years, young girls in the New Glarus area who owned horses kept them in the barn shown here.

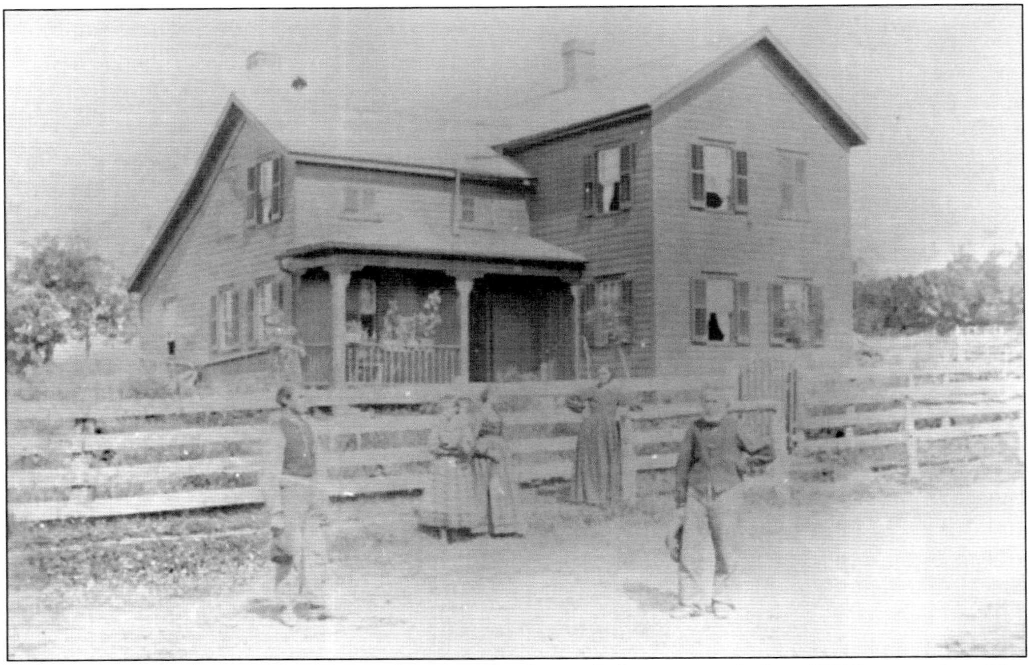

Originally located at 215–217 Second Street, this house belonging to Joshua Wild, an early miller in New Glarus, was later moved to its current location at 118 First Avenue. Shown from left to right in this photograph are John Wild, Maria Wild, Barbara Wild, Mrs. Wild, and Joshua Wild.

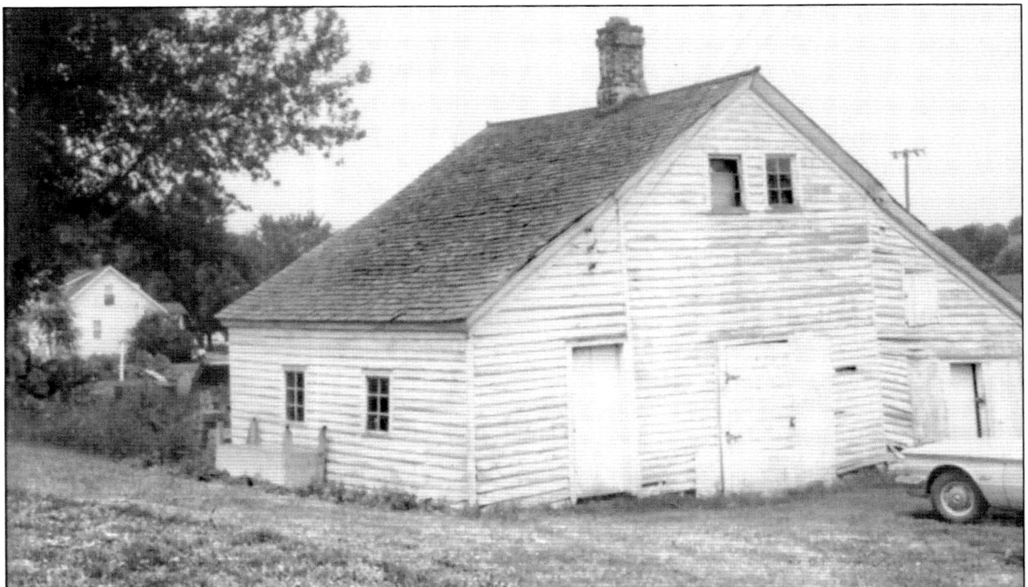

This building was located at 409 Third Street where the New Glarus EMS is now located. Bachelor brothers Peter and Hum (Abraham) Disch lived here for many years. Peter was the last Civil War veteran living in New Glarus, passing away in 1927. Peter always occupied a place of honor during Memorial Day exercises. This building was probably constructed as a town barn, and a section of it was turned into living quarters.

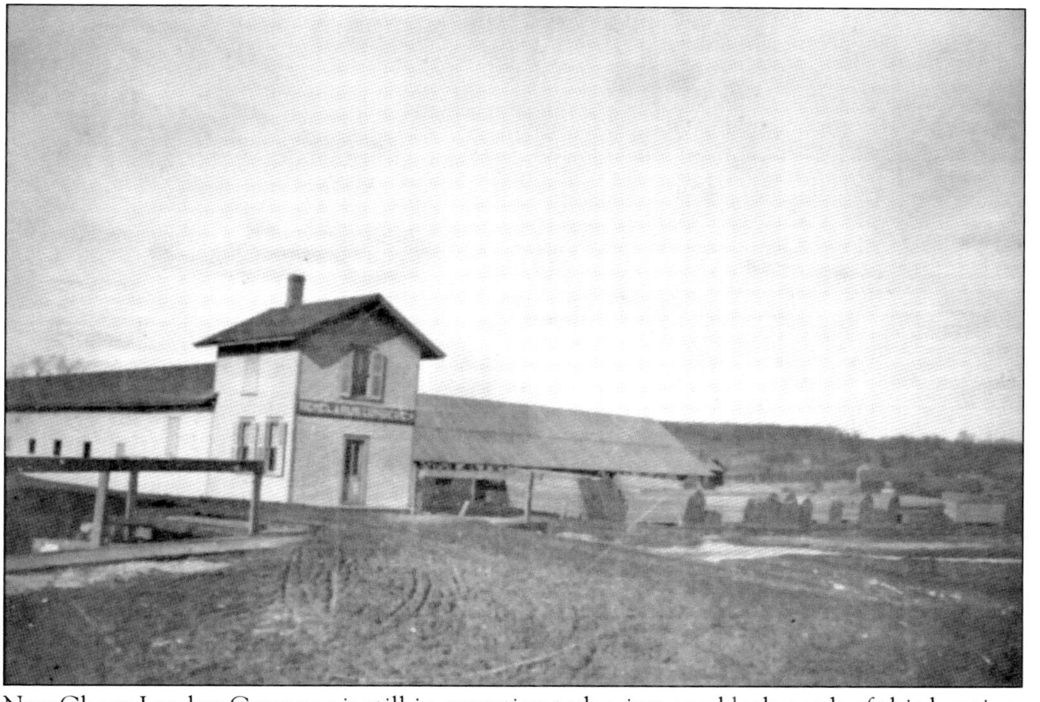

New Glarus Lumber Company is still in operation today, just one block north of this location. The downtown village park now occupies the former lumberyard location. Part of this building was moved to the new location and today serves as the lumberyard office.

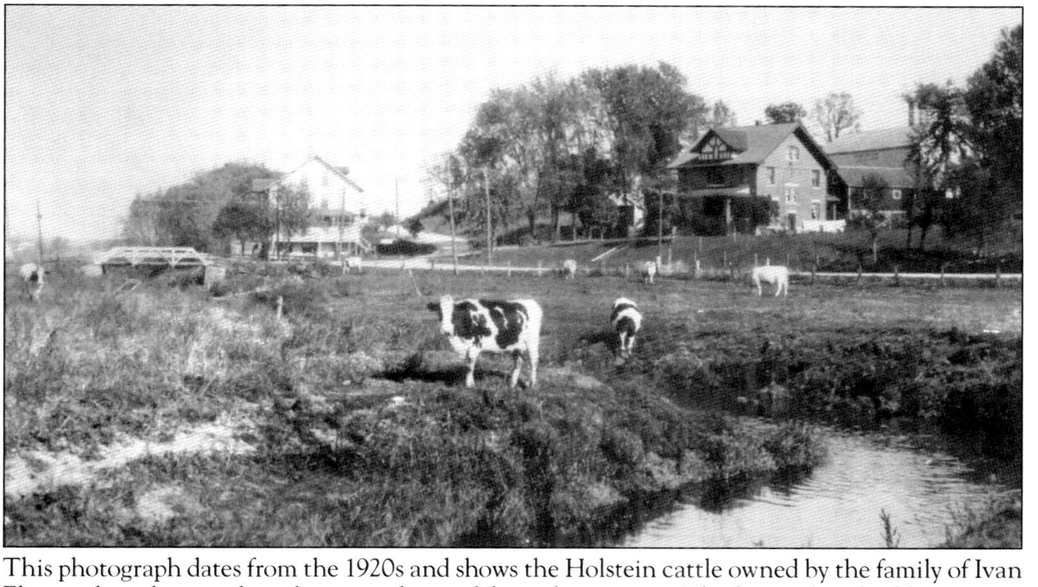

This photograph dates from the 1920s and shows the Holstein cattle owned by the family of Ivan Elmer, whose barn is directly across the road from this pasture. The large white building just to the right of the bridge was constructed as a railroad hotel but never opened as such because the railroad chose to locate two blocks west of here. This building burned in the early 1970s and was demolished.

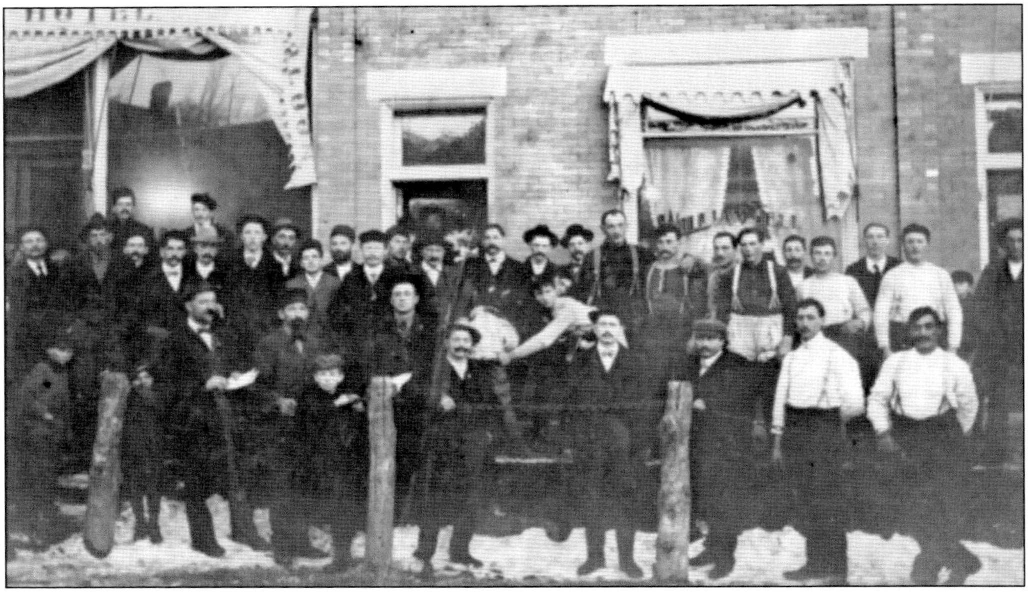

This photograph was taken in front of the Wilhelm Tell Hotel located at 114 Second Street. The men posing for the camera are area cheese makers who moved into town each year during the winter layoff when no cheese was being made. To entertain themselves, they would hold Swiss Wrestling matches that drew big crowds.

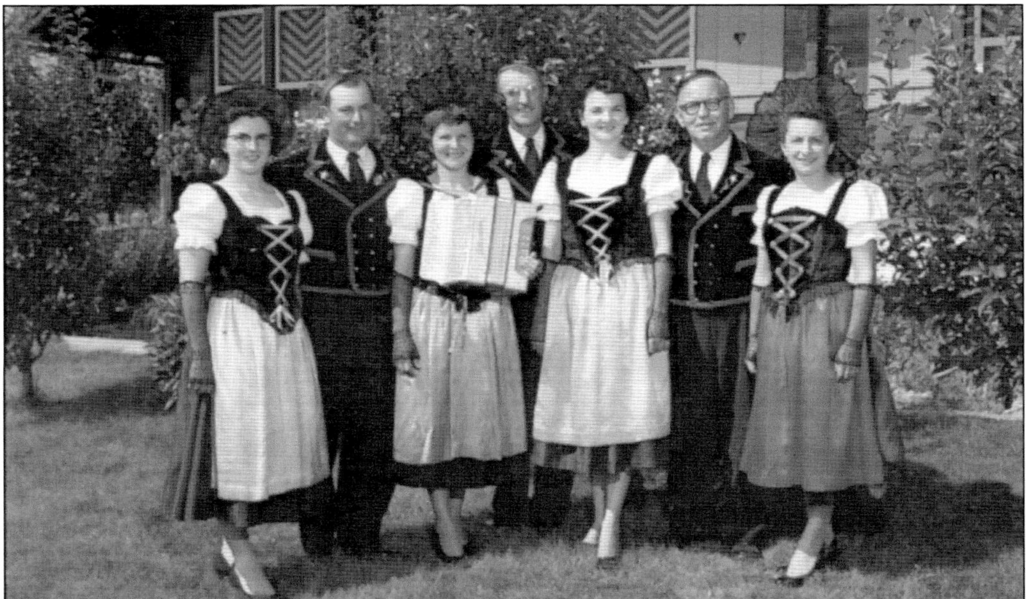

The Edelweiss Stars performed all over the United States during their years of singing together. In 1956, they appeared in a Disney series, *Adventures in Dairyland*, which was filmed near Verona, Wisconsin. Seen here from left to right are group members Marion Streiff, Clayton Streiff, Dorthea Widmer, Ernest "Red" Zentner, Kathleen Ingwell, Paul Grossenbacher, and Margaret Wild. Other New Glarus residents appearing in *Adventures in Dairyland* were William Ruef Sr. and Karl Luescher. (Schroeder.)

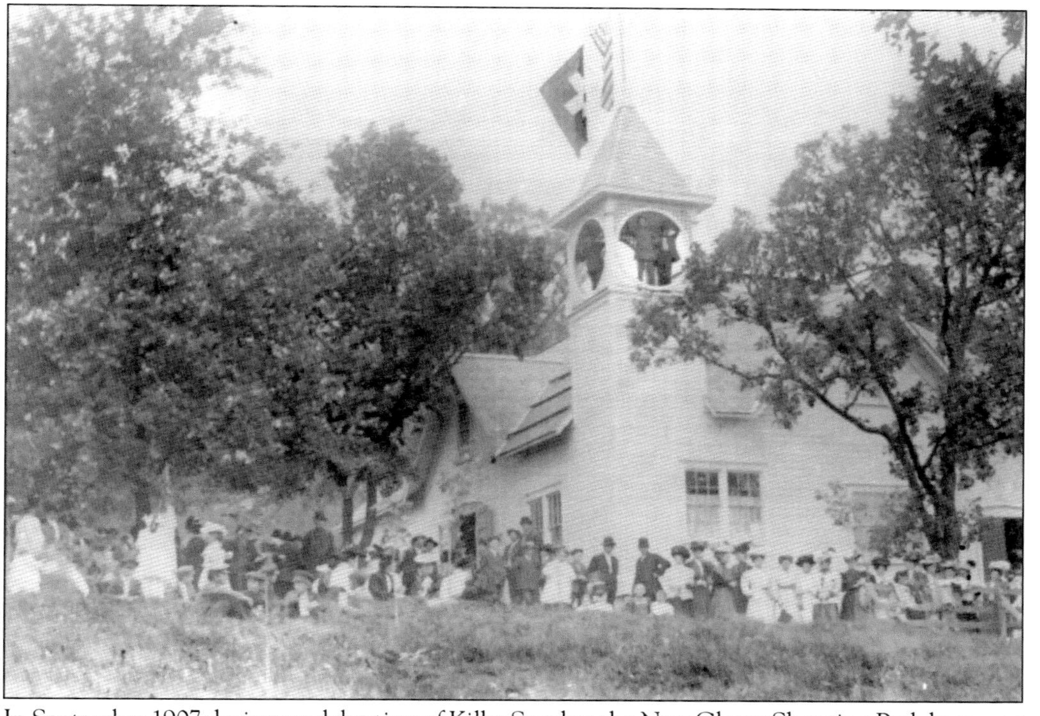

In September 1907 during a celebration of Kilby Sunday, the New Glarus Shooting Park barn was dedicated. Hundreds of area people joined in the festivities of the day with picnics, speeches, and entertainment. The local Swiss United Church of Christ still celebrates Kilby Sunday each year. Kilby is a Swiss celebration to welcome back to the villages the Swiss farmers who are returning with their cattle from the high Alpine meadows where the cattle have summered.

September 1965 saw the dedication of Swiss floral clock in New Glarus. New Glarus Hotel owner Robbi Schneider went to Switzerland and made all the arrangements for the clock to be shipped to New Glarus. The clock was donated by New Glarus–area farmers Lawrence and Lucinda Arnes, who were helped by local citizens when their family lost their farm buildings to a 1928 tornado.

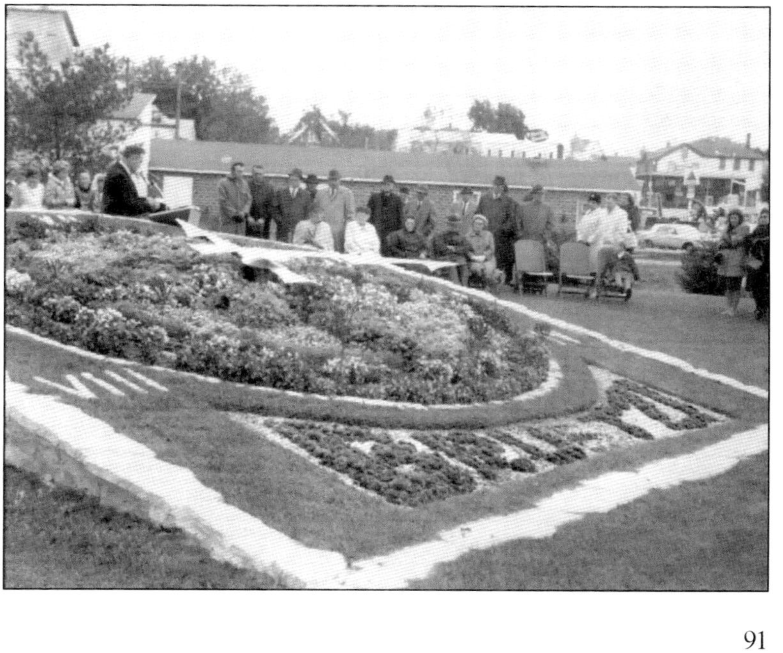

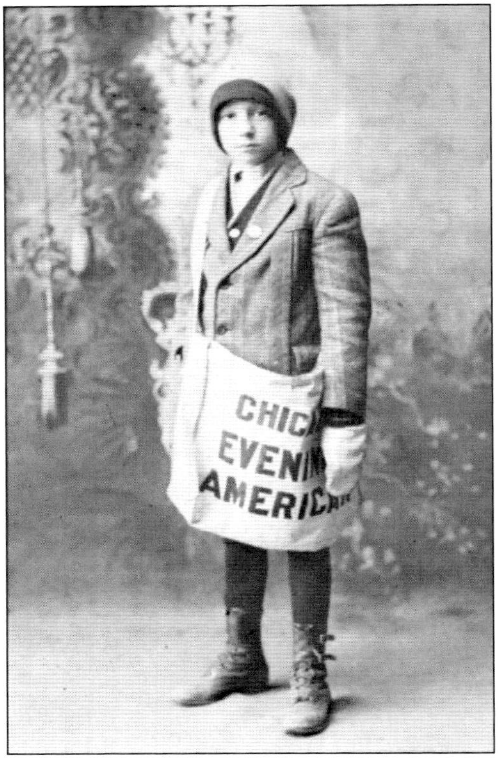

This young man, John Schindler, would grow up to become one of the founders of the Monroe Clinic, the largest medical clinic in the area. Schindler's popular 1954 book, *How to Live 365 Days a Year*, is still in print. He gave a keynote address for the centennial event at the University of Wisconsin that was broadcast by the university radio station. His talk was so popular that requests for copies of his address quickly came into the station. Schindler's recorded talk was shared with other public radio stations across the United States. This was the first time in public radio history that a locally produced broadcast was shared with other public radio stations.

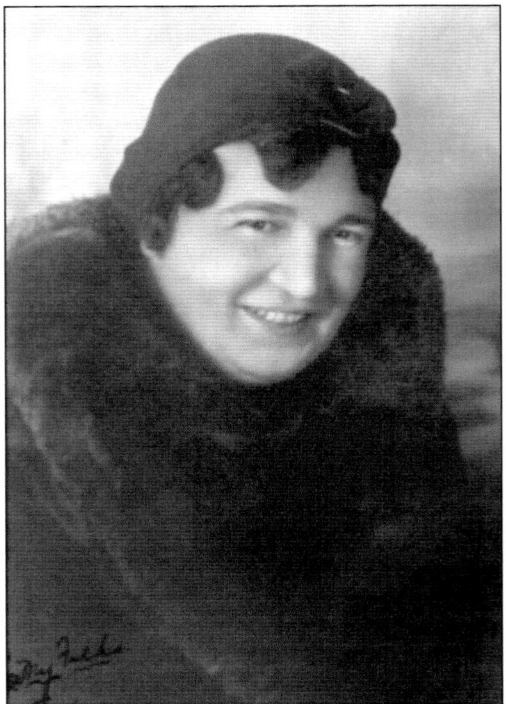

Esther Streiff Stauffacher, during her short life, was one of New Glarus's most influential citizens. A farm wife, she was active in forming the New Glarus Historical Society and served as its first curator. Esther was the town's hostess for important visitors, foreign and domestic. She used her beautiful voice for funerals and weddings and was active in all community endeavors. When Edwin Barlow conceived of the idea of presenting Schiller's *Wilhelm Tell*, Esther was the person Barlow sought out for assistance. (Pauline Ott.)

Eight

Ghost Towns of Green County

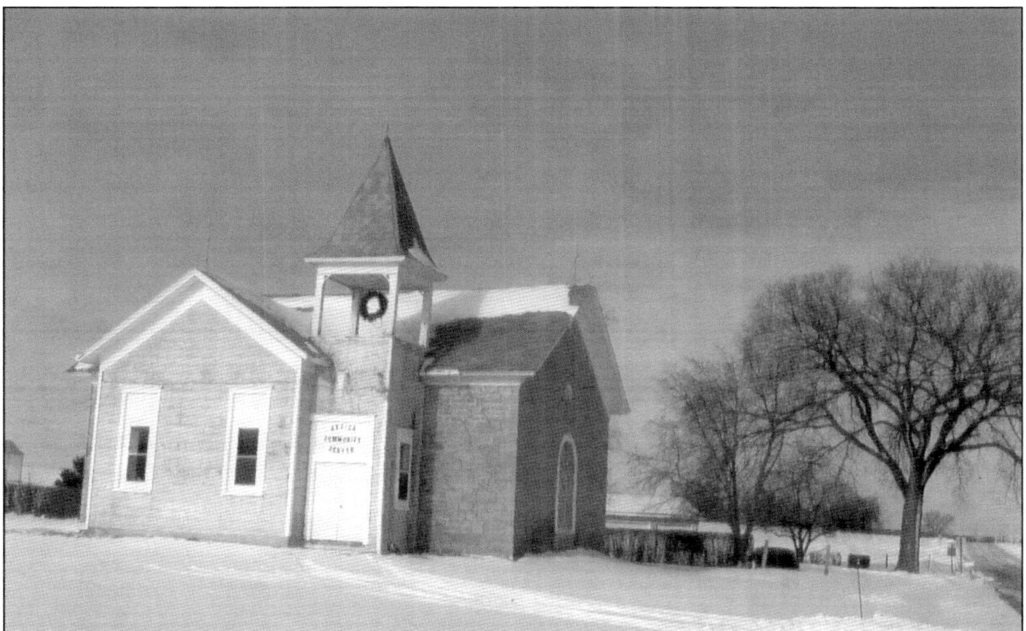

The "new" Attica Methodist Church was built in 1906 and 1907 after lightning destroyed the first church. Services continued in the church until 1953 when the congregation disbanded. In 1955, the church was sold to 19 area families, each putting up $25 toward the purchase of the property, which would be used as a community center. Wayne and Jan Albertson of Attica recently restored the interior of the church.

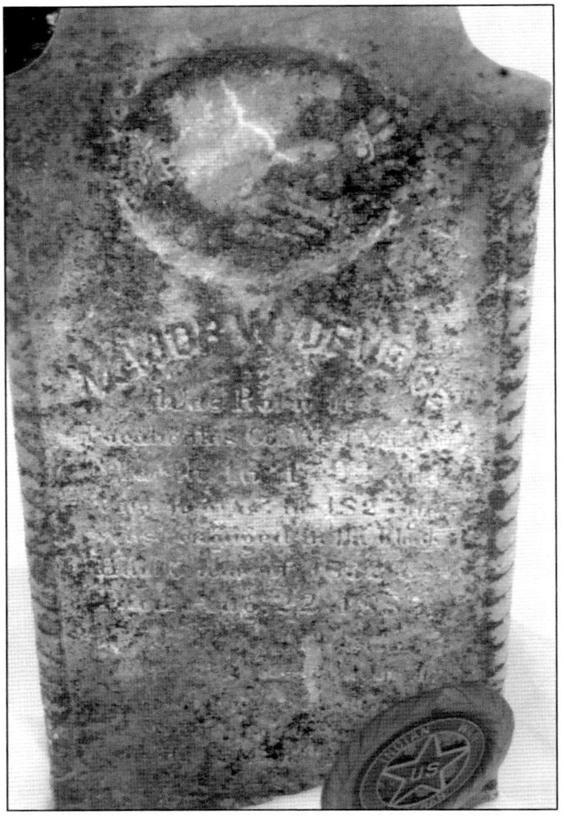

This is the grave of Maj. William Deviese, the first permanent settler in Green County. Deviese, a native of Pocahontas County, West Virginia, arrived in Green County in 1828. Four years later, he enlisted in the militia and served as Gen. Henry Atkinson's aide-de-camp during the Black Hawk War of 1832.

This photograph shows the students of the Exeter School celebrating the armistice ending World War I. This school was still standing in the 1950s, but it is now gone. (Belleville Area Historical Society.)

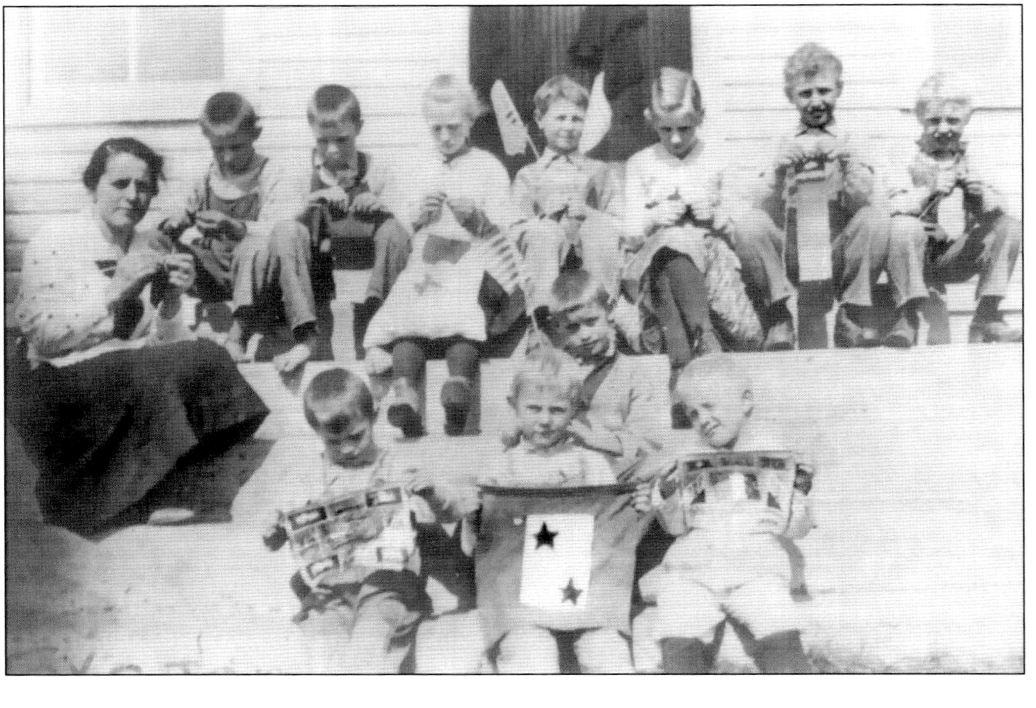

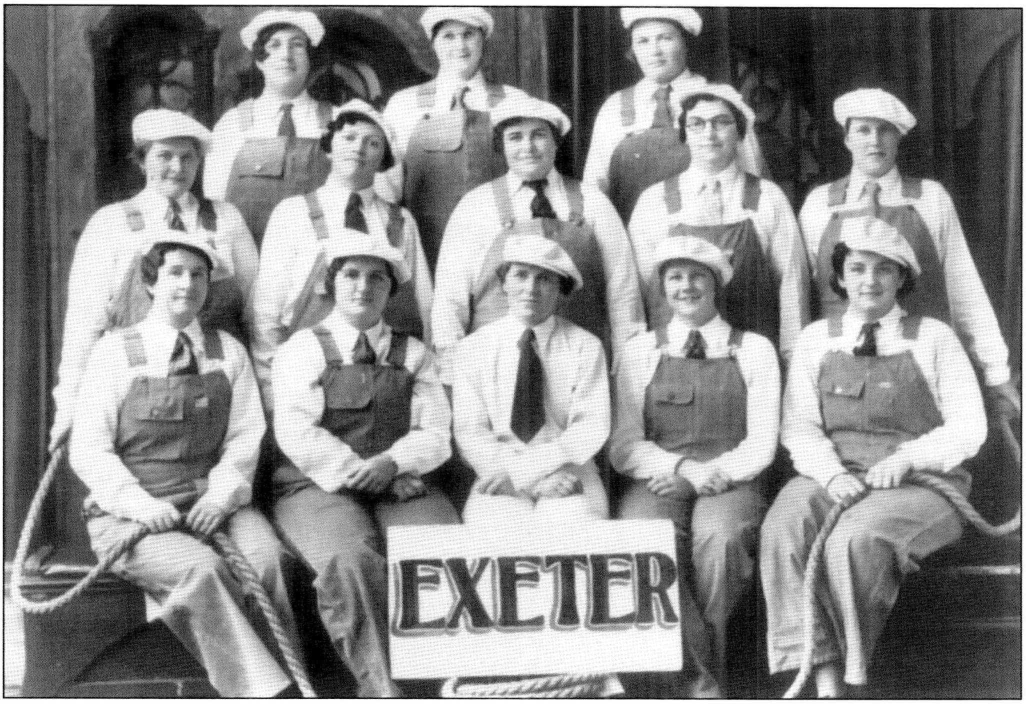

This 1934 photograph shows the Exeter Women's Rope Pulling Team. From left to right the members are (first row) Mrs. Freddie Zunker, Mrs. Walter Richards, Katherine Zentner, Lena Buol, and Florence Voegeli; (second row) Edna Marty, Alma Babler, Katie Schrepfer, Ida Voegeli, and Mrs. Earle McChire; (third row) Elsie Richards, Mrs. Herman Schupback, and Mrs. John Schilt. (Belleville Area Historical Society.)

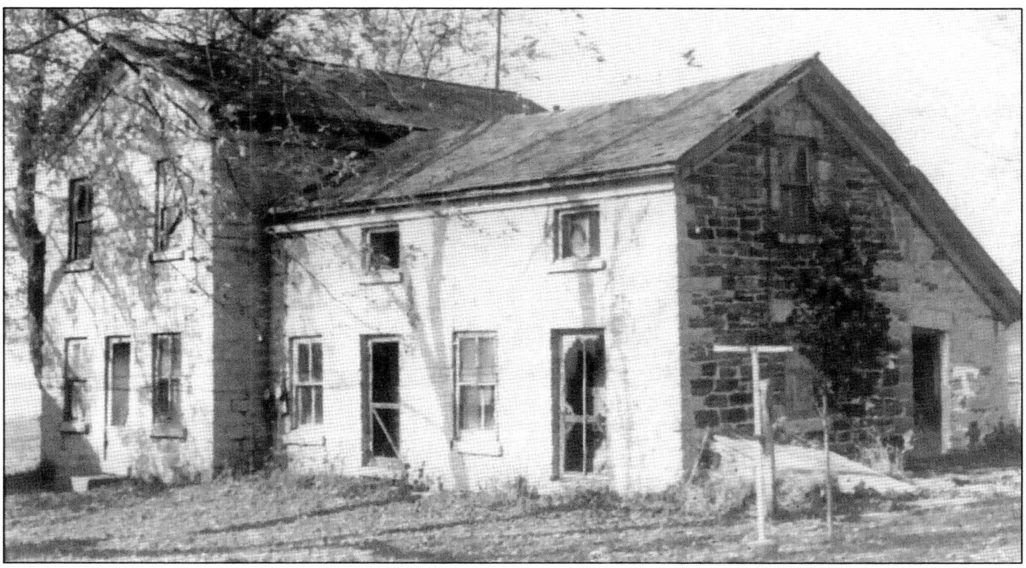

This stone house was probably built by one of the owners of the Exeter Store next door. The two-story portion of the house was the original house. The 1.5-story addition housed a kitchen and dining room, with two small bedrooms in the half story. (Belleville Area Historical Society.)

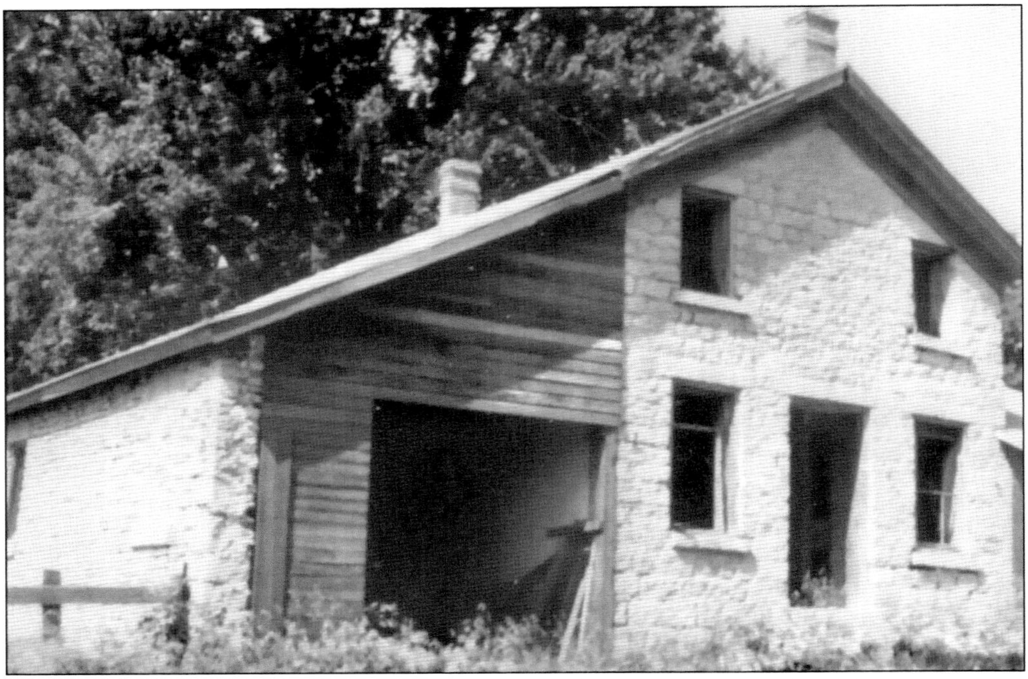

This photograph shows the Exeter Store, which was built in the late 1850s. The second story served as a dance hall. A grand opening for the store and dance hall attracted people from as far away as Janesville and Beloit, Wisconsin, and Rockford, Illinois. This building is still standing. (Belleville Area Historical Society.)

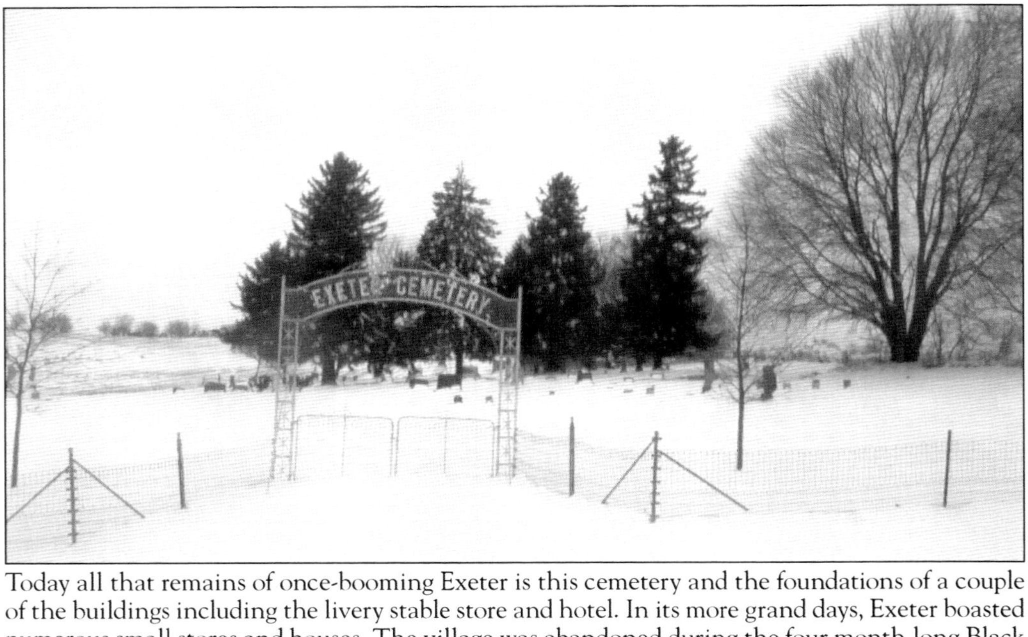

Today all that remains of once-booming Exeter is this cemetery and the foundations of a couple of the buildings including the livery stable store and hotel. In its more grand days, Exeter boasted numerous small stores and houses. The village was abandoned during the four-month-long Black Hawk War of 1832, when residents fled to Fort Blue Mounds, 25 miles northwest of Exeter. (Belleville Area Historical Society.)

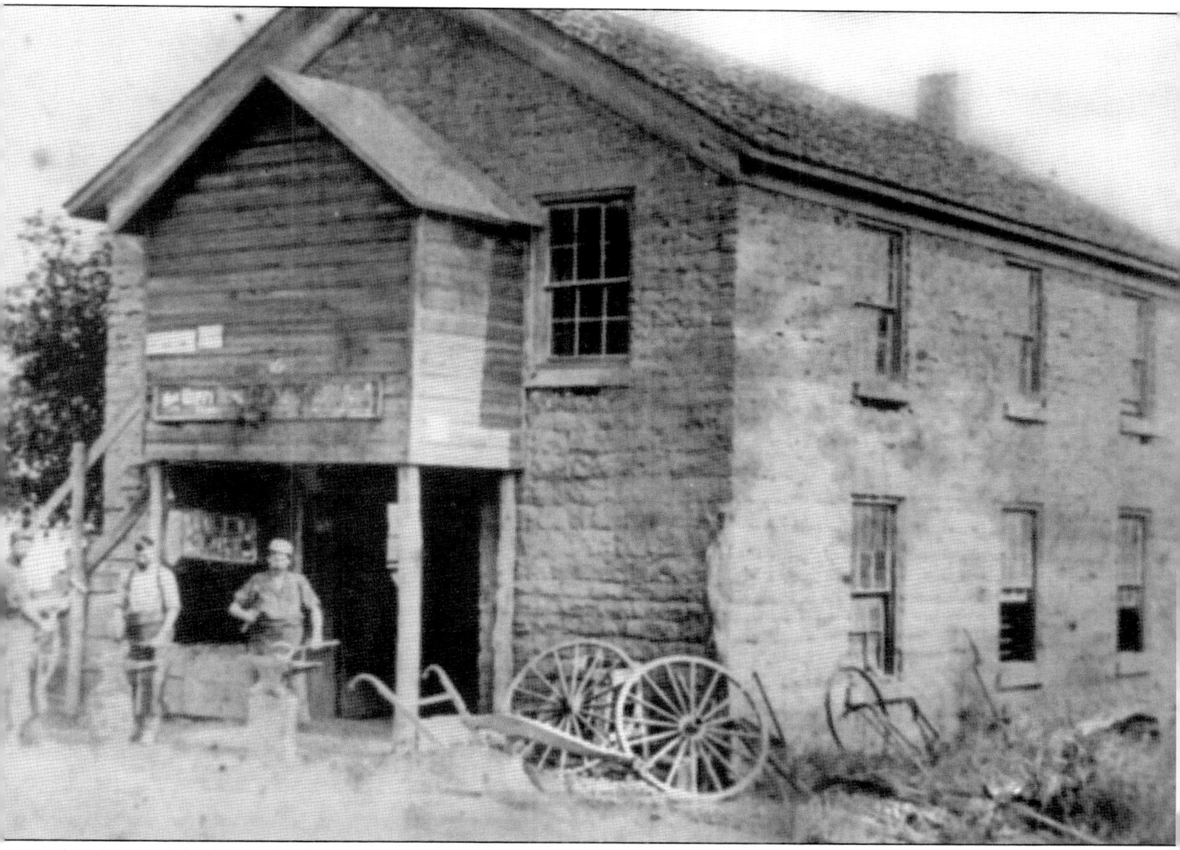

The Attica blacksmith shop was a rather substantial shop for its day. It had more than enough work to keep its blacksmiths busy, as can be seen by the use of the outside anvils. The upstairs of this building served as a fraternal hall for the Modern Woodmen of America. This building was recently restored and will be open to the public. (Augie Keehn.)

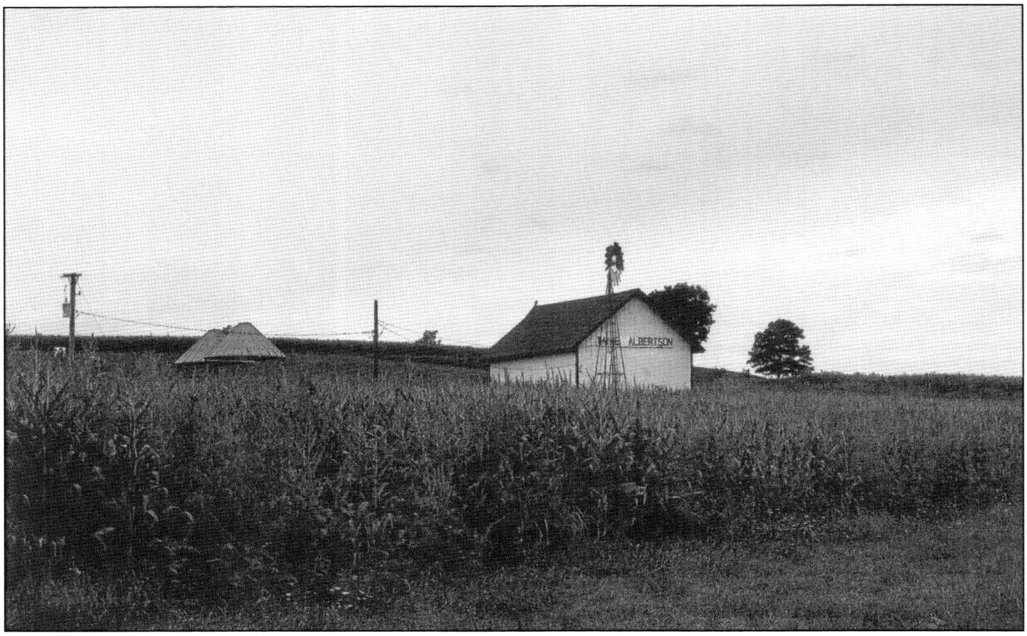

The Albertson family's roots in the Attica area date back to the 1850s. Shown here is the barn on the Albertson farm, which features a hand-laid foundation of lime fieldstone. Many area farms still have large piles of the same type of stone. The rocks were gathered each spring during "rock picking," which had to be done before the crops were planted. (Augie Keehn.)

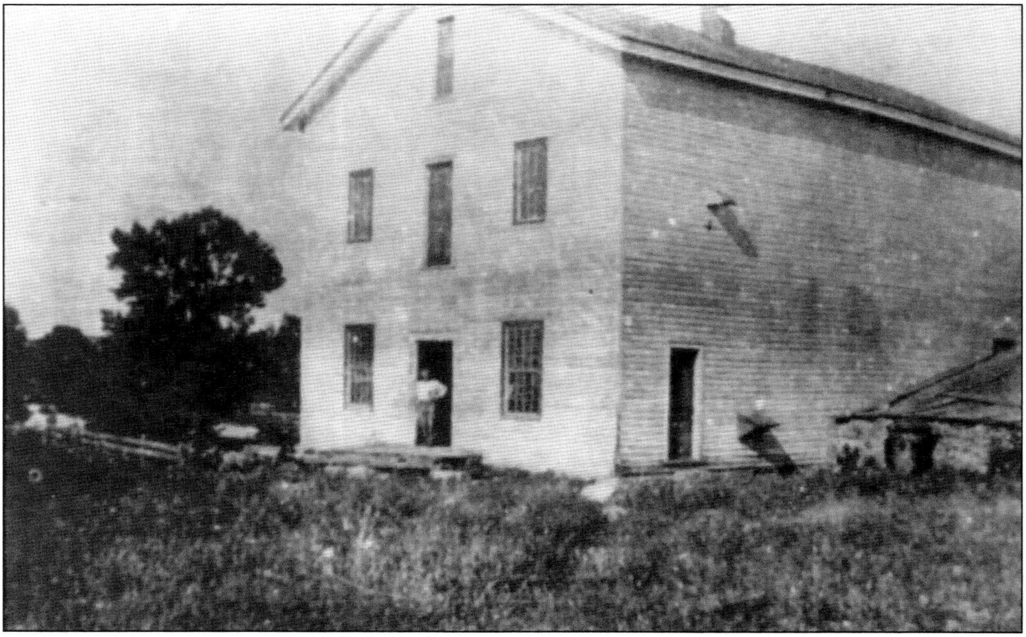

Because of the volume of water flow on the Sugar River, this mill did a good business. Most often, the success of a town depended on waterpower or the railroad. Because Attica had sufficient waterpower, it drew residents of nearby Exeter to move into Attica. (Augie Keehn.)

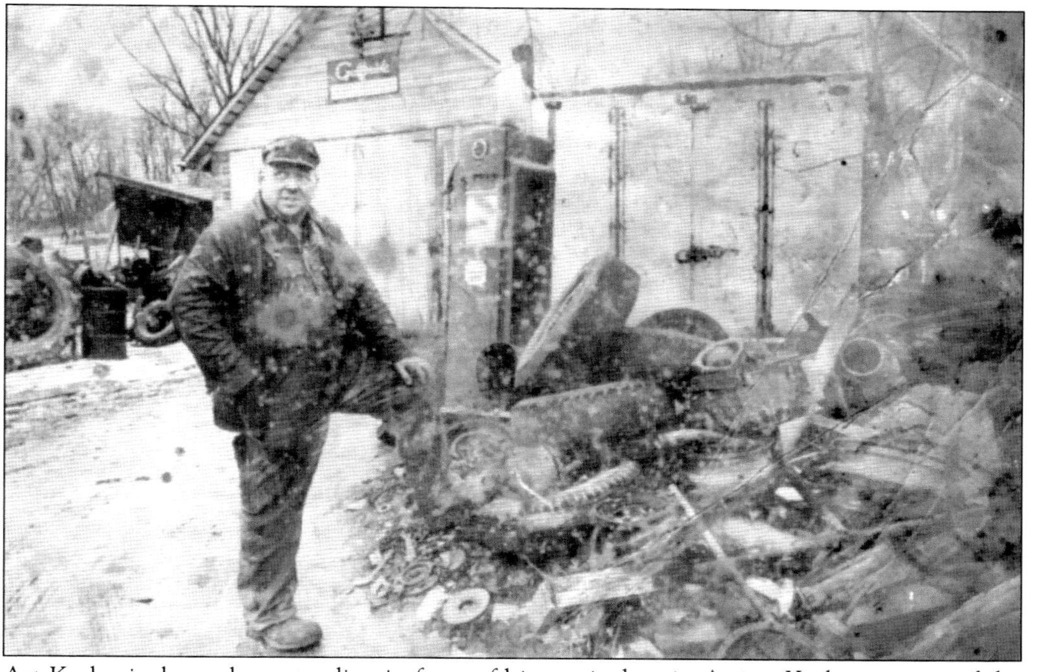

Art Keehn is shown here standing in front of his repair shop in Attica. Keehn was one of the last full-time businesses in Attica. His repair shop maintained and kept running area residents' cars, trucks, tractors, and other motorized equipment. Today Keehn's son Augie continues the business. (Augie Keehn.)

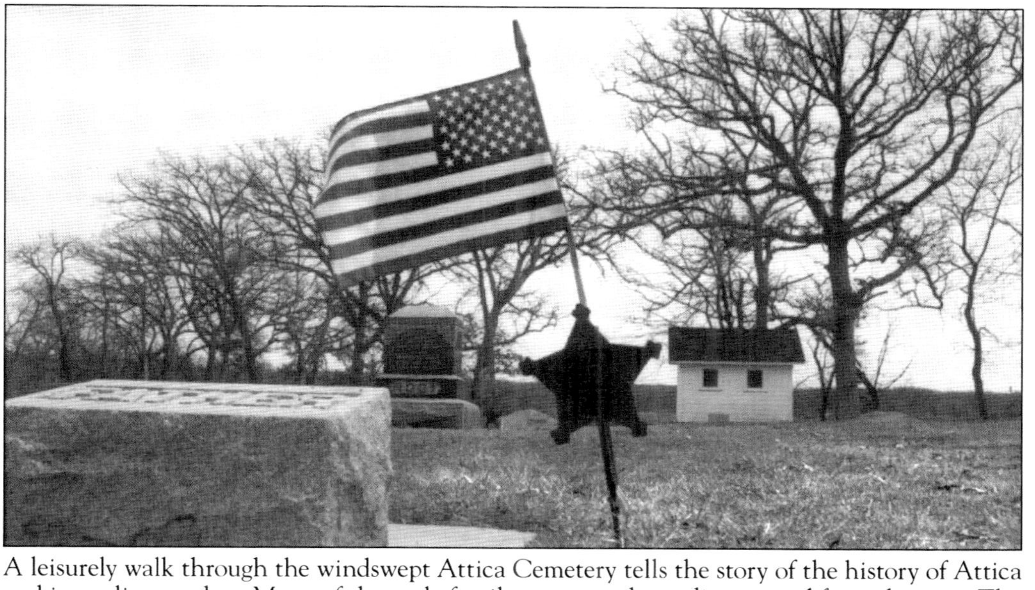

A leisurely walk through the windswept Attica Cemetery tells the story of the history of Attica and its earliest settlers. Many of the early family surnames have disappeared from the area. The cemetery, which overlooks the Sugar River, has in recent years been restored by a group of area residents who have lovingly reset and repaired damaged and fallen headstones. This dedicated group holds a cemetery walk each fall, which features the life histories of several of the deceased. (Augie Keehn.)

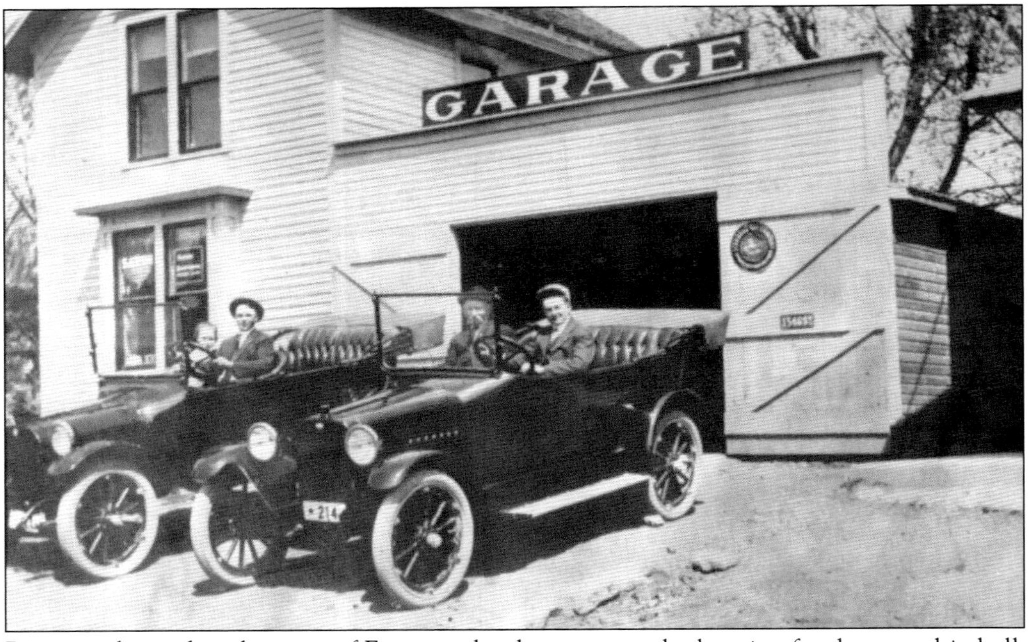

Dayton is located in the town of Exeter and today serves as the location for the township hall. In its heyday, Dayton boasted a main street with numerous businesses including a mill, stores, and tavern. The garage shown in this photograph sold both Dodge and Saxon automobiles. Jim Dooley is in the Dodge on the left, and Charles Richardson is in the Saxon on the right. (Belleville Historical Society.)

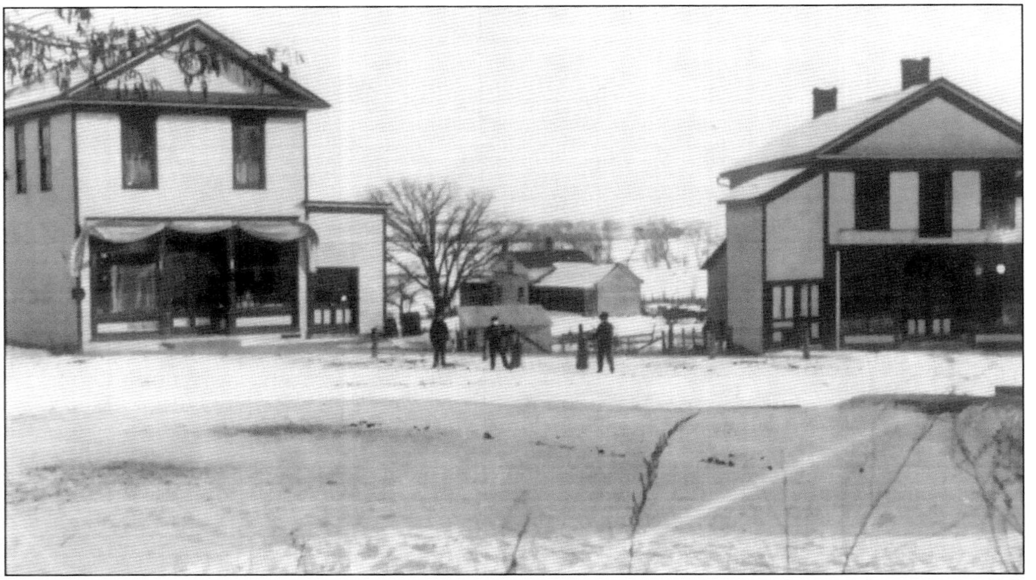

These two buildings front the Sugar River to the rear of the buildings. The building on the left was the Dayton grocery store, which provided food and other staple items for area farmers as well as a gathering place for the talk of politics and weather. The grocery store was in business through the late 1950s and housed a tavern for a number of years after that. (Belleville Historical Society photograph.)

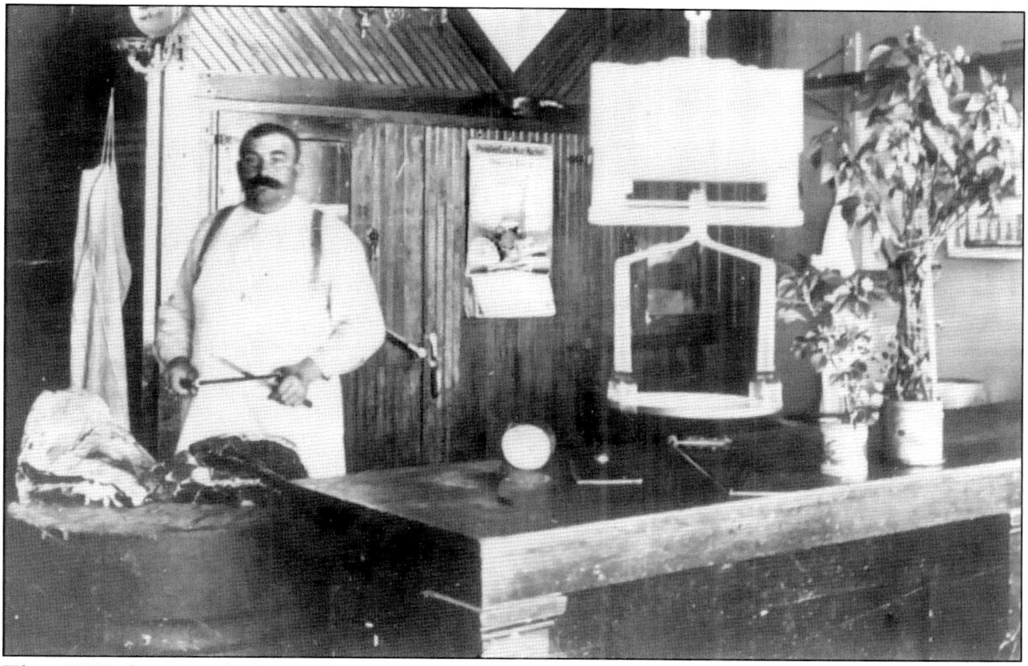

This 1915 photograph shows the Dayton Meat Market and Otto Weber. He is standing in front of the walk-in cooler. (Belleville Historical Society.)

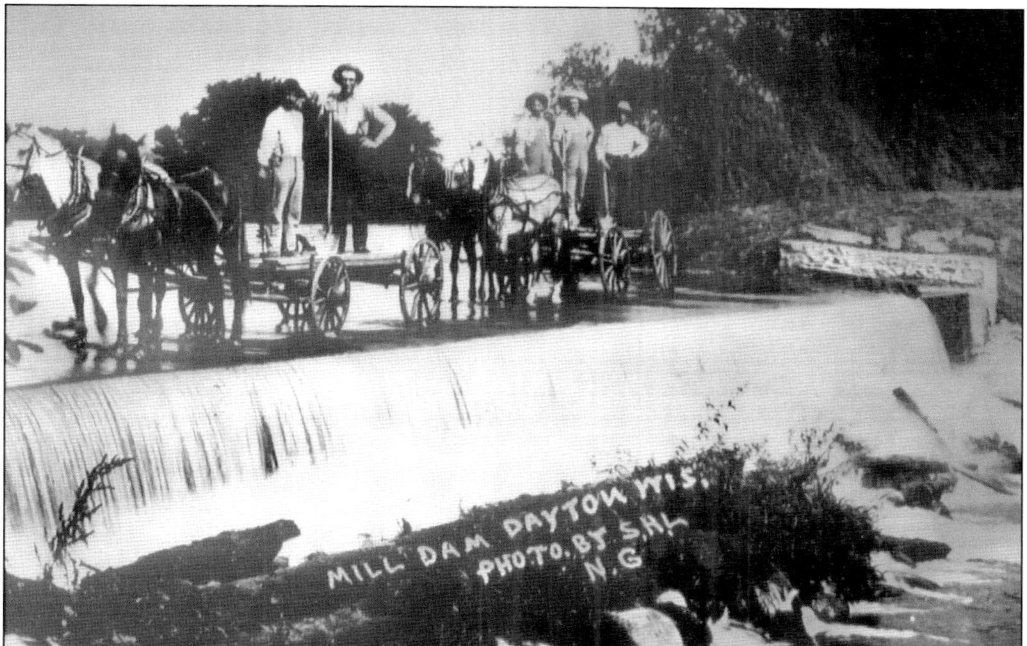

This interesting photograph shows the milldam. What makes the picture interesting is the size of the dam top and the presence of the horses and wagons on top of the dam. This is possibly the second dam on the river at this location. The photographer who took this image was Samuel H. Luchsinger of New Glarus. (Town of Exeter.)

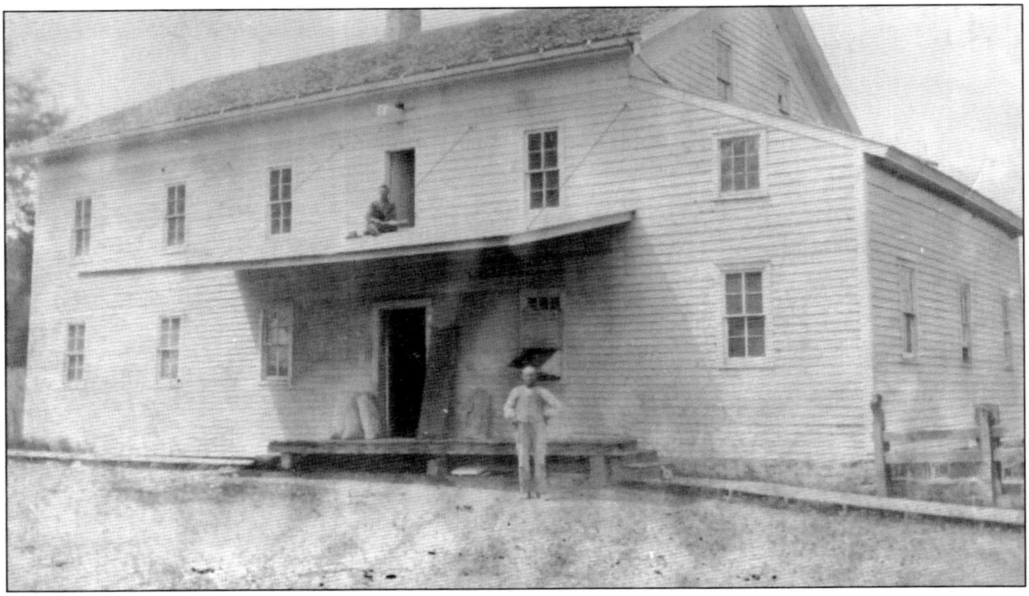

The Dayton mill building was located north of the present Highway 92 next to the Exeter Town Hall. Nothing remains of the mill building, but portions of the mill flume can still be seen. The man in the photograph is Joseph Jackson. He leased the mill from 1880 to 1888. The boy sitting on the porch roof is Fred B. Jackson, the mill operator's son. (Town of Exeter.)

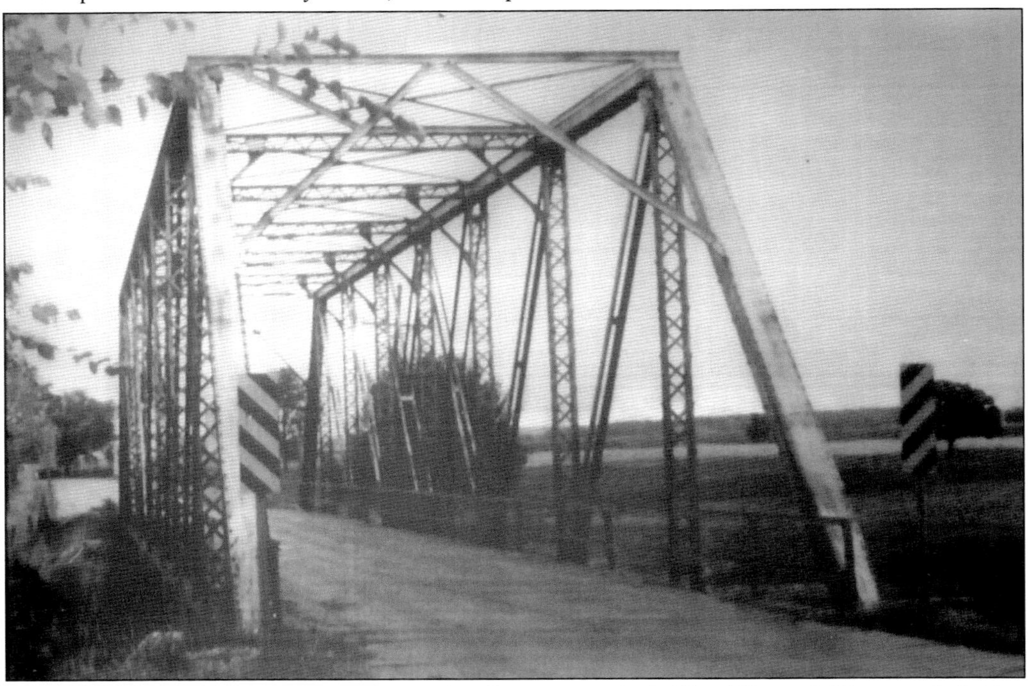

The old bridge saw several generations of traffic over its deck. This Through Truss–style bridge was in use until 1982, when it was replaced by the current concrete bridge as part of a large public works project that also reconstructed the highway through Dayton. One bridge of this style stands on private land near Monticello. (Belleville Historical Society.)

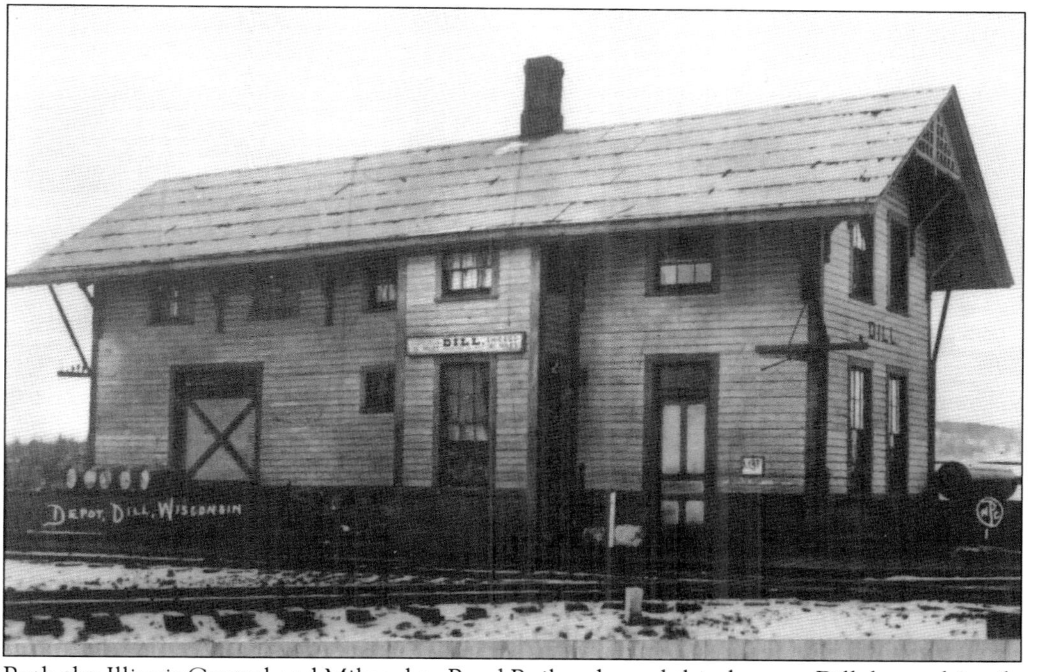

Both the Illinois Central and Milwaukee Road Railroads used this depot at Dill, located 1 mile west of Browntown. Built by the Illinois Central, this is a common design used on the Illinois Central Railroad. The depot was moved from one side of the Pecatonica River to the other. Once the river was frozen solid, men and horses pulled the depot to its new location.

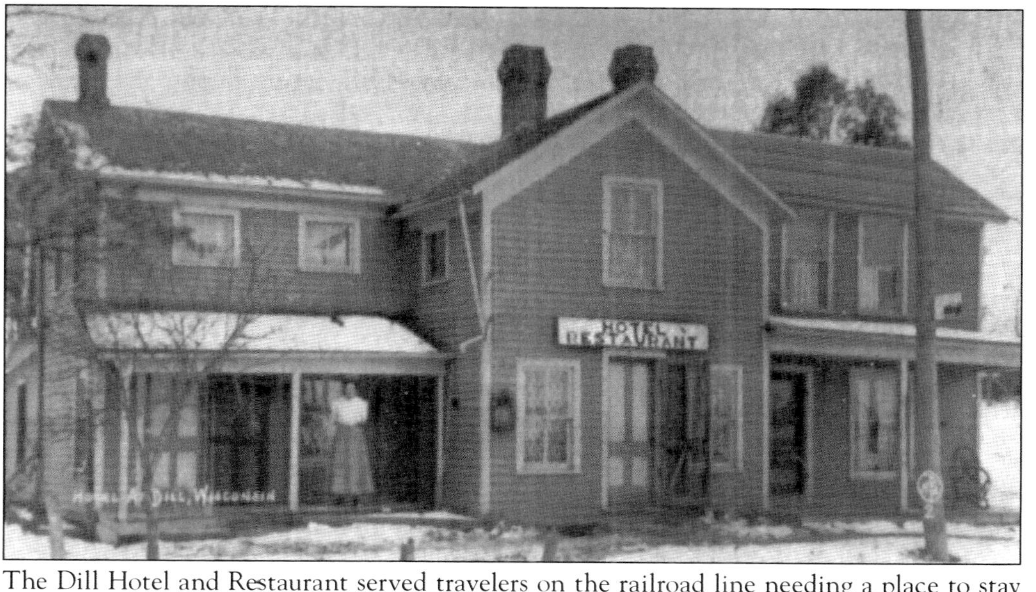

The Dill Hotel and Restaurant served travelers on the railroad line needing a place to stay overnight while waiting for their connection from one rail line to the other. The hotel boasted 10 to 12 overnight rooms as well as a post office. The post office was known as Ramona. (Marion McGuire.)

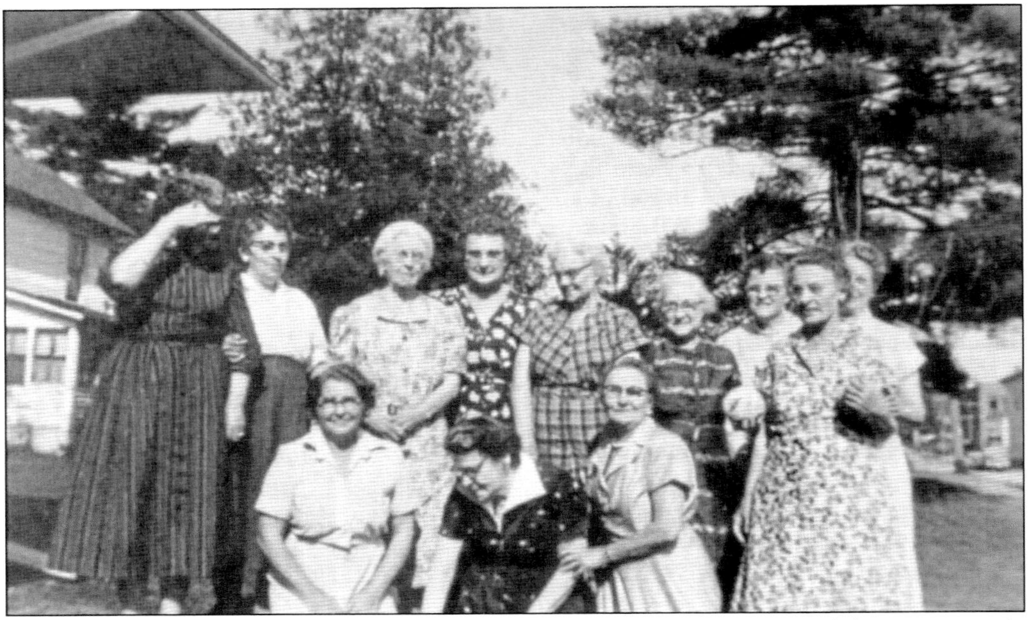

Despite Dill's small size, the women of Dill had their own homemakers club, appropriately named the Dill Homemakers. Shown in this photograph from left to right are (kneeling) Esther Cook, Effie Vincent, and Hulda Bechtolt; (standing) Minnie Shager, Ella Bechtolt, unidentified, Theda Mau, unidentified, Mrs. Martin, Leona DeVoe, Hattie Mani, and Cora Bock. (Browntown Historical Society.)

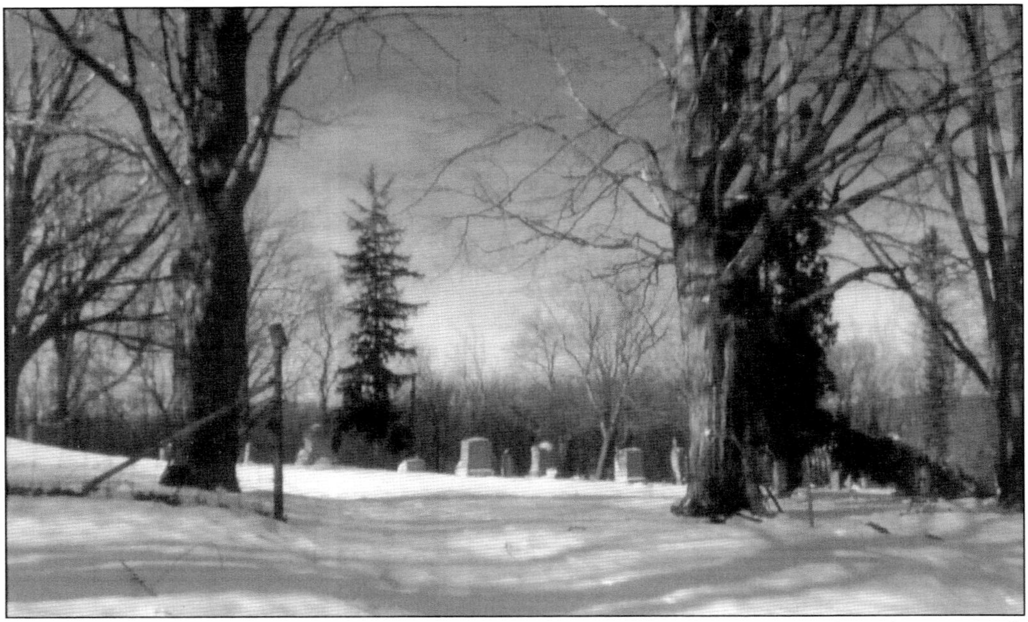

Sometimes all that remains of a ghost town is a lonely country cemetery. Such is the case with Dutch Hollow, located several miles southeast of Monticello. The first residents were New York Dutch descendants and were followed by New Englanders and finally Swiss. There were four primary Swiss families: Norder, Elmer, Stauffacher, and Zentner.

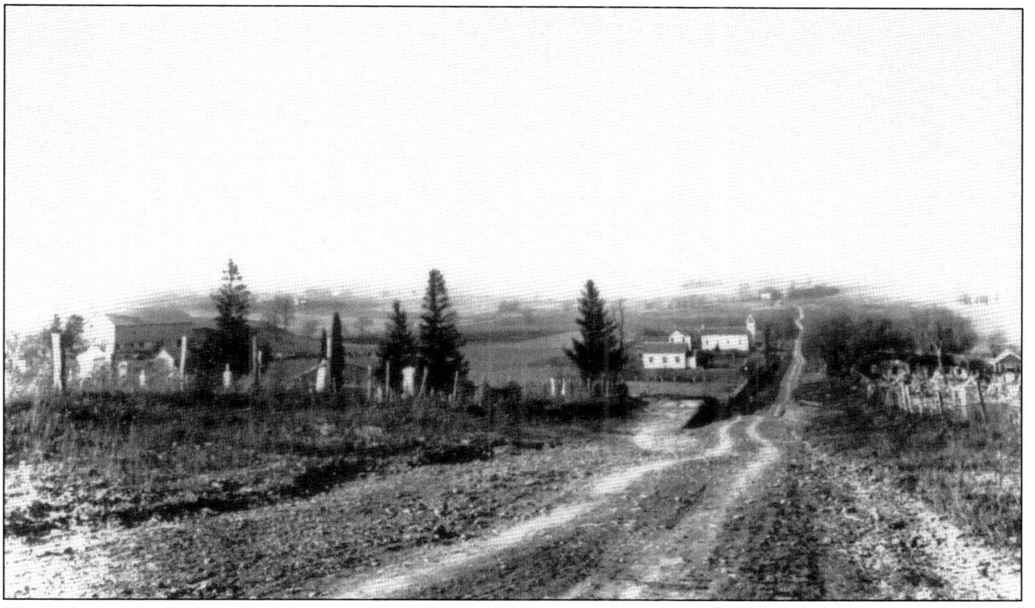

This photograph shows an overview of Dutch Hollow looking north from the cemetery showing the Elmer School and Dutch Hollow Church. In 1896, the school had 43 pupils; over 30 were Elmers or Stauffachers. Today the school and church are gone. It is thought that the church was moved to the east end of Monticello Prairie and was attached to the Gap Church. (Monticello Historical Society.)

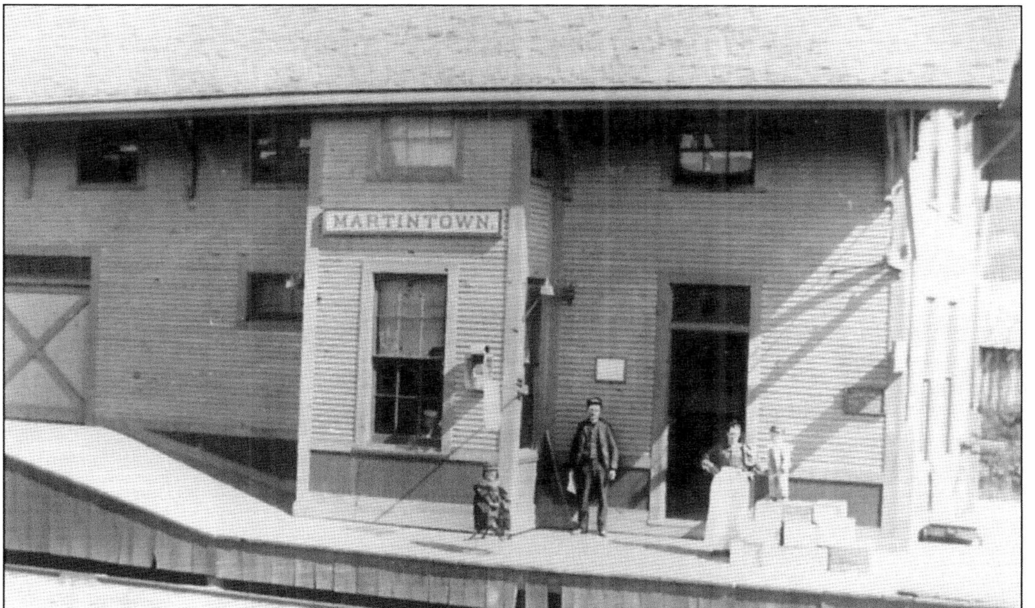

Martintown is located on the Wisconsin-Illinois border in the town of Cadiz, south of Browntown. The Illinois Central Railroad arrived in Martintown in 1888 and brought with it prosperity. Shown on the depot platform are the depot agent, his wife, and young daughter. This depot is the only one of its once-popular style surviving in Wisconsin. It is now being used as a house.

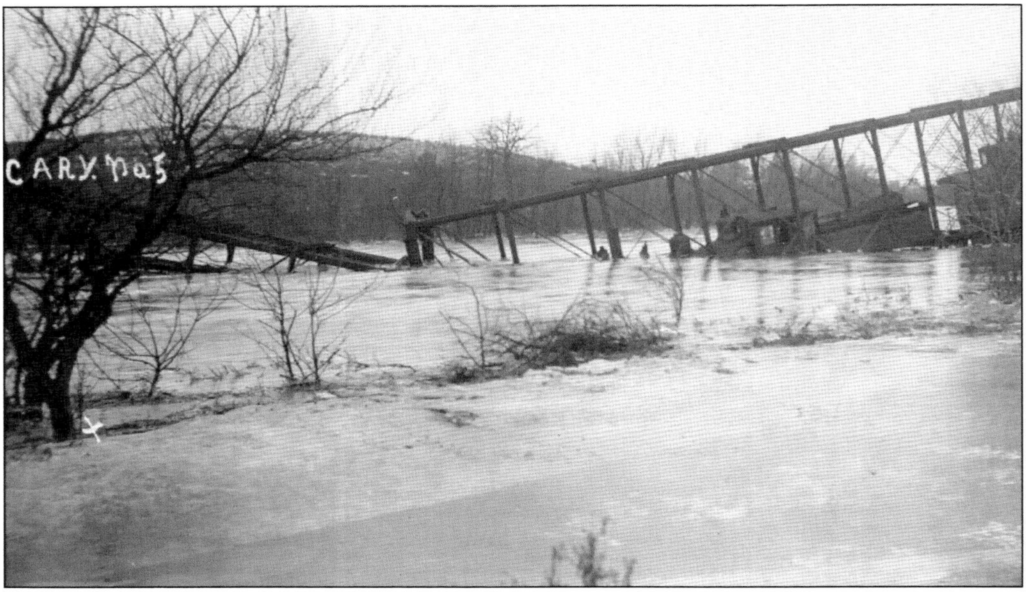

Severe spring floods on February 19, 1911, caused the abutments on this railroad bridge to give way and send the bridge crashing into the Pecatonica River. The railroad quickly brought a crane and other recovery equipment in to extract the engine from the raging water. The railroad also had to use a diver to do underwater rigging to the locomotive before lifting it from the river.

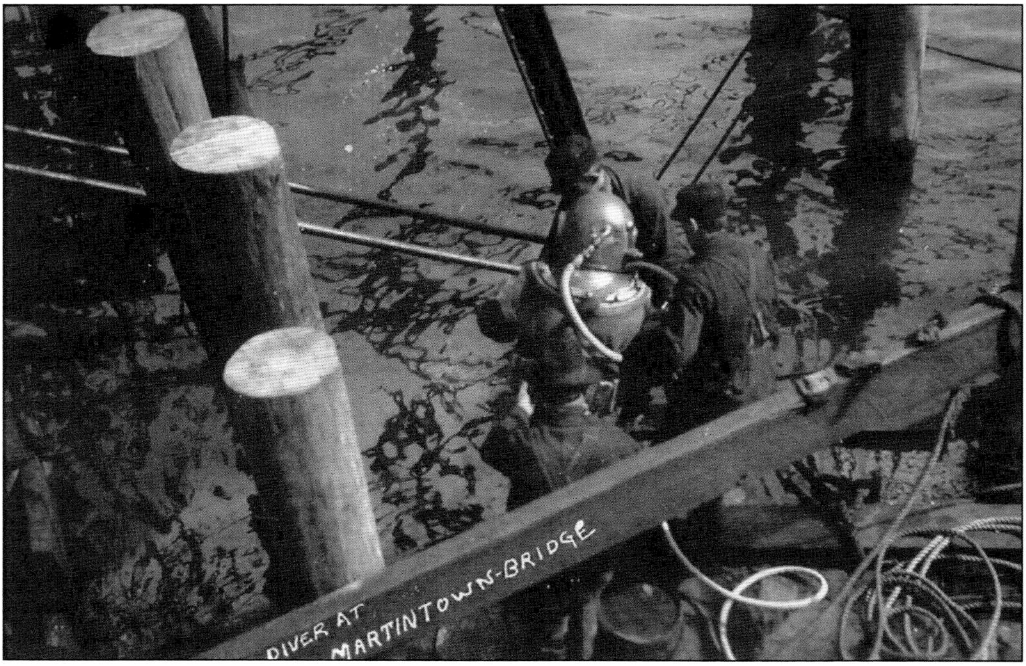

This photograph shows the collapsed railroad bridge and the diver who was brought in to inspect the underwater structure of the bridge. The diver was looking for damage from the flooding that caused the bridge to collapse during the spring 1911 floods. This was dangerous work considering the underwater currents brought on by the rushing waters.

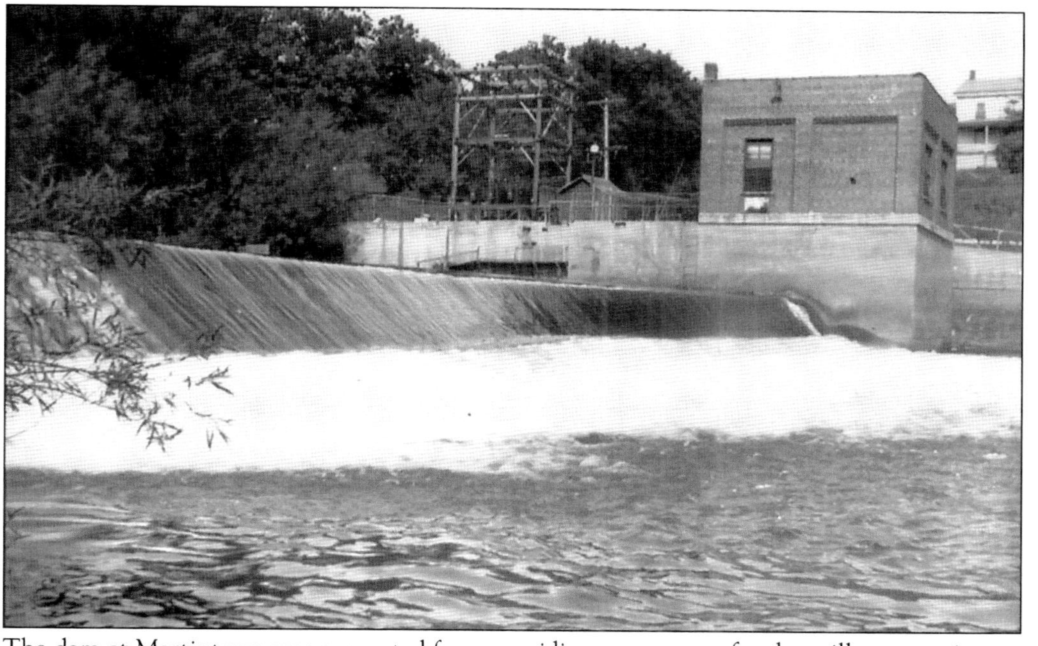

The dam at Martintown was converted from providing waterpower for the mill to powering an electric-generation plant. Because of the size of the river at Martintown, this generation plant was the largest on the Pectonica River in Wisconsin. One other waterpower plant on this river is still in operation at Argyle.

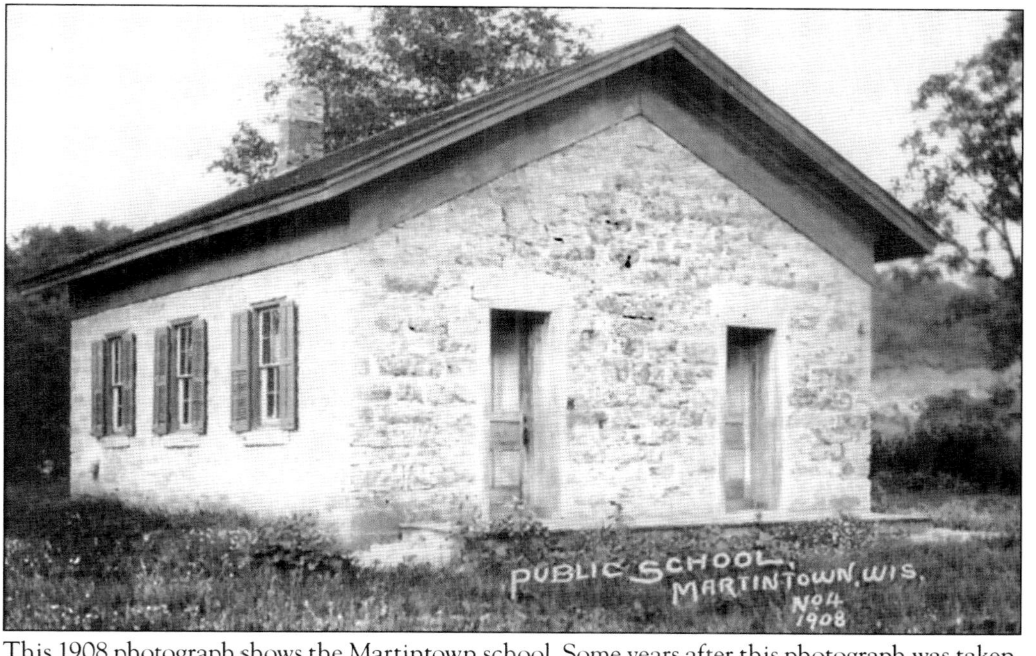

This 1908 photograph shows the Martintown school. Some years after this photograph was taken, a small addition was added to the front and the building was entered from the right side. Notice the two front doors, one for the boys and one for the girls. The stone used in this building was probably taken from a nearby quarry.

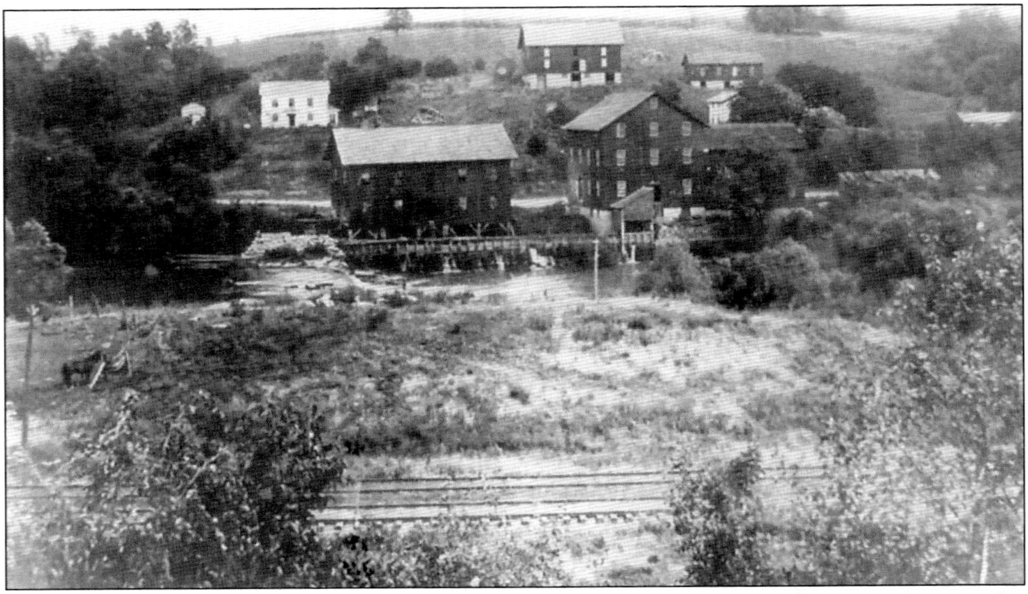

This overview of Martintown is looking north from above the business district and across the Pecatonica River. The two large buildings across the river are associated with the mill. Nathaniel Martin and a partner built the first mill in Martintown in 1854. Several years later, Martin's brother Isaiah formed a partnership to operate the mill.

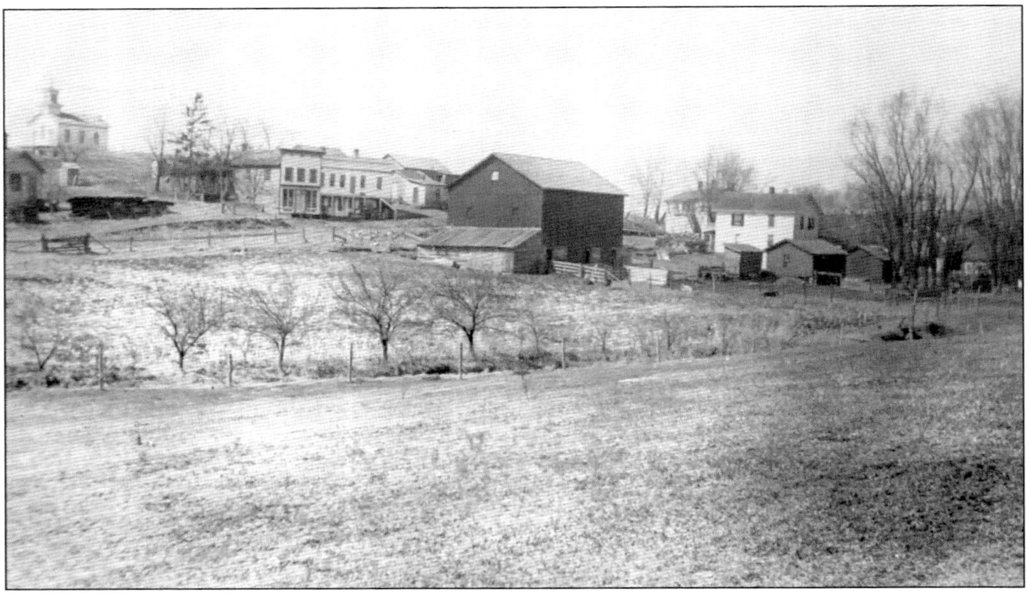

This undated photograph shows an overview of Postville, located about 7 miles east of Blanchardville in the town of York. Postville was originally called Stewart, but because of a post office name conflict, the name was changed to Postville. The building in the upper left corner was one of the three churches that served Postville. (Pat Elmer.)

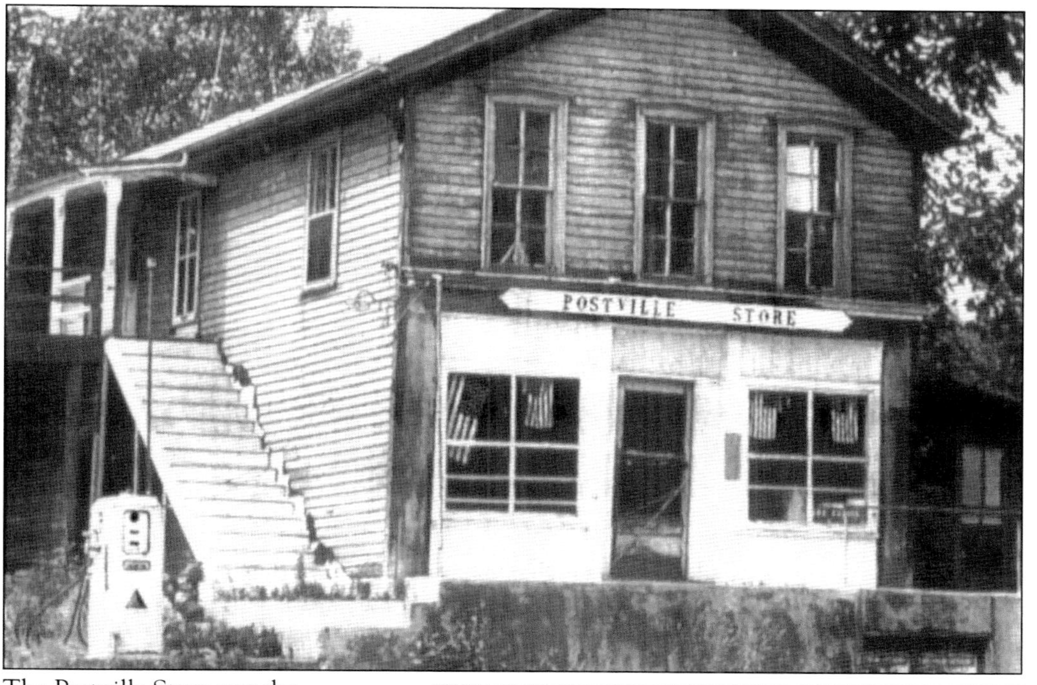

The Postville Store was the stereotypical country store depicted in old-time paintings. The store sold groceries, light hardware, and gas. Earl and Helen Erickson were the last full-time operators of the store, which remained open until the 1970s. (Pat Elmer.)

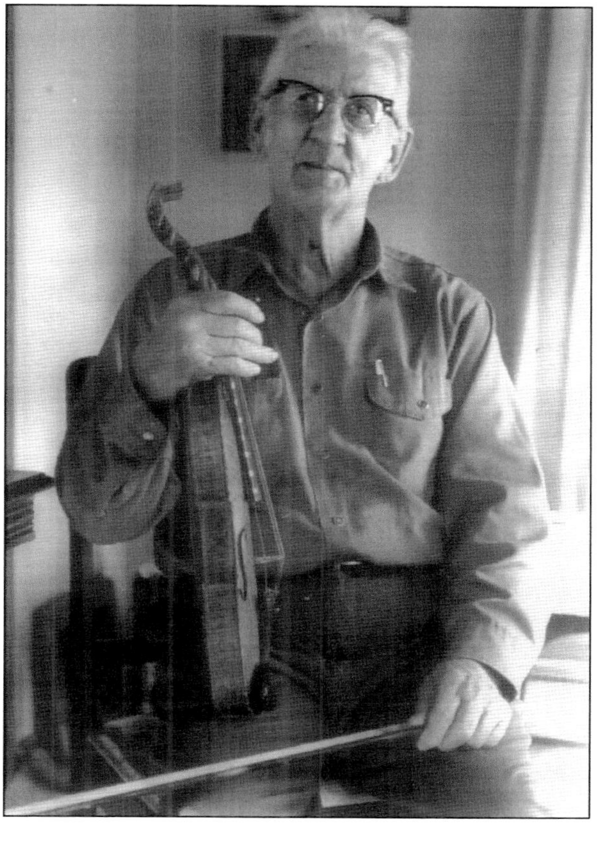

Thomas Kammerud, a retired farmer who lived a couple of miles south of Postville, was one of the regulars who frequented the Postville Store. Several days a week, an interesting and eclectic collection of old men gathered at the store to tell stories and listen to Thomas play his fiddle. (Bob Bergman.)

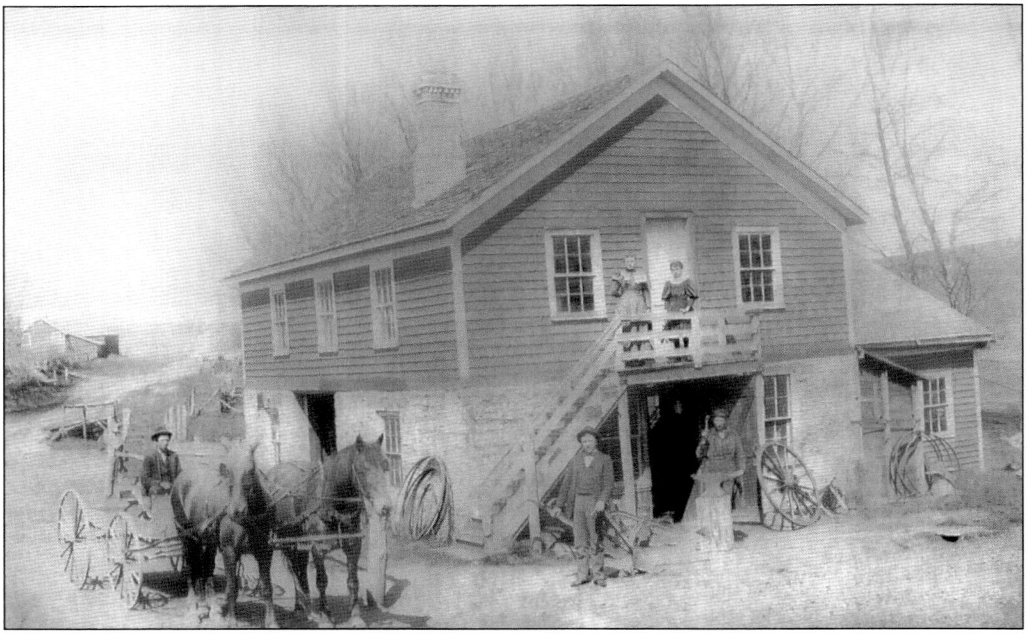

This early view of the Postville Blacksmith shop shows a busy operation. Blacksmith shops in these small crossroads communities were often the busiest place in town. With the exception of the blacksmith, all other people in this photograph are dressed up for a day in town. Notice the ornate brickwork at the top of the chimney. (Bob Bergman.)

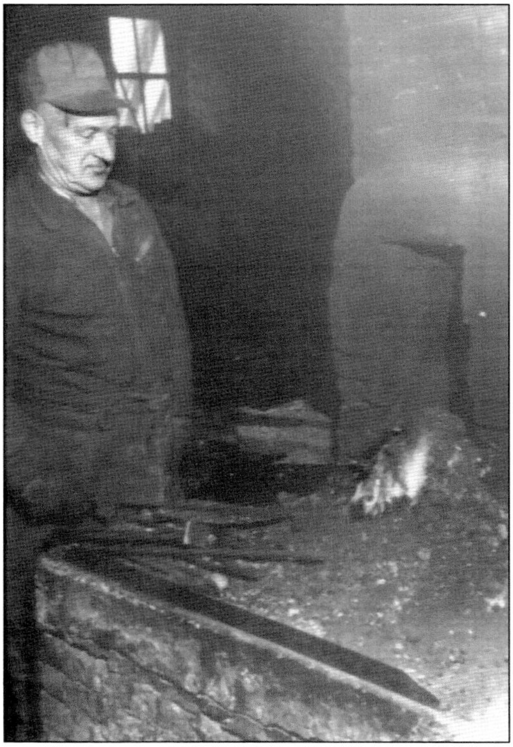

Carl Blaser owned the Postville Blacksmith shop for over 50 years before selling it in 1969 to the current owner, Bob Bergman. Blaser is shown here working at the forge possibly heating up a horseshoe to be bent slightly to make it better fit the horse. (Bob Bergman.)

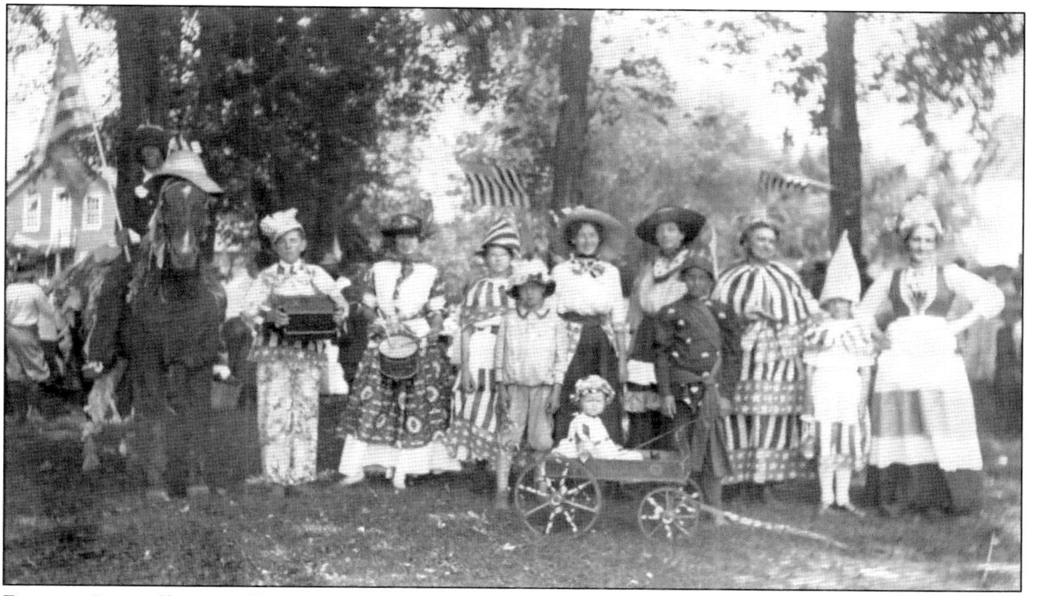

Despite Postville's small population, the residents of the area took national holidays seriously. Residents of Postville and the surrounding area took the day off to celebrate the Fourth of July in grand style. Judging from the costumes, the community put on some type of play for the entertainment of adults and children. The woman on the left is Jennie Massee, and the woman on the right is Mrs. Lillidahl. (Pat Elmer.)

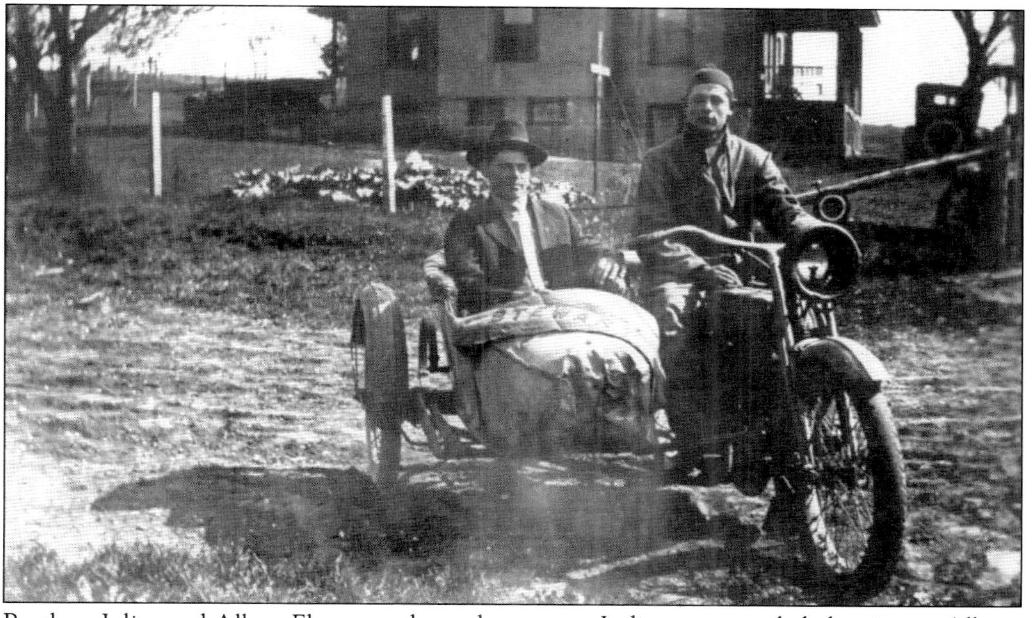

Brothers Julius and Albert Elmer are shown here on an Indian motorcycle belonging to Albert, who built the sidecar Julius is riding in. Notice the banner, reading "STEWART," on the front of the sidecar. The Elmer brothers were about to leave home to participate in a parade in Postville. (Pat Elmer.)

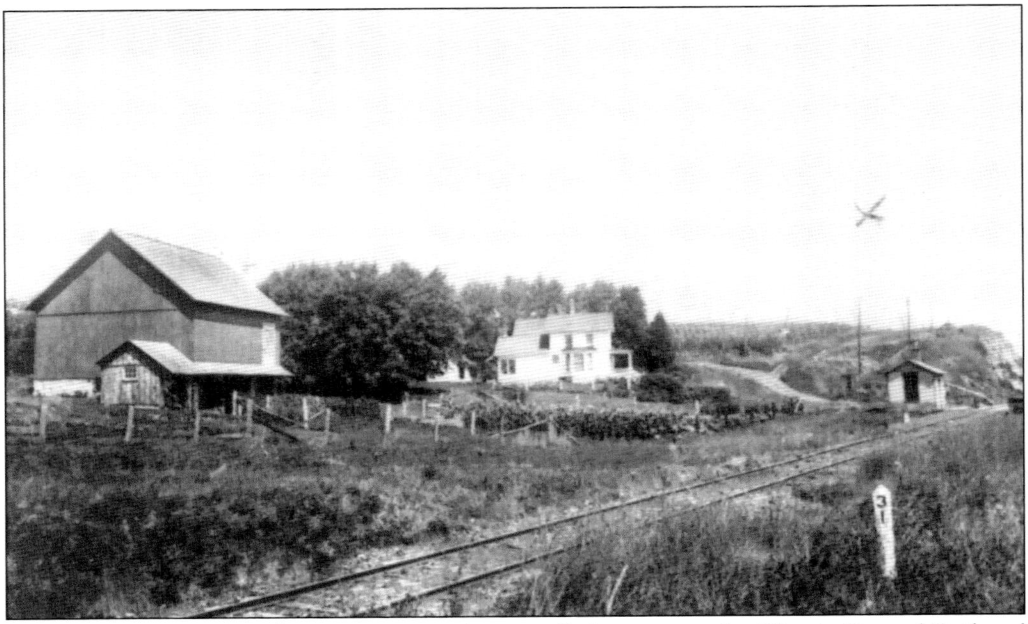

Schultz will not be found on many maps, but it will show up on the Illinois Central Railroad timetable as a stop at milepost 31 on its line from Freeport, Illinois, to Madison, Wisconsin. Schultz consisted of a small general store and train depot, which can be seen in this photograph. (Monticello Area Historical Society.)

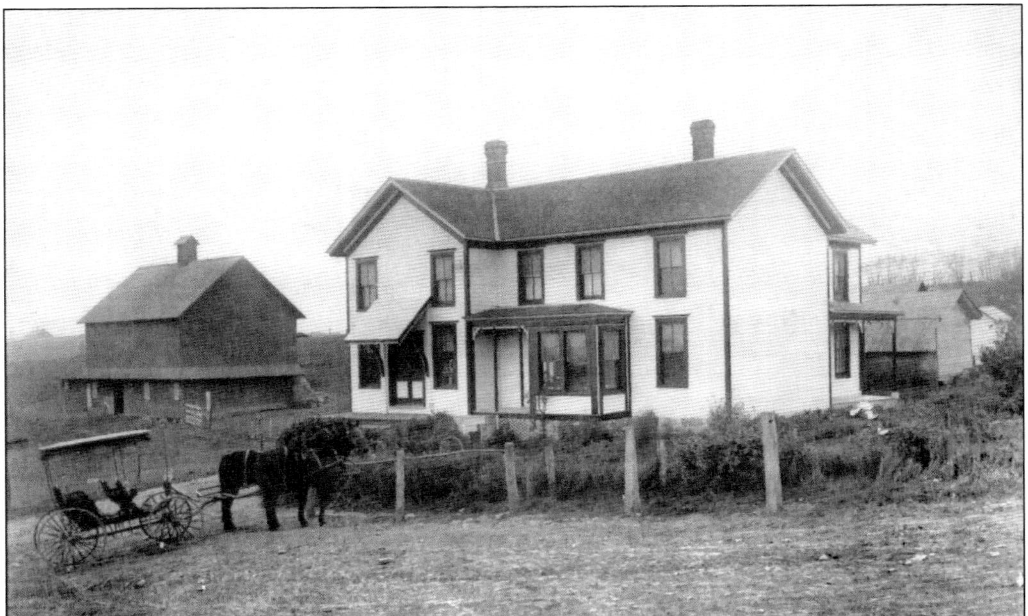

The Schultz store was located in this house. The store, which sold a general line of goods necessary for rural life, saved local residents many trips into Monticello, the closest village. Businesses such as the Schultz store dotted the rural landscape for many years with the last ones closing in the 1950s and early 1960s. (Monticello Area Historical Society.)

Nine

Around Green County

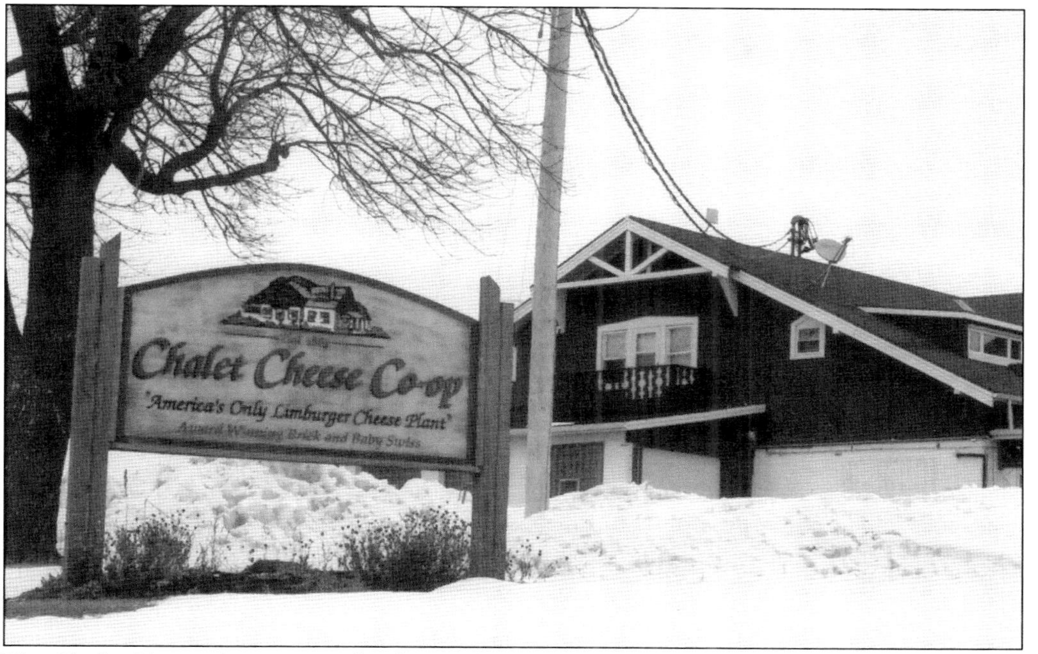

The Chalet Cheese Co-op, several miles north of Monroe, is the only cheese factory in the United States that makes Limburger cheese. At one time, Limburger was produced at many of the cheese factories in Green County. The popularity of Limburger is growing, and in 2009 Chalet produced 600,000 pounds of Limburger, which was up from a low of 250,000 pounds 15 years ago.

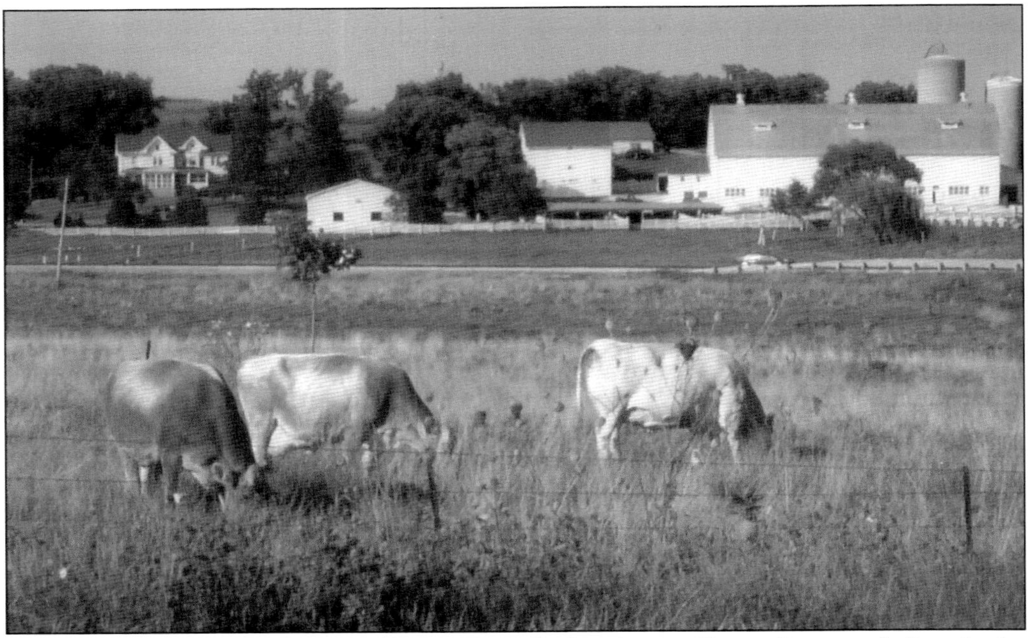

Voegeli Farm just north of Monticello is perhaps the best-known Brown Swiss cattle farm in the world. Five generations of Voegelis have been raising purebred Brown Swiss cattle that are highly sought after by other Brown Swiss breeders who want to improve their herds. (Voegeli Farm.)

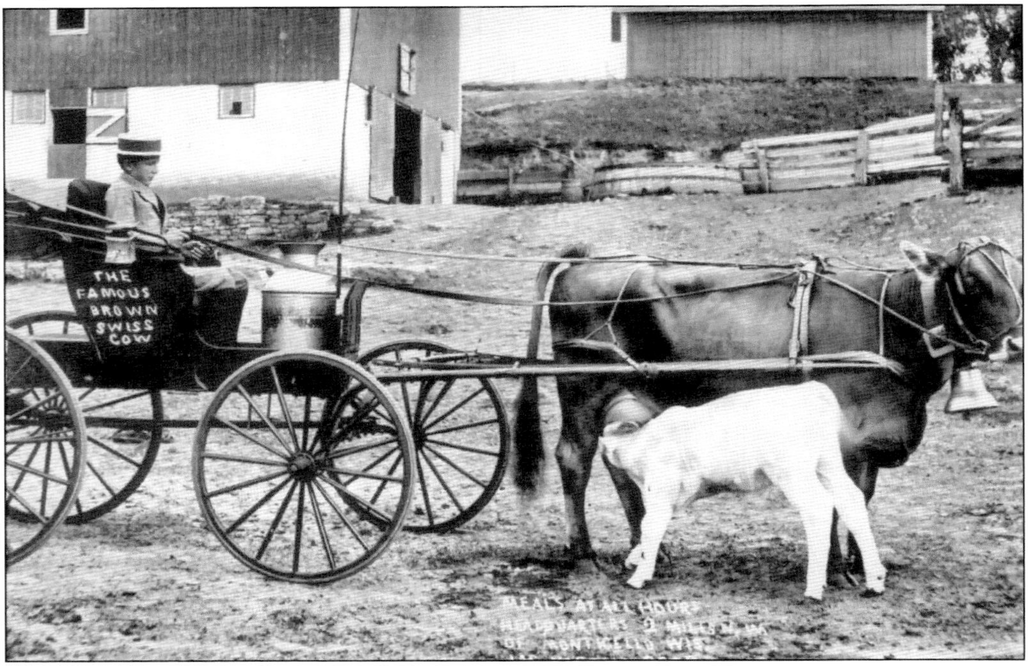

The notation at the bottom of this photograph states, "Meals at all hours, headquarters 2 miles NW of Monticello, WI Jac Voegeli Prop." Someone at Voegeli Farm took the time to train this Brown Swiss cow to pull a buggy, which no doubt caused numerous double takes from motorists when they saw this unlikely pair.

Howard Voegeli is shown milking one of the championship Brown Swiss cattle the family farm is noted for. Howard and Alice Voegeli were among the founders of the World Dairy Expo. (Voegeli family.)

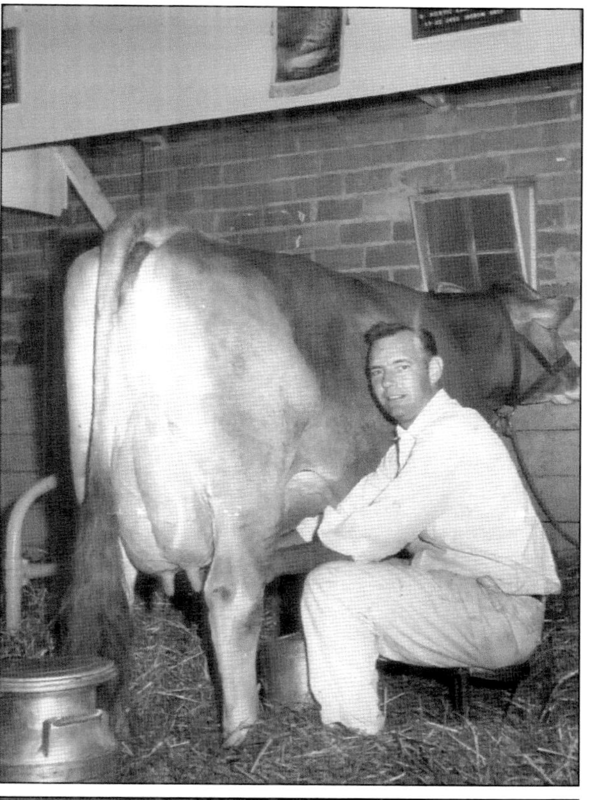

Beth Voegeli is shown here introducing the next generation of Voegelis, Brittany Innes and Brienna Voegeli, to the family dairy herd. The Voegeli family members are no doubt the best goodwill ambassadors and friends that the Wisconsin dairy industry has. (Voegeli family.)

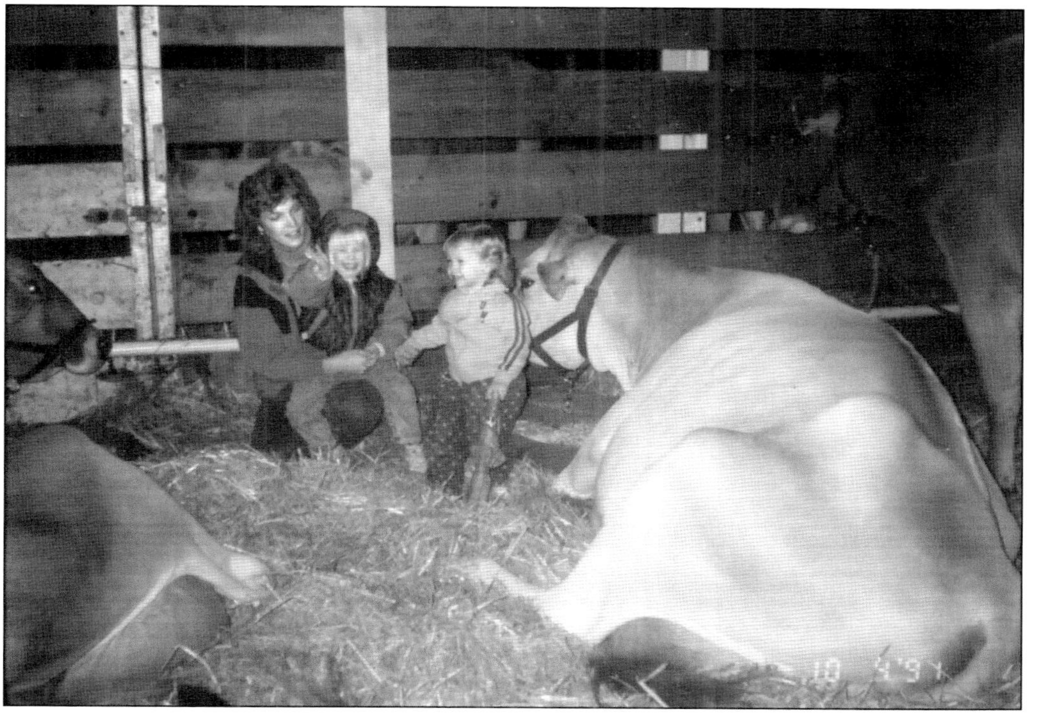

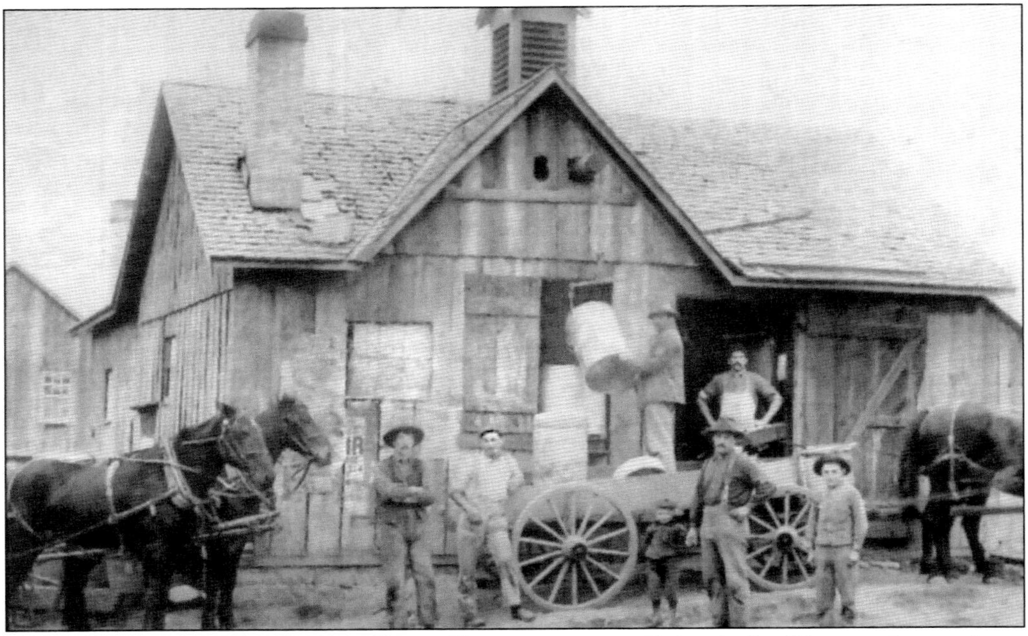

It is early morning at the Zentner Cheese Factory just east of Monticello. The area farmers have completed the morning milking and chores and are hauling their milk to the factory for processing into cheese. The cans that the milk is hauled in weigh well over 200 pounds each. The little boy in the center of this photograph is probably enjoying a day with his dad. (Monticello Area Historical Society.)

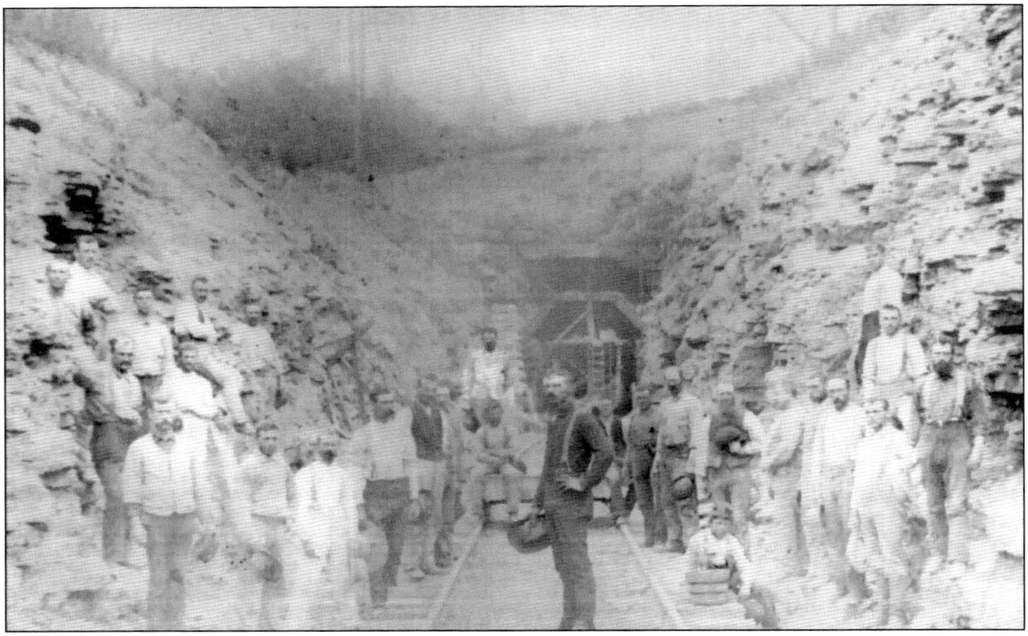

In this c. 1887 photograph, workers are taking a break at the Steward Tunnel, located in the town of Exeter. Within a year, the Chicago, Madison, and Northern Railroad will be bringing its first train north from Freeport, Illinois, to the end of the line in Madison, Wisconsin.

Since the Steward Tunnel opened in 1888, it has been an attraction for the public. This photograph of the south portal shows a pair of well-dressed young women posing for a photograph on the large rocks brought in to hold back the hillside. During World War II, the federal government stationed armed guards at each end of the tunnel to protect it from Nazi sympathizers in the area.

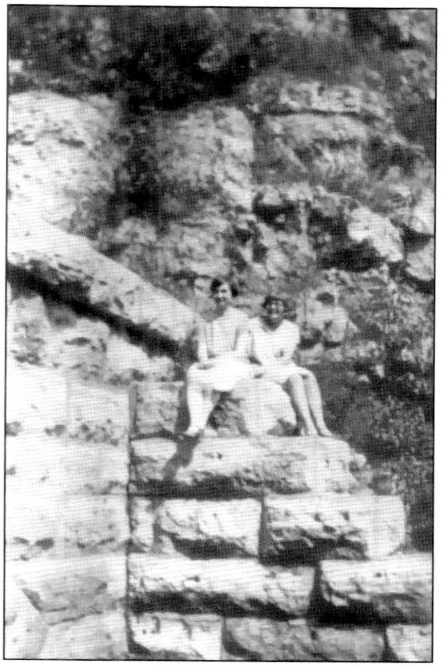

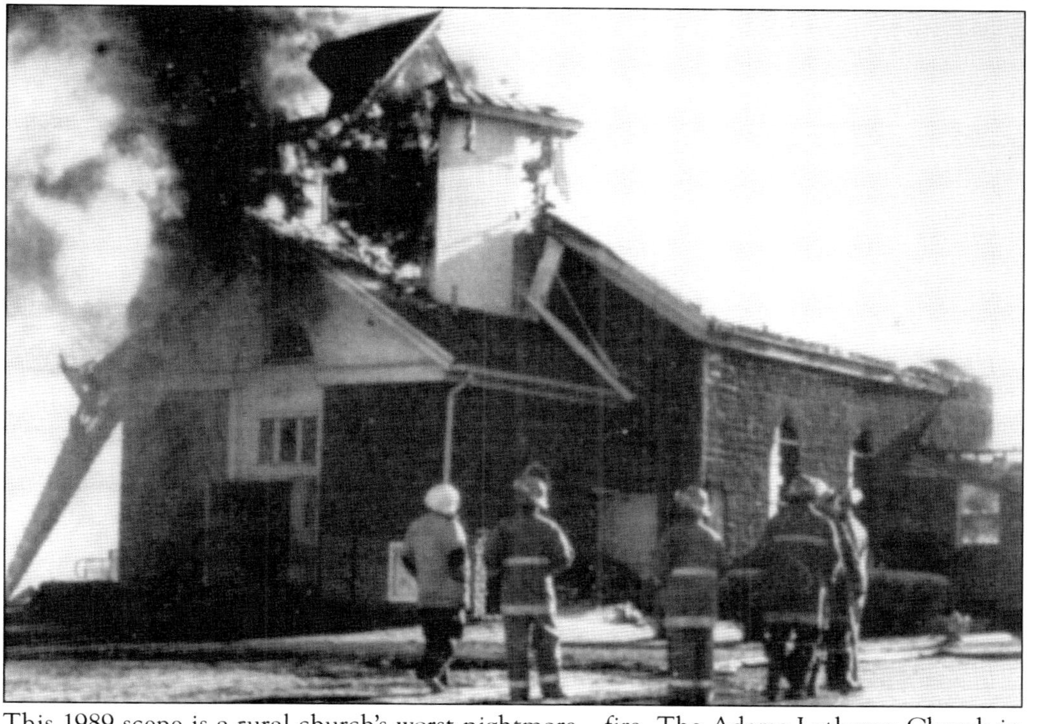

This 1989 scene is a rural church's worst nightmare—fire. The Adams Lutheran Church in November 1863 hired Arne K. Lien and Christian Almsengen to do the stonework for their new church for $300. The pair completed their work on the 18-foot-high, 45-foot-long limestone walls in October 1864. The stone was quarried a quarter mile away. The men of the congregation hauled it to the church site with stone boats. (Blanchardville Women's Club.)

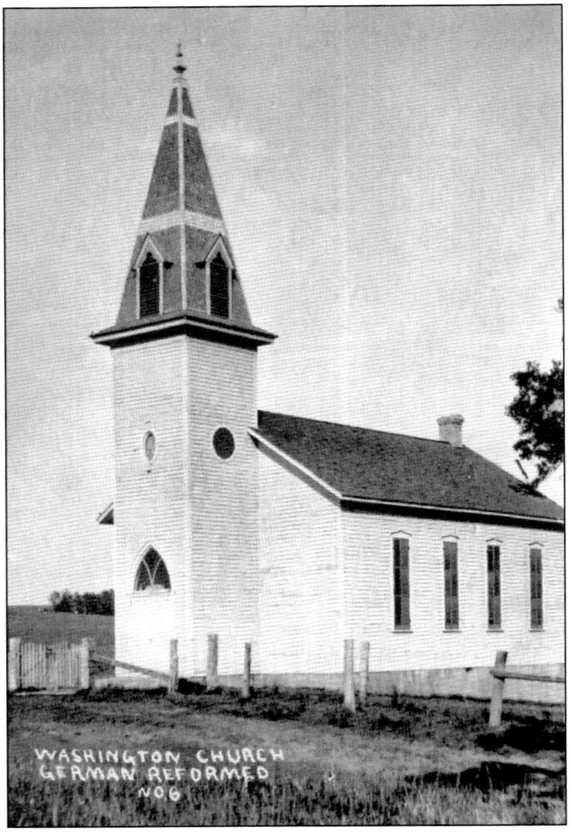

The Washington German Reformed Church several miles west of Monticello served the Swiss- and German-speaking settlers in the town of Washington. This church was struck by lightning and destroyed. The current church on this site is active in the community. (Monticello Area Historical Society.)

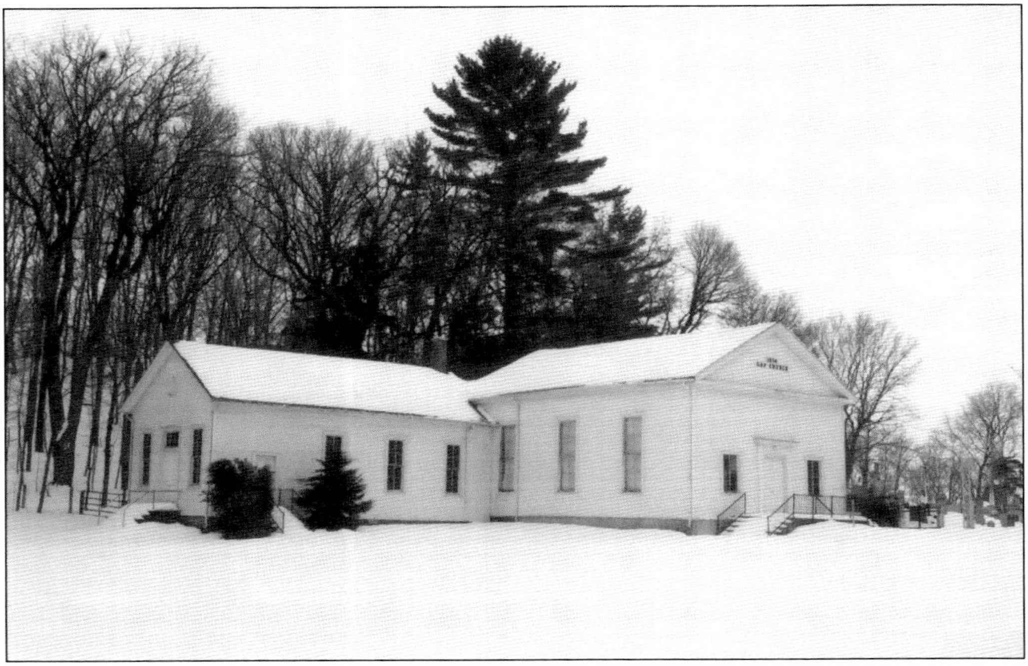

Gap Church, built on Monticello Prairie several miles west of Albany, has not been used as a church for many years, but a dedicated group of volunteers keep up the building and grounds out of respect for the past. The interior of this church has been beautifully maintained. The church was built with no steeple, which made it less of a target for a lightning strike. The addition to the back of the church on the left side may be the former Dutch Hollow Church.

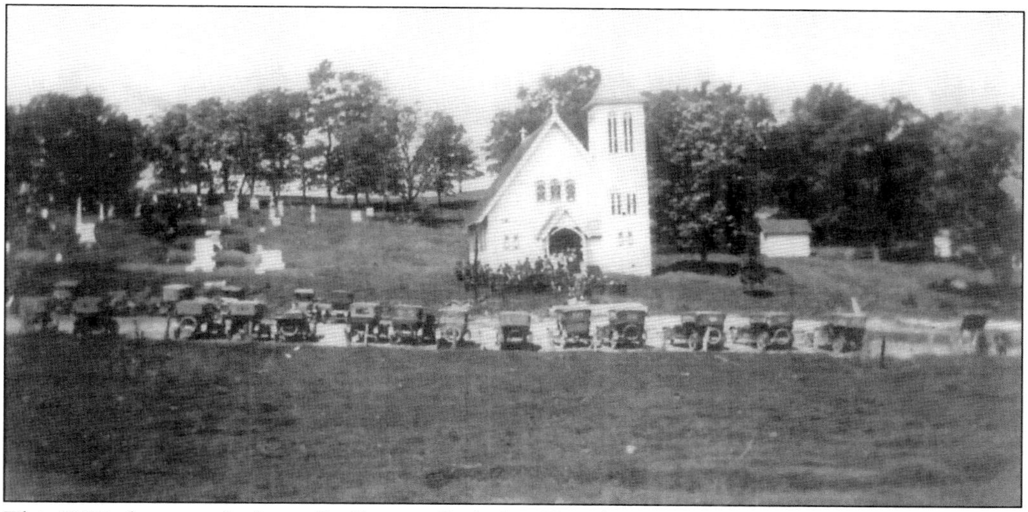

This 1920 photograph shows St. Francis Catholic Church on Biggs Road in the town of Adams, which served the area until the 1950s. Changing rural dynamics in agriculture slowly eroded away the multi-generation families that supported St. Francis. (Anna and Robert Keough.)

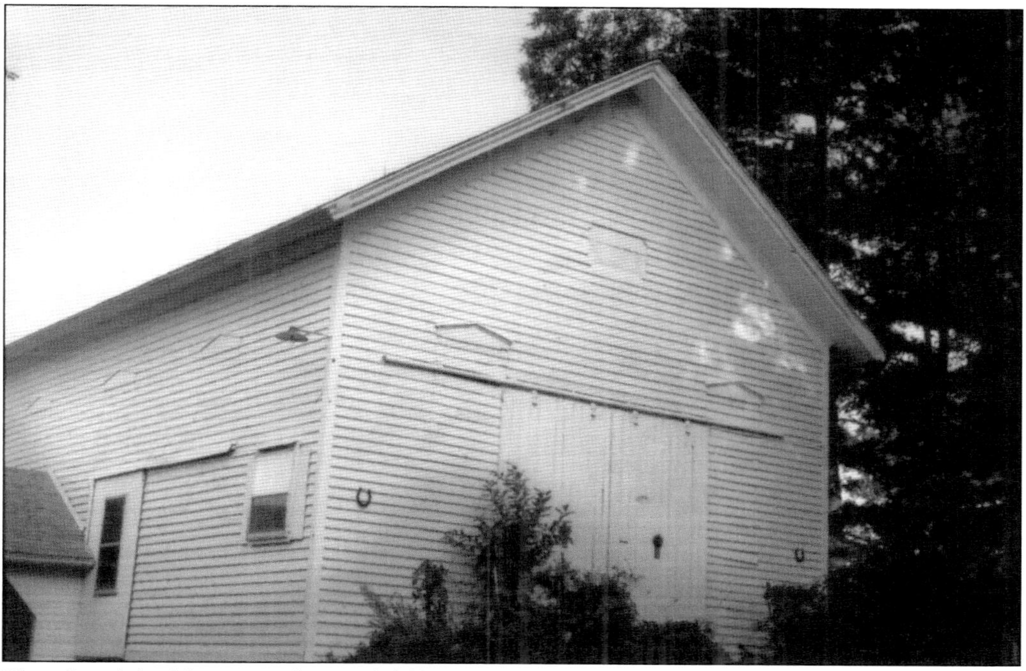

This church building served several different groups of Swiss settlers in the town of Washington, who decided in 1874 to build a joint church that came to be known informally as "Berner Church." Ministers from both the evangelical and reformed churches in Monroe served the group. This structure is now used as a storage building.

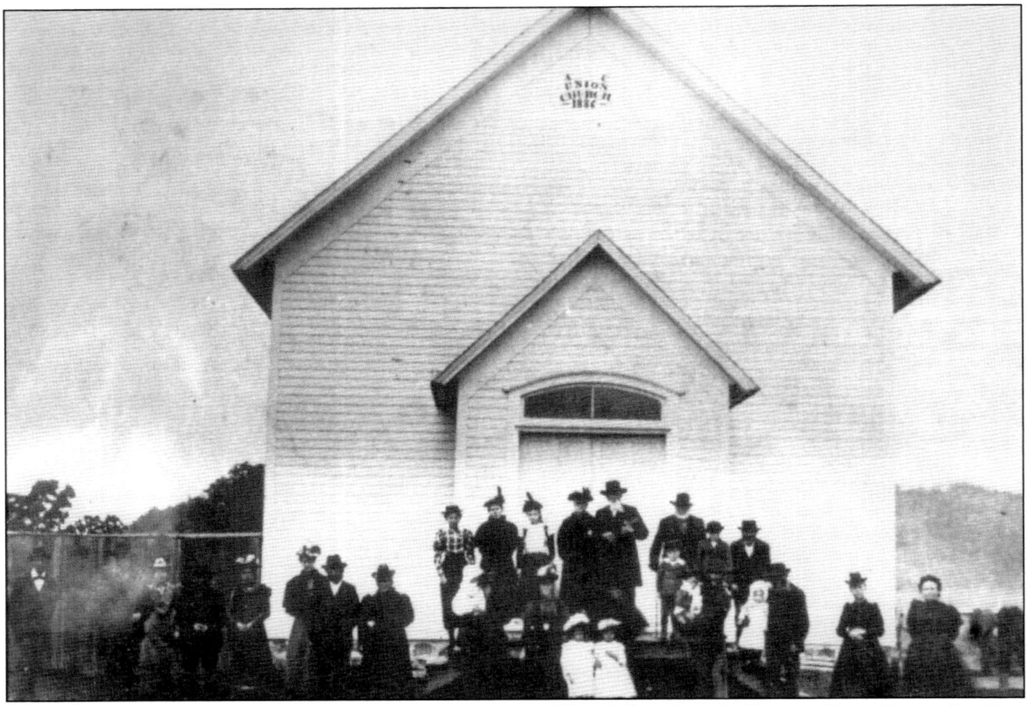

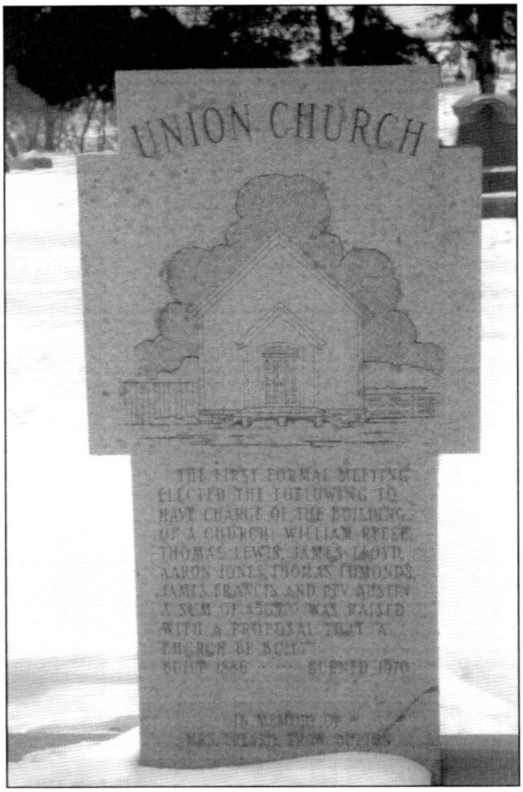

The Allen Creek Union Church was built in 1886 to serve as the neighborhood church for the Allen Creek settlement, known at the time as the English settlement, several miles north of Albany. The structure was used by many different religious groups that lacked enough members to build their own churches. (Albany Historical Society.)

Today all that remains of the Allen Creek Union Church are memories and this stone commemorating the history of the burned church.

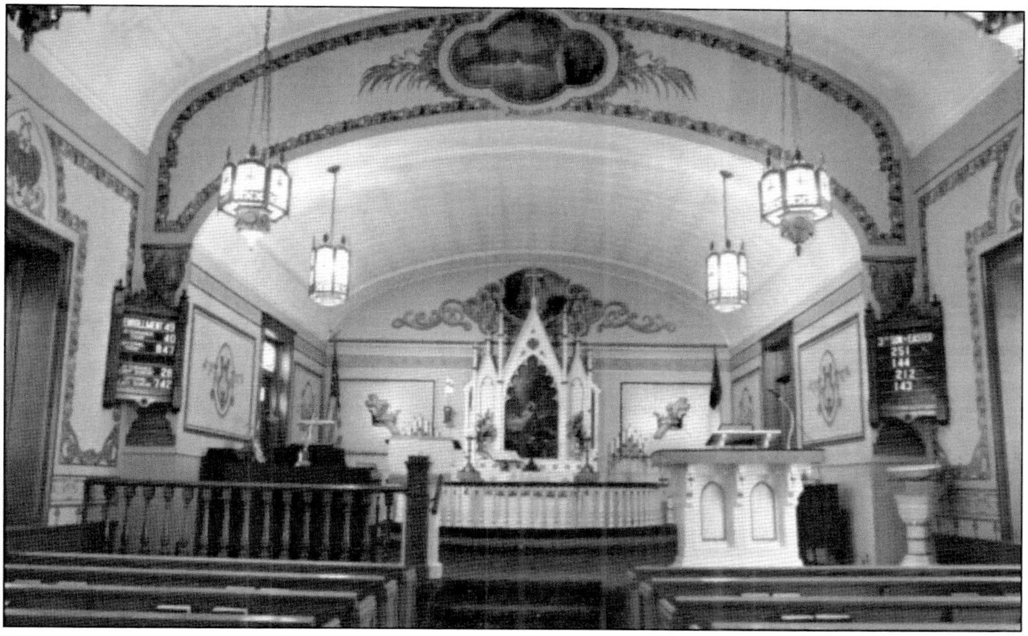

The stark stone exterior of the Jordan Lutheran Church indicates little about the beauty of the sanctuary. This 1985 photograph shows the pride the congregation takes in its church building, where in 2010 they will celebrate the 150th anniversary of the founding of the church. (Browntown Historical Society.)

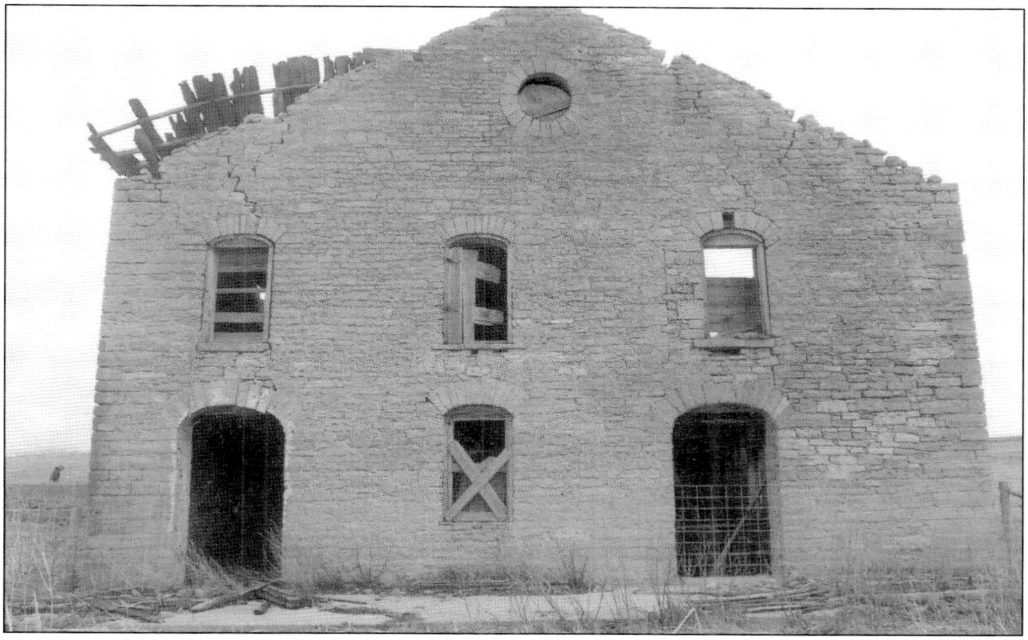

Constructed in 1833, this building was used as a lead smelter until 1866. Lead was mined near this building and brought in for smelting into more pure lead before being shipped either to Milwaukee or Galena, from which it was shipped to manufacturing plants in larger cities.

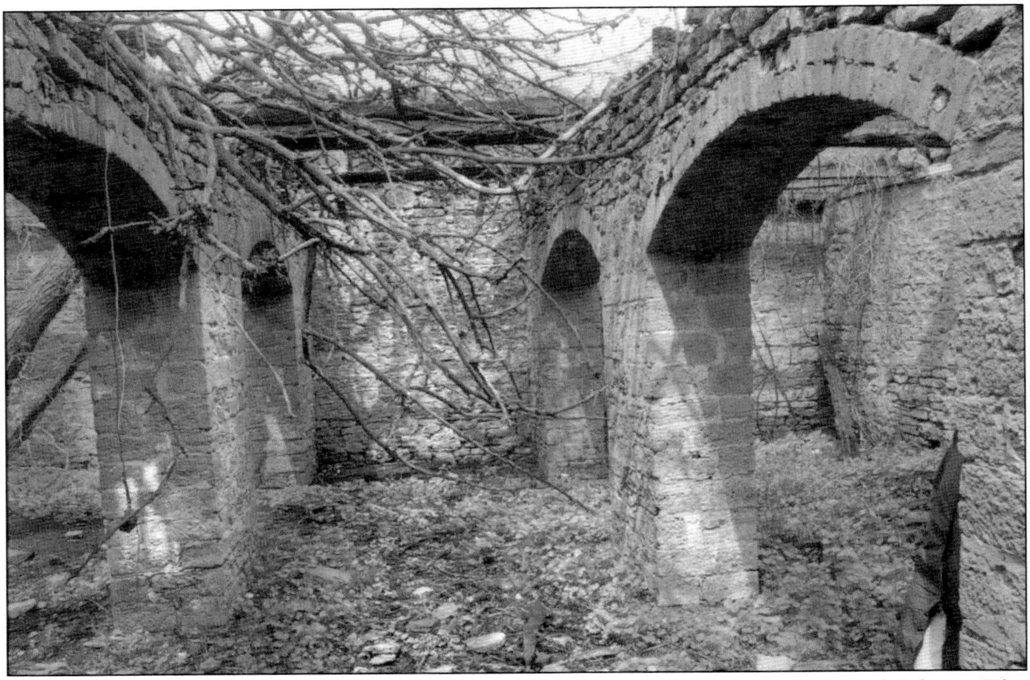

This photograph shows the interior of the lead smelting building in the town of Adams. The brick and stonework in this building is very interesting; handmade bricks were used along with cut stone and field rubble stone. Nearby lead mines used both vertical (the most common) as well as horizontal mine shafts.

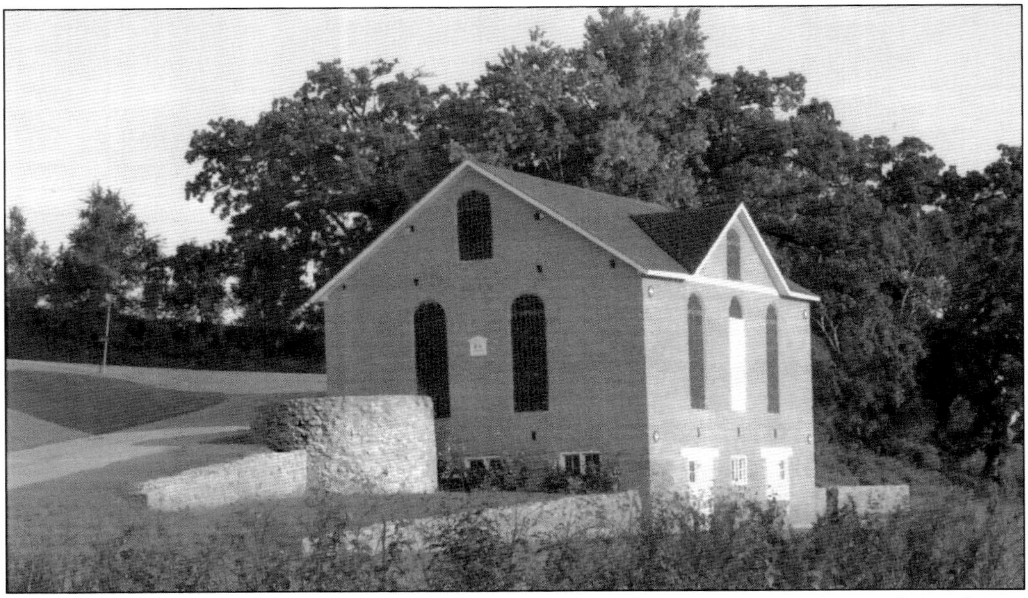

The Hefty-Blum Homestead farm dates to the early 1850s, and the beautiful stone barn shown here was built in 1863. In the 1950s, the silo in the front of the barn was hit by a tornado that took off the silo roof. This barn was used until recent years. It has been fully restored, and the entire farm is on the National Register of Historic Places. The Blum family still resides here.

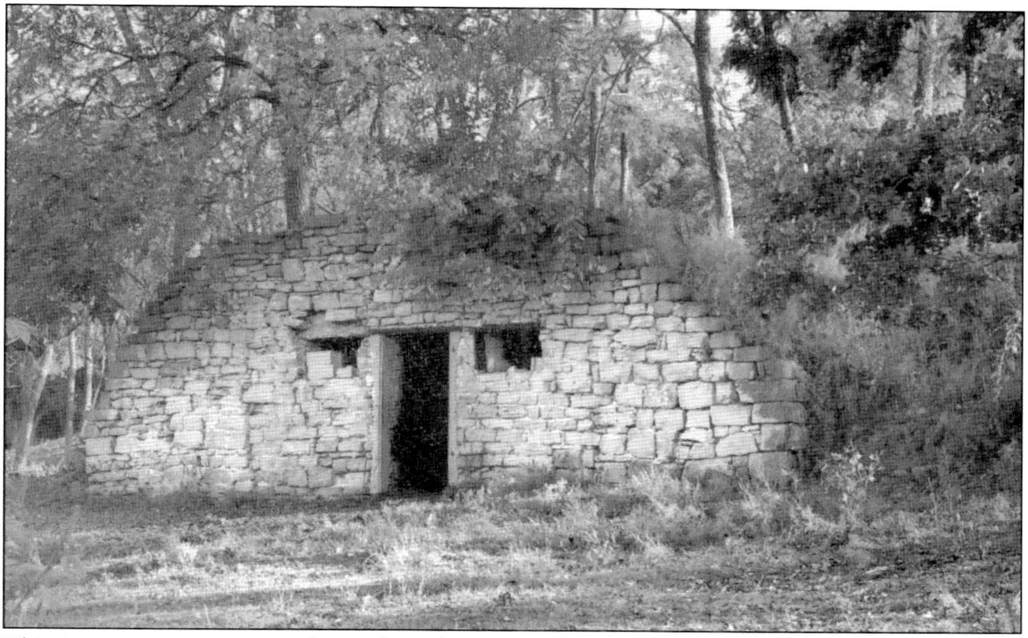

This interesting structure is located on County Highway H west of New Glarus. In its original form, the building was used as a cheese storage warehouse. Built deep into the hillside, the structure kept the same temperature year round.

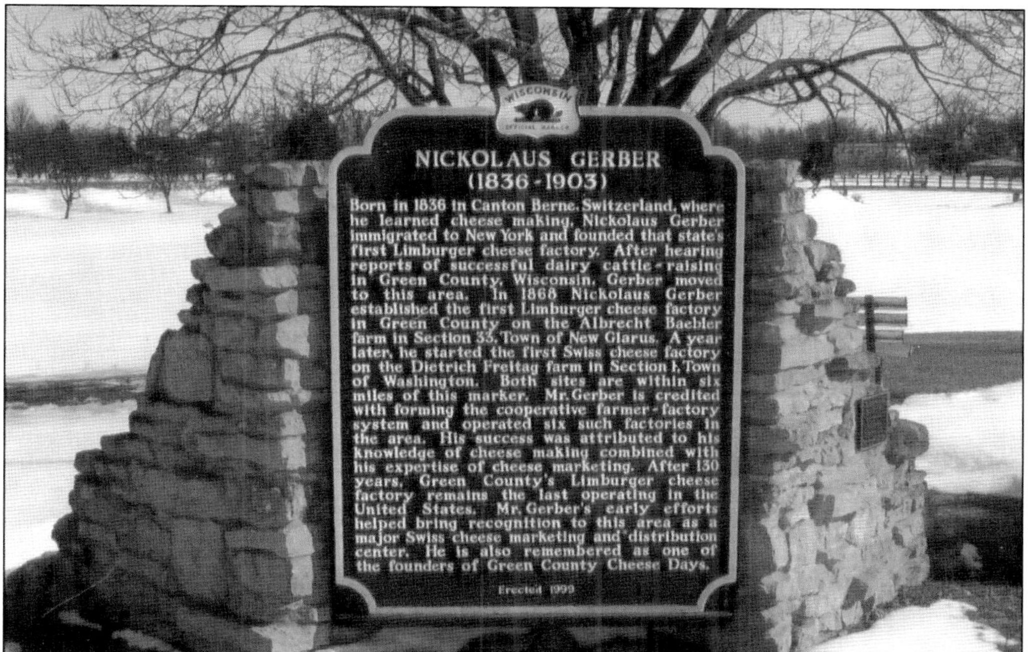

This Wisconsin historical marker located at Lake Montesian in Monticello commemorates the work of Nickolaus Gerber, a native of Switzerland who developed the first Swiss cheese factory in the United States. The equipment Gerber used in his factory on the Freitag Estate Farm 1 mile north of here can be seen at the Swiss Historical Village cheese factory in New Glarus.

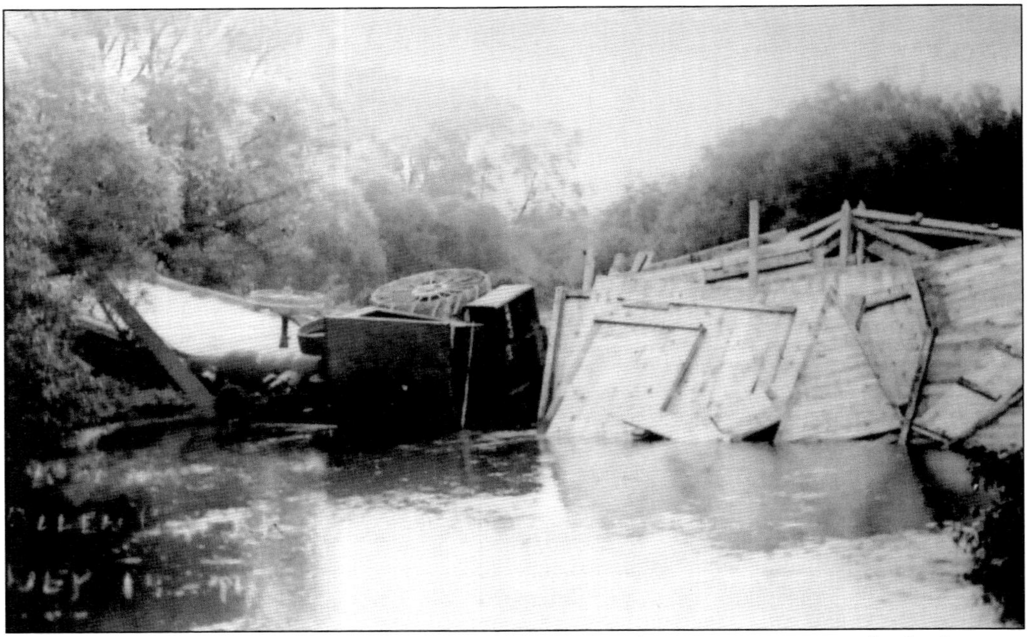

Imagine the surprise the driver had when his steam-powered tractor was crossing this bridge over Allen Creek, and the weight of the tractor sent the bridge into the creek. It appears that this was a covered bridge. Allen Creek runs north and east of Albany. (Albany Historical Society.)

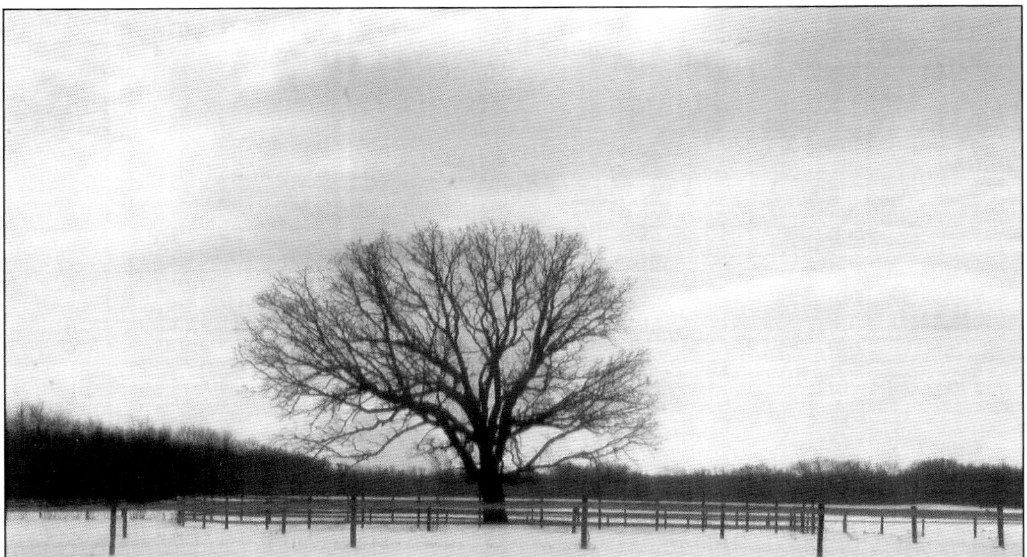

This burr oak tree located on Half Way Tree Road south of Brodhead was identified by local Native Americans as the halfway point between Lake Michigan and the Mississippi River. The Native Americans were correct—years later, surveys indicated that the Half Way Tree was only off by 1 mile.

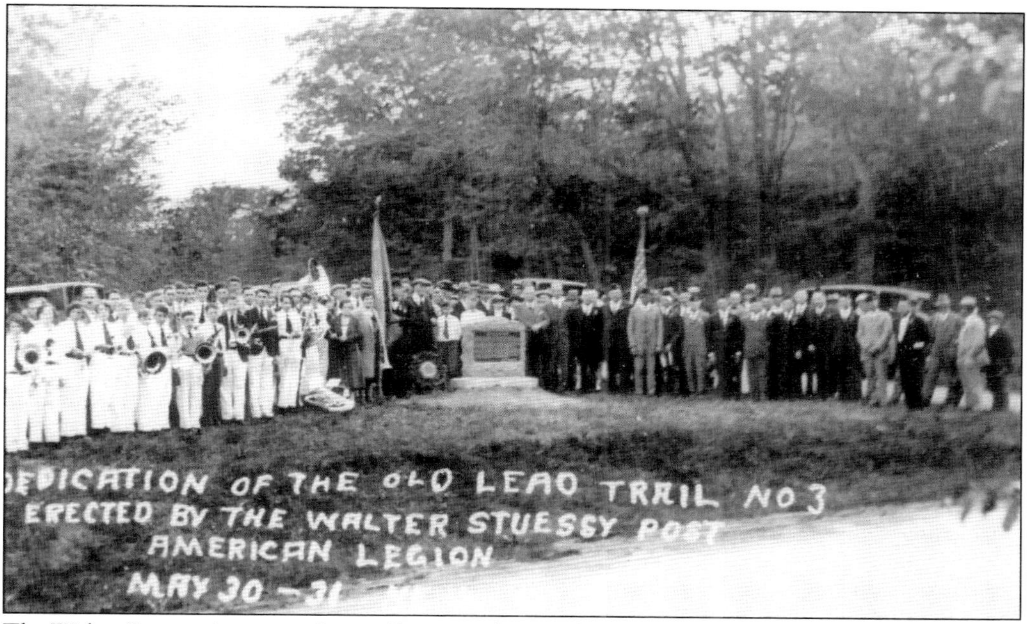

The Walter Stuessy American Legion Post 141 of New Glarus dedicated a memorial commemorating the Old Lead Road that connected Milwaukee with Galena. This event played out over two days. Local bands played, and speeches were made. At one time, a World War I field gun was also placed at this site.

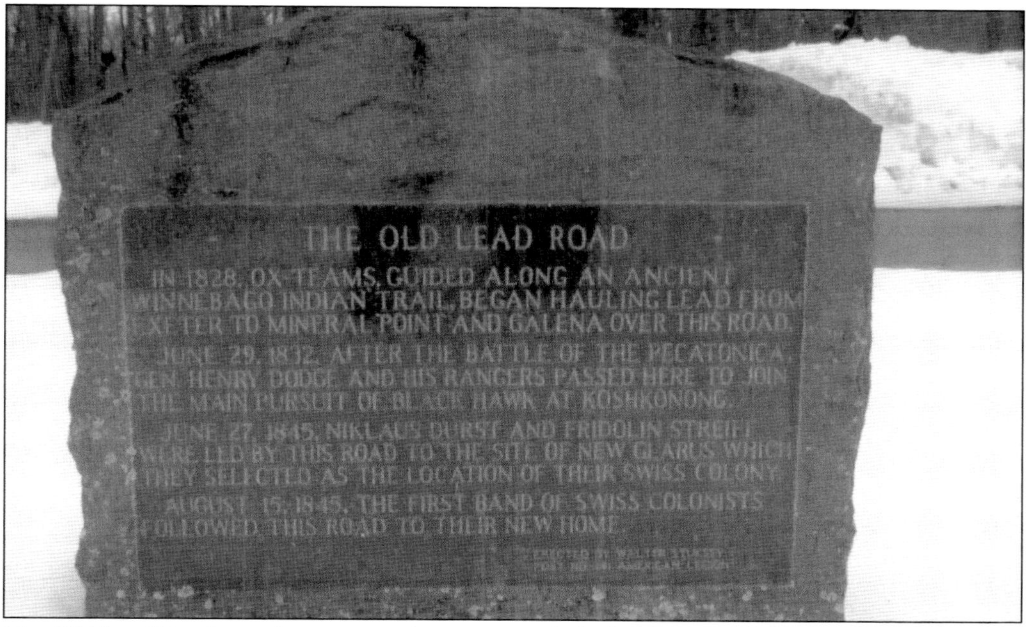

The Old Lead Road was the main road connecting Lake Michigan and the Mississippi River. In April of 1832, the drumbeat of war was loud. In late April 1832, one of the last Indian Wars east of the Mississippi River was fought in southern Wisconsin and northern Illinois. The nearby ghost town of Exeter was abandoned during the war, which lasted until early August of 1832, bringing a sad event in American history to an end.

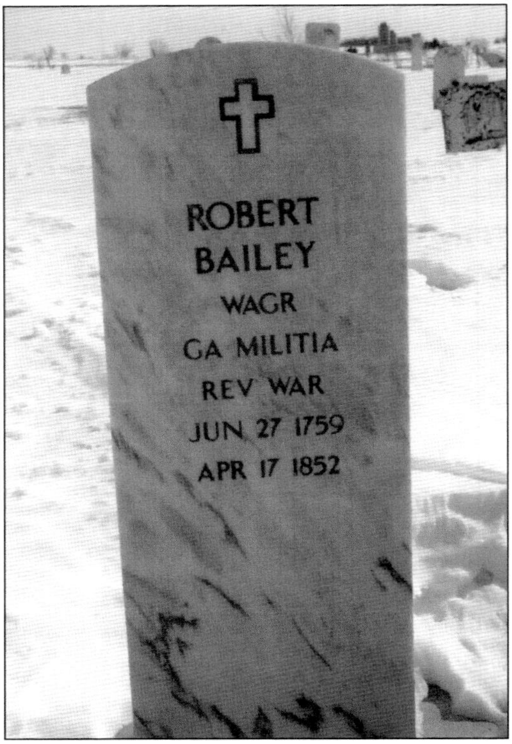

Robert Bailey is the only Revolutionary War veteran buried in Green County. A man of conscience, Bailey realized that slavery was wrong in 1814, and he gave the slaves who worked on his farm their freedom. Bailey and his wife moved to Green County in 1838 to be with their son.

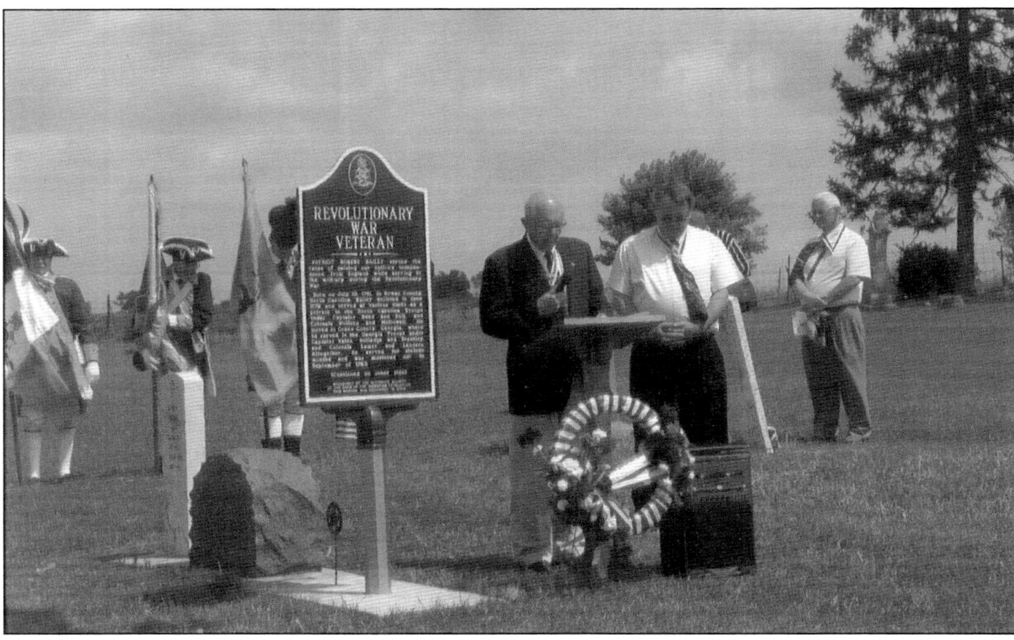

In August 2009, the Sons of the Revolutionary War dedicated a historical marker commemorating the life of Robert Bailey at Shooks Prairie Cemetery in the town of Adams. Ancestors of Robert Bailey were present for the touching ceremony, which included men dressed in Revolutionary War uniforms.

ORGANIZATIONS

The following is a list of Green County Historical Societies and their contact information:

Albany Historical Society
117–119 Water Street
Post Office Box 464
Albany, WI, 53502
Phone: (608) 862-3423
Hours: year-round on Saturday, 9:00 a.m.–12:00 p.m.
June–September on Saturday, 9:00 a.m.–2:00 p.m.

Belleville Area Historical Society
Post Office Box 202
Belleville, WI, 53508

Brodhead Historical Society
1108 First Center Avenue
Brodhead, WI, 53520
Phone: (608) 897-4150
Hours: Memorial Day–September on Wednesdays, Saturdays, and Sundays, 1:00 p.m.–4:00 p.m.

Browntown Historical Society
110 South Mill Street
Browntown, WI, 53522
Phone: (608) 966-3273

Green County Historical Society
1619 Ninth Street
Post Office Box 804
Monroe, WI, 53566-0804
Phone: (608) 325-4301
Hours: late May–September on Saturdays and Sundays, 1:00 p.m.–4:00 p.m.

Monticello Area Historical Society
206 Main Street
Monticello, WI, 53570
Phone: (608) 938-4216
Hours: May–October on Saturdays, 10:00 a.m.–2:00 p.m.

New Glarus Historical Society
Post Office Box 745
New Glarus, WI, 53574
Phone: (608) 527-2317

New Glarus Historical Village
612 Seventh Avenue
New Glarus, WI, 53574
Hours: May 1–October 31, 10:00 a.m.–4:00 p.m.